# Advancing Maths for AQA
# PURE MATHS I

Sam Boardman, David Evans, Tony Clough and Maureen Nield

**Series editors**
**Sam Boardman   Ted Graham   Keith Parramore**
**Roger Williamson**

**Heinemann Educational Publishers**

a division of Heinemann Publishers (Oxford) Ltd,
Halley Court, Jordan Hill, Oxford OX2 8EJ

OXFORD   MELBOURNE   AUCKLAND   JOHANNESBURG
BLANTYRE   GABORONE   PORTSMOUTH NH (USA)   CHICAGO

First published in 2000

Reprinted with corrections 2001

01 10 9 8 7 6 5 4 3 2

ISBN 0 435 51300 1

Typeset and illustrated by Tech-Set Limited, Gateshead, Tyne & Wear.

Printed and bound by Bath Press in the UK.

**Acknowledgements**
The publishers' and authors' thanks are due to the AEB for permission to
reproduce questions from past examination papers.

The answers have been provided by the authors and are not the responsibility
of the examining board.

# About this book

This book is one in a series of textbooks designed to provide you with exceptional preparation for AQA's new Advanced GCE Specification B. The series authors are all senior members of the examining team and have prepared the textbooks specifically to support you in studying this course.

## Finding your way around

The following are there to help you find your way around when you are studying and revising:

- **edge marks** (shown on the front page) – these help you to get to the right chapter quickly;
- **contents list** – this identifies the individual sections dealing with key syllabus concepts so that you can go straight to the areas that you are looking for;
- **index** – a number in bold type indicates where to find the main entry for that topic.

## Key points

Key points are not only summarised at the end of each chapter but are also boxed and highlighted within the text like this:

$$\text{Gradient of chord} = \frac{\delta y}{\delta x}$$

## Exercises and exam questions

Worked examples and carefully graded questions familiarise you with the syllabus and bring you up to exam standard. Each book contains:

- Worked examples and Worked exam questions to show you how to tackle typical questions; Examiner's tips will also provide guidance;
- Graded exercises, gradually increasing in difficulty up to exam-level questions, which are marked by an [A];
- Test-yourself sections for each chapter so that you can check your understanding of the key aspects of that chapter and identify any sections that you should review;
- Answers to the questions are included at the end of the book.

# Contents

## 5 Functions and graphs

## 6 Introduction to differentiation

# CHAPTER 1

# Indices

## Learning objectives

After studying this chapter, you should be able to:

■ use the language of indices

■ simplify expressions involving indices

■ know the laws of indices

■ interpret negative, zero and fractional indices.

## 1.1 Introduction

At the end of the twentieth century, the English mathematician Andrew Wiles solved a problem involving powers of whole numbers that had perplexed people for hundreds of years. From his childhood he had learned that certain whole numbers could satisfy Pythagoras' relationship $a^2 + b^2 = c^2$, such as $a = 3$, $b = 4$ and $c = 5$ (or $a = 5$, $b = 12$ and $c = 13$, etc.). In 1637, the French mathematician Pierre de Fermat stated that, although this was true for squares, he had found a proof that this could never be done for cubes or any higher powers. Fermat wrote in the margin of his book that it was too small to contain the proof. This is not surprising because it took Andrew Wiles seven years research and 200 pages to present a proof of Fermat's Last Theorem, namely that there are no whole numbers $a$, $b$, and $c$ that satisfy $a^n + b^n = c^n$ when the power $n$ is greater than two.

During your mathematics course, you will combine some ideas discovered centuries ago with those that will inspire great minds of the twenty-first century. Some of the concepts in this chapter you may have met in your GCSE course but others will be new.

## 1.2 Index notation

**Index** is simply another word for **power**.
The plural of index is **indices**.

You should recall that $a \times a \times a$ can be written as $a^3$
in a shorthand way

Similarly

$a \times a \times a \times a$      can be written as $a^4$ ($a$ to the power 4)

$\underbrace{a \times a \times \ldots a \times a}_{n \text{ of these}}$   can be written as $a^n$ ($a$ to the power $n$)

> In this expression, $a$ is called the **base** and 3 is called the power or **index**.

> read as $a$ cubed or $a$ to the power 3

> The name for the fourth power is biquadrate, but, whereas we regularly use the terms square and cube, we never really use this obscure word.

## 1.3 The laws of indices

There are three rules which will help us to simplify complicated expressions involving indices.

**1** Consider the expression   $a^4 \times a^5$

$$a^4 \times a^5 = (a \times a \times a \times a) \times (a \times a \times a \times a \times a)$$
$$= a \times a \times a \times a \times a \times a \times a \times a \times a$$
$$= a^9$$

So we have

$$a^4 \times a^5 = a^{9`}$$

By now (probably long ago!) you will have spotted that we can simply add the powers in the expression to get the new power.

In general we have,

> $a^4 = a \times a \times a \times a$
> and
> $a^5 = a \times a \times a \times a \times a$

**Law 1 (the multiplication rule)**

$$a^m \times a^n = a^{m+n}$$

**2** What about division?

Consider    $a^5 \div a^2$

Now

$$a^5 \times a^2 = \frac{a \times a \times a \times a \times a}{a \times a} = a \times a \times a = a^3$$

So    $a^5 \div a^2 = a^3$

> $a \times a$ cancels in both the top and in the bottom.

> Again there is a simple rule – when dividing expressions with indices, you can subtract the indices to find the new power.

In general we have,

**Law 2 (the division rule)**

$$a^m \div a^n = a^{m+n}$$

**Note.** The expressions $a^m + a^n$ and $a^m - a^n$ **cannot** be simplified to a single power of $a$.

**3** Consider the expression $(a^3)^4$

Now

$$(a^3)^4 = a^3 \times a^3 \times a^3 \times a^3$$
$$= (a \times a \times a) \times (a \times a \times a) \times (a \times a \times a) \times (a \times a \times a)$$
$$= a^{12}$$

> Four lots of $a^3$

> Again, a simple rule is that you can multiply the two indices to find the new index, i.e. $3 \times 4 = 12$.

In general we have

**Law 3 (the power rule)**

$$(a^m)^n = a^{m \times n}$$

## Worked example 1.1

Simplify:   **1** $3x^4 \times 7x^6$,   **2** $3x^5 \times 4y^3 \times 2y^2 \times 5x^3$,

**3** $(3p^4q)^3$,   **4** $2x^4y^3 \times (x^2y^3)^4$.

## Solution

**1** $3x^4 \times 7x^6 = 3 \times x^4 \times 7 \times x^6 = 3 \times 7 \times x^4 \times x^6 = 21x^{10}$

> Add the indices $4 + 6 = 10$.

> The order in which we multiply is not important.

**2** $3x^5 \times 4y^3 \times 2y^2 \times 5x^3 = 3 \times 4 \times 2 \times 5 \times x^5 \times x^3 \times y^3 \times y^2$
$$= 120x^8y^5$$

> Notice that there are two different bases and they must be handled separately.

**3** $(3p^4q)^3 = 3^3 \times (p^4)^3 \times q^3$
$$= 27 \times p^{12} \times q^3 = 27p^{12}q^3$$

> Each term is raised to the power 3.

**4** $2x^4y^3 \times (x^2y^3)^4$
$$= 2x^4y^3 \times x^8y^{12}$$
$$= 2x^{8+4}y^{3+12}$$
$$= 2x^{12}y^{15}$$

> Both $x^2$ and $y^3$ are raised to the power 4.

## EXERCISE IA

Simplify the following as far as possible.

1  $3 \times m \times m \times m \times m \times 2 \times m$,

2  $2 \times b \times b \times b$,

3  $6 \times 4 \times p \times p \times p \times q \times q$,

4  $r^5 \times r^4$,

5  $7t^2 \times 8t^6$,

6  $4a^3 \times 9b^6$,

7  $9a^4 \times 2a \times 3a^7$,

8  $4a^4 \times 2b^3 \times a^8 \times 3b^2$,

9  $10p^3 \times 3p^2 \times 2q^3 \times q$,

10  $2pq^2 \times 5p^3q^4 \times p^6 \times q^2$,

11  $6a^3p \times 2aq^3 \times 3p^2q$,

12  $(m^3)^5$,

13  $(m^5)^3$,

14  $(a^2b^2)^5$,

15  $(2x^2)^3$,

16  $(a^2b^4)^3$,

17  $(p^2q^2)^4 \times 3p$,

18  $2m^2 \times 5n^3 \times (mn)^4$,

19  $4r^2t \times (r^3t^2)^3$,

20  $10p^2q^5 \times (q^3)^2 \times 2(p^4)^3$.

> **Note.** In general, expressions involving indices can only be simplified when the numbers involved have the **same base**. The expression $a^2 \times b^2$, for example, cannot be simplified since one base is $a$ while the other is $b$.

## Worked example 1.2

Simplify:   1  $8p^2 \div 4p^7$,

2  $21x^3y^4 \div 3x^2y$,

3  $\dfrac{(3s^3t^4)^2 \times s^2t^5}{(s^2t^3)^4}$.

## Solution

1  $8p^2 \div 4p^7 = \dfrac{8}{4}p^{2-7}$
    $= 2p^{-5}$

> First, we deal with the numbers 8 divided by 4, then we subtract the indices $2 - 7 = -5$.

We will explain what is meant by a negative index in the next section and show an alternative form in which the answer may be written.

2  $21x^3y^4 \div 3x^2y$
    $= \dfrac{21}{3}x^{3-2}y^{4-1}$
    $= 7xy^3$

> The numbers give 21 divided by 3. Now we subtract the indices for each of the bases $x$ and $y$ separately.

> **Note.** $3 - 2 = 1$ so we have $x^1$ but this is normally written simply as $x$.

3  $\dfrac{(3s^3t^4)^2 \times s^2t^5}{(s^2t^3)^4} = \dfrac{9s^6t^8 \times s^2t^5}{s^8t^{12}} = \dfrac{9s^8t^{13}}{s^8t^{12}} = 9t$

**Note.**  It may be that you obtained an answer $9s^0t$. This is still correct as you will see in a later section.

## EXERCISE 1B

Simplify the following as far as possible.

**1** $a^5 \div a^2$,      **2** $8p^3 \div 2p$,      **3** $20t^6 \div 4t^5$,

**4** $60h^7 \div 6h^7$,      **5** $(x^2)^4 \div x^5$,      **6** $12(a^2)^7 \div 4a^{11}$,

**7** $5p^2q^3 \div 15pq^2$,      **8** $10a^{15} \div 20a^7$,      **9** $60p^2q^5 \div 30pq^2$,

**10** $25a^2b^9 \div 30a^2b^8$,      **11** $\dfrac{5t^5 \times 2t^6}{t^7}$,      **12** $\dfrac{4a^4 \times 5a^7}{2a^3}$,

**13** $\dfrac{8p^5q \times 3p^2q^3}{12p^3q}$,      **14** $\dfrac{(x^2)^5 \times x^3y^4}{x^2y^5}$,

**15** $\dfrac{(m^3)^2 \times m^3n}{m^8n^3}$,      **16** $\dfrac{5a^2c \times 2ac^3}{30a^3c^9}$,

**17** $\dfrac{9(mn)^3 \times 2(m^2n)^2}{24m^8n^2}$,      **18** $\dfrac{(x^2y^3)^3 \times (xy^3)^2}{x^8y^{15}}$,

**19** $\dfrac{6x^3y^2z \times 5x^2yz^4}{(x^2yz^3)^2}$,      **20** $\dfrac{4(ab)^4 \times (2ab^2)^3}{16(abc)^5}$.

# 1.4 Negative indices

Consider the expression      $a^4 \div a^6$

Now

$$a^4 \div a^6 = \frac{a \times a \times a \times a}{a \times a \times a \times a \times a \times a} = \frac{1}{a \times a} = \frac{1}{a^2}$$

but if we use **the division rule** and subtract the powers we get

$$a^4 \div a^6 = a^{4-6} = a^{-2}$$

> We have simplified the expression using two different methods but the answers must be the same.

Therefore      $a^{-2} = \dfrac{1}{a^2}$

Similarly, we can show that

$$a^{-1} = \frac{1}{a} \quad a^{-3} = \frac{1}{a^3} \quad a^{-4} = \frac{1}{a^4} \text{ etc.}$$

In general, we have

---
the negative index rule

$$a^{-n} = \frac{1}{a^n}$$

---

You often make use of the fact that when there is a negative power you take the reciprocal. For example because $2^3 = 8$, we can write $2^{-3} = \dfrac{1}{8}$.

# 1.5 The zero index

Consider the expression $a^5 \div a^5$

Now

$$a^5 \div a^5 = \frac{a \times a \times a \times a \times a}{a \times a \times a \times a \times a}$$

> Everything cancels top and bottom.

but using **the division law** we can simply subtract the indices to find the new index.

$$a^5 \div a^5 = a^{5-5} = a^0$$

$$a^0 = 1$$

> In other words, any non-zero number raised to the power of 0 is equal to 1.

We can apply these rules to expressions involving numbers rather than letters.

## *Worked example 1.3*

Without using a calculator, evaluate

**1** $73^0$,            **2** $\left(\dfrac{3}{4}\right)^{-2}$,            **3** $(-4)^{-3}$

## *Solution*

**1** $73^0 = 1$

> Any non-zero number raised to the power of 0 is equal to 1.

**2 Method 1**    $\left(\dfrac{3}{4}\right)^{-2} = \dfrac{3^{-2}}{4^{-2}} = \left(\dfrac{1}{9}\right) \div \left(\dfrac{1}{16}\right) = \dfrac{16}{9}$

     **Method 2**    Since $\left(\dfrac{3}{4}\right)^2 = \dfrac{16}{9}$ we can use the reciprocal idea

                 and so $\left(\dfrac{3}{4}\right)^{-2} = \dfrac{16}{9}$

> $a^{-2} = \dfrac{1}{a^2}$

**3** $(-4)^{-3} = (-1)^{-3}(4)^{-3} = -1 \times \dfrac{1}{4^3} = -\dfrac{1}{64}$

> Make sure you deal with the negative sign.

## *Worked example 1.4*

Simplify

**1** $\dfrac{2^7 \times 2^3}{4^3}$,            **2** $\dfrac{15^3}{5^2 \times 3^5}$

     without using a calculator

## Solution

1
$$\frac{2^7 \times 2^3}{4^3} = \frac{2^7 \times 2^3}{(2^2)^3} = \frac{2^{10}}{2^6} = 2^4 = 16$$

[ Multiplication rule ]
[ 4 is a power of 2 ]
[ Power rule ]
[ Division rule ]

Notice that we have not had to use a calculator!

2
$$\frac{15^3}{5^2 \times 3^5} = \frac{(5 \times 3)^3}{5^2 \times 3^5} = \frac{5^3 \times 3^3}{5^2 \times 3^5} = \frac{5^1}{3^2} = \frac{5}{9}$$

We could have worked with negative indices here and obtained $5^1 \times 3^{-2} = \dfrac{5}{9}$.

You can check your answer using a calculator but be careful to use brackets for the denominator.

Back to algebra again.

## Worked example 1.5

Simplify the following expressions as much as possible

1 $\dfrac{(x^2)^{-2}}{x^{-7}}$,

2 $\dfrac{(p^{-2}q^3)^{-3}}{p^4 q^{-7}}$.

## Solution

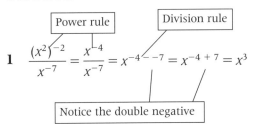

1
$$\frac{(x^2)^{-2}}{x^{-7}} = \frac{x^{-4}}{x^{-7}} = x^{-4 - -7} = x^{-4 + 7} = x^3$$

[ Power rule ]
[ Division rule ]
[ Notice the double negative ]

Cannot be simplified any further.

2
$$\frac{(p^{-2}q^3)^{-3}}{p^4 q^{-7}} = \frac{p^6 q^{-9}}{p^4 q^{-7}} = p^{6-4}q^{-9 - -7} = p^2 q^{-9 + 7}$$
$$= p^2 q^{-2}$$

You may not like leaving your answer with negative indices and might prefer $\dfrac{p^2}{q^2}$.
Either form is acceptable for your final answer.

## EXERCISE 1C

1 Write each of the following as a prime number raised to a particular power

(a) 16,     (b) 27,     (c) 125,     (d) 1,

(e) 49,     (f) $\dfrac{1}{8}$,     (g) $\dfrac{1}{81}$,     (h) $\dfrac{1}{3}$,

(i) $\dfrac{1}{121}$,     (j) $\dfrac{1}{289}$,     (k) $\dfrac{1}{128}$.

**2** Express each of the following in a form without indices, without using your calculator

(a) $2^{-1}$,      (b) $3^0$,      (c) $5^4$,      (d) $7^{-2}$,

(e) $(-13)^0$,      (f) $(-5)^{-3}$,      (g) $12^{-1}$,      (h) $(-3)^{-2}$,

(i) $(5^2)^{-1}$,      (j) $(3^{-2})^{-1}$.

**3** Simplify each of the following without using a calculator

(a) $\dfrac{2^3}{4^2}$,      (b) $\dfrac{(3^2)^3}{9^5}$,      (c) $\dfrac{2^3 \times 3^4}{6^3}$,

(d) $\dfrac{5^7}{125^3}$,      (e) $\dfrac{12^3}{4^2 \times 3^5}$,      (f) $\dfrac{20^7 \times 5^5}{4^{10} \times 25^6}$.

**4** Simplify each of the following

(a) $(x^5)^{-2}$,                     (b) $(a^{-3})^{-7}$,

(c) $(a^3 b^2)^0$,                (d) $(c^{-3} d^4)^5$,

(e) $x^{-9} \div x^3$,              (f) $a^{-9} \div a^{-7}$,

(g) $p^{-8} \div p^3$,              (h) $25p^5 \div (5p^{-7})$,

(i) $28a^{-3} \div 7a^{-5}$,        (j) $13a^{14} \div (a^6)^3$,

(k) $14(a^{-3})^5 \div 2a^{-9}$,    (l) $16(p^{-2})^4 \div 8p^{-8}$,

(m) $8(y^2)^3 \div 2y^{-6}$,       (n) $28(x^2)^{-9} \div 4(x^{-2})^{10}$,

(o) $15p^{-2}q^{-7} \div (5pq^{-3})$,    (p) $21a^3 b^{-5} c \div (7a^{-4} bc^{-3})$,

(q) $15(a^3 b)^{-3} \div (5ab^{-5})$,    (r) $16a^{-2} b^2 c^{-3} \times 2(abc)^{-2}$,

(s) $3a^{-2} bc^{-3} \times a^{-2} bc \div (2a^{-2} bc^{-5})$,

(t) $9xy^{-4} \times 4x^{-5} yz^{-4} \div [6(x^{-2} yz)^{-2}]$.

**5** Simplify

(a) $\dfrac{x^{-5} \times x^7}{x^{-3}}$,      (b) $\dfrac{y^{-3} \times y \times y^2}{y^3}$,      (c) $\dfrac{(p^{-2})^3}{p^{-5}}$,

(d) $\dfrac{r^5 \div r^8}{r^3}$,      (e) $(t^5 u^6)^{-3} \times (t^7 u^{20})$,      (f) $\dfrac{(pq)^7}{(pq^2)^4}$,

(g) $\dfrac{(a^2 b^3)^{-2}}{(a^{-3} \div b^5)}$

# 1.6 Fractional indices

It is very useful to be able to write $\sqrt{\phantom{a}}$ and $\sqrt[3]{\phantom{a}}$, and so on, as powers so that you can use the rules that we have already obtained.

Assume that $\sqrt{a}$ can be written using a power as $a^x$.
We need to find the value of $x$.

We know that

$$\sqrt{a} \times \sqrt{a} = a$$

so

$$a^x \times a^x = a^1$$

Using one of the index laws that we know gives

$$a^{2x} = a^1$$

This means that

$$2x = 1$$

and so

$$x = \frac{1}{2}.$$

Therefore, $\sqrt{a}$ can be written as $a^{\frac{1}{2}}$

So, we know that $\qquad a^{\frac{1}{2}} = \sqrt{a} \quad$ (square root)

similarly $\qquad\qquad a^{\frac{1}{3}} = \sqrt[3]{a} \quad$ (cube root)

In general

$$a^{\frac{1}{n}} = \sqrt[n]{a} \quad (n\text{th root})$$

## Worked example 1.6

**1** Write down the exact value of $27^{\frac{1}{3}}$ and $16^{\frac{1}{4}}$.

**2** Find the value of the fifth root of 1200 giving your answer to three significant figures.

## Solution

**1** $27^{\frac{1}{3}} = \sqrt[3]{27} = 3 \qquad$ (since $3 \times 3 \times 3 = 27$)

$16^{\frac{1}{4}} = \sqrt[4]{16} = 2 \qquad$ (since $2 \times 2 \times 2 \times 2 = 16$)

Notice that we did not need a calculator to evaluate these expressions.

**2** We need to express the fifth root as an index before we can work out its value on a calculator.

$$\sqrt[5]{1200} = 1200^{\frac{1}{5}} = 4.1289179\ldots$$

$$\approx 4.13 \text{ (to three significant figures)}$$

If you did not obtain this answer then you almost certainly forgot to put the power $\frac{1}{5}$ in brackets. Of course you could always use the index 0.2

## Other fractional indices

What about $a^{\frac{2}{3}}$?

$$a^{\frac{2}{3}} = a^{2 \times \frac{1}{3}} = (a^2)^{\frac{1}{3}} \qquad \text{(using the fact that } a^{m \times n} = (a^m)^n)$$

$$\Rightarrow \qquad a^{\frac{2}{3}} = \sqrt[3]{a^2}$$

or
$$a^{\frac{2}{3}} = a^{\frac{1}{3} \times 2} = (a^{\frac{1}{3}})^2$$

$$\Rightarrow \qquad a^{\frac{2}{3}} = (\sqrt[3]{a})^2$$

In general

$$a^{\frac{m}{n}} = \sqrt[n]{a^m} \text{ or } (\sqrt[n]{a})^m$$

## Worked example 1.7

Evaluate the following without using a calculator

**1** $64^{-\frac{1}{3}}$,              **2** $\left(\dfrac{25}{9}\right)^{-\frac{3}{2}}$,            **3** $\left(\dfrac{16}{81}\right)^{\frac{1}{4}}$.

## Solution

**1** $64^{-\frac{1}{3}} = \dfrac{1}{64^{\frac{1}{3}}} = \dfrac{1}{\sqrt[3]{64}} = \dfrac{1}{4}$,

**2** $\left(\dfrac{25}{9}\right)^{-\frac{3}{2}} = \left(\dfrac{9}{25}\right)^{\frac{3}{2}} = \left(\sqrt{\dfrac{9}{25}}\right)^3 = \left(\dfrac{3}{5}\right)^3 = \dfrac{27}{125}$,

**3** $\left(\dfrac{16}{81}\right)^{\frac{1}{4}} = \dfrac{16^{\frac{1}{4}}}{81^{\frac{1}{4}}} = \dfrac{\sqrt[4]{16}}{\sqrt[4]{81}} = \dfrac{2}{3}$.

## Worked example 1.8

Simplify each of the following expressions as far as possible.

**1** $\sqrt[3]{a^4 b^5} \times \dfrac{b^{\frac{1}{3}}}{a}$,          **2** $\dfrac{\sqrt[4]{xy^2} \times \sqrt[3]{xy}}{x^2 y}$

## Solution

**1** $\sqrt[3]{a^4 b^5} \times \dfrac{b^{\frac{1}{3}}}{a} = \sqrt[3]{a^4} \times \sqrt[3]{b^5} \times \dfrac{b^{\frac{1}{3}}}{a}$

$$= a^{\frac{4}{3}} \times b^{\frac{5}{3}} \times b^{\frac{1}{3}} \times a^{-1} = a^{\frac{1}{3}} b^2$$

**2** $\dfrac{\sqrt[4]{xy^2} \times \sqrt[3]{xy}}{x^2y} = \dfrac{x^{\frac{1}{4}} \times y^{\frac{2}{4}} \times x^{\frac{1}{3}} \times y^{\frac{1}{3}}}{x^2y}$

$$= \dfrac{x^{\frac{7}{12}} \times y^{\frac{5}{6}}}{x^2y} = x^{\frac{7}{12}-2} \times y^{\frac{5}{6}-1} = x^{-\frac{17}{12}}y^{-\frac{1}{6}}$$

# 1.7 Solving equations with indices

We are now in a position to solve certain equations where the unknown quantity is either a power or forms part of the power.

## Worked example 1.9

Solve the following equations.

**1** $9^{x+1} = 3$,  **2** $2^{3x} \times 4^{(x+1)} = 64$.

## Solution

**1** $9^{x+1} = 3$

So,  $9^{x+1} = 9^{\frac{1}{2}}$

$\Rightarrow x + 1 = \dfrac{1}{2}$.

Giving $x = -\dfrac{1}{2}$.

> Considering the RHS of the equation, 3 can be expressed as a power of 9, since $9^{\frac{1}{2}} = 3$, (or $\sqrt{9} = 3$).

> Both sides of the equation now have the same **base**.

> Equating the powers.

## Alternative solution:

We could also express 9 as a power of 3 as follows:

$9^{x+1} = 3 \Rightarrow (3^2)^{(x+1)} = 3$

so that $2(x + 1) = 1$

and $x = -\dfrac{1}{2}$, as before.

> Don't forget that 3 can be written as $3^1$.

**2** $2^{3x} \times 4^{(x+1)} = 64$

$2^{3x} \times 2^{2(x+1)} = 64$   $\boxed{4 = 2^2}$

and hence $2^{5x+2} = 64$.

But $64 = 2^6$

and so we can equate the indices

$$5x + 2 = 6 \Rightarrow x = \dfrac{4}{5}.$$

> If you expressed every term as a power of 4 ($4^{\frac{1}{2}} = 2$) then you would still get the same answer. Try it and see.

## EXERCISE 1D

**1** Work these out without using a calculator.

(a) $4^{\frac{3}{2}}$,

(b) $100^{\frac{5}{2}}$,

(c) $27^{\frac{2}{3}}$,

(d) $1000^{1\frac{1}{3}}$,

(e) $16^{\frac{5}{4}}$,

(f) $32^{0.4}$.

**2** Write these as fractions.

(a) $16^{-\frac{1}{2}}$,

(b) $4^{-1\frac{1}{2}}$,

(c) $125^{-\frac{4}{3}}$,

(d) $\left(\dfrac{4}{49}\right)^{-\frac{1}{2}}$,

(e) $\left(\dfrac{125}{8}\right)^{\frac{2}{3}}$,

(f) $\left(1\frac{7}{9}\right)^{\frac{1}{2}}$,

(g) $\left(\dfrac{16}{25}\right)^{-\frac{1}{2}}$,

(h) $\left(\dfrac{27}{64}\right)^{\frac{2}{3}}$,

(i) $\left(2\frac{7}{81}\right)^{\frac{1}{2}}$.

**3** Simplify the following as far as possible.

(a) $\dfrac{\sqrt[3]{x} \times \sqrt[3]{x^4}}{x^{-\frac{1}{3}}}$,

(b) $(\sqrt{a})^3 \times (\sqrt{a^7})$,

(c) $\dfrac{x^2 \times \sqrt{x^5}}{x^{-\frac{1}{2}}}$,

(d) $\dfrac{(\sqrt[3]{y})^2 \times (y^2)^{\frac{1}{3}}}{\sqrt[3]{y}}$,

(e) $\dfrac{\sqrt[6]{a} \times a^{\frac{2}{3}}}{\sqrt[4]{a}}$,

(f) $\dfrac{\sqrt{xy} \times \sqrt[3]{x} \times 2\sqrt[4]{y}}{(x^{10}y^9)^{\frac{1}{12}}}$.

**4** Solve the following equations

(a) $3^{x-2} = \dfrac{1}{27}$,

(b) $5^{3x} \times 25^{x-2} = 1$,

(c) $7^{3x+1} = 49$,

(d) $2^{3x-1} \times 8^{x-1} = 128$.

**5** Solve the equation

$$\dfrac{81^x}{27^{2x+1}} = \dfrac{9^{2x-5}}{729}.$$

**6** Fermat stated that every whole number could be expressed as the sum of no more than four squares, so that, for example

$$15 = 3^2 + 2^2 + 1^2 + 1^2$$
$$139 = 9^2 + 7^2 + 3^2$$
$$327 = 13^2 + 10^2 + 7^2 + 3^2$$

Do you think he was correct? Can you find a general formula for those numbers that require the sum of at least four squares to make up the number itself?

## Key point summary

1  $a^m \times a^n = a^{m+n}$ $\qquad$ p2

2  $a^m \div a^n = a^{m-n}$ $\qquad$ p3

3  $(a^m)^n = a^{m \times n}$ $\qquad$ p3

4  $a^{-n} = \dfrac{1}{a^n}$ $\qquad$ p5

5  $a^0 = 1$ $\qquad$ p6

6  $a^{\frac{1}{n}} = \sqrt[n]{a}$ $\qquad$ p9

7  $a^{\frac{m}{n}} = \sqrt[n]{a^m}$ or $(\sqrt[n]{a})^m$ $\qquad$ p10

| Test yourself | What to review |
|---|---|
| **1** Simplify each of the following: | *Section 1.3* |

  **(a)** $7 \times s \times s \times s \times s \times t \times t \times t$,

  **(b)** $5y^4 \times 4y^6 \times 3y^2$,

  **(c)** $3a^3 \times 4b^3 \times b \times 6a^2$,

  **(d)** $5p^2q^7 \times q^6 \times 2q^2 \times 3p^4$.

| | |
|---|---|
| **2**  Simplify each of the following: | *Section 1.4* |

  **(a)** $x^{-8} \times x^3$, $\qquad$ **(b)** $y^7 \div y^{-3}$, $\qquad$ **(c)** $\dfrac{p^7 q^{-2}}{p^{-4} q^{-3}}$.

| | |
|---|---|
| **3** Evaluate each of the following without using a calculator: | *Sections 1.5 and 1.6* |

  **(a)** $27^{\frac{1}{3}}$, $\qquad$ **(b)** $\left(\dfrac{5}{8}\right)^{-1}$,

  **(c)** $8^{-\frac{2}{3}}$, $\qquad$ **(d)** $(-23)^0$.

| | |
|---|---|
| **4** Solve the equation: | *Section 1.7* |

$$3^{x+1} \times 9^{1-x} = \dfrac{1}{27}.$$

## Test yourself ANSWERS

**4** $x = 6$.

**3 (a)** 3, $\qquad$ **(b)** $\dfrac{8}{5}$, $\qquad$ **(c)** $\dfrac{1}{4}$, $\qquad$ **(d)** 1.

**2 (a)** $x^{-5}$, $\qquad$ **(b)** $y^{10}$, $\qquad$ **(c)** $p^{11}q$,

**1 (a)** $7s^4t^3$, $\qquad$ **(b)** $60y^{12}$, $\qquad$ **(c)** $72a^5b^4$, $\qquad$ **(d)** $30p^6q^{15}$.

# CHAPTER 2

# Surds

---

## Learning objectives

After studying this chapter, you should be able to:
- distinguish between rational and irrational numbers
- understand what is meant by a surd
- simplify expressions involving surds
- perform arithmetic involving surds.

---

## 2.1 Special sets of numbers

When you learned to count, you started to use the numbers 1, 2, 3, 4, … which are known as natural numbers and denoted by the symbol $\mathbb{N}$.

As the need arose to use zero and negative numbers the set of integers, denoted by $\mathbb{Z} = \{\ldots -3, -2, -1, 0, 1, 2, 3, 4, \ldots\}$, was constructed.

Some numbers such as fractions cannot be written as a whole number. Those which can be written in the form $\frac{a}{b}$, where $a$ and $b$ are integers and $b$ is not equal to zero, are called **rational** numbers and are denoted by $\mathbb{Q}$, since they can be written as the quotient of two integers.

Are these sensible or reasonable numbers?

The term rational is used because these numbers can be written as the **ratio** of two integers

When rational numbers are written as decimals they either terminate such as $\frac{3}{4} = 0.75$ or $\frac{71}{1000} = 0.071$ or they have a sequence of recurring digits such as $\frac{5}{11} = 0.45454545\ldots$ or $\frac{5}{7} = 0.714285714285714\ldots.$

However, numbers that cannot be written as a fraction in the form $\frac{a}{b}$, where $a$ and $b$ are integers, are called **irrational**.

The decimal representation of an irrational number neither terminates nor has a recurring pattern of digits, no matter how many decimal places we write down.

Examples include $\sqrt{3} = 1.73205\ldots$ and $\sqrt[3]{5} = 1.709975947\ldots$ and $\pi = 3.14159\ldots$ which each has a non-repeating pattern of digits in its decimal representation.

The set of rationals combined with the set of irrationals gives us the set of **real numbers** and is denoted by $\mathbb{R}$.

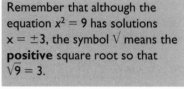

## 2.2 Surds

In mathematics, we often arrive at answers that contain root signs (they may be square roots, cube roots, etc).

We will find that some of these numbers with a root sign are easy to deal with since they have an exact decimal representation.

For instance $\sqrt{16} = 4$, $\sqrt[3]{8} = 2$, $\sqrt{11.56} = 3.4$, $\sqrt[5]{\dfrac{1}{32}} = 0.5$.

This is because each of these numbers is **rational**.

> Expressions with root signs involving irrational numbers such as $\sqrt{7} - 2$ or $\sqrt[3]{5}$ are called **surds**.

Remember that although the equation $x^2 = 9$ has solutions $x = \pm 3$, the symbol $\sqrt{\phantom{x}}$ means the **positive** square root so that $\sqrt{9} = 3$.

*EXERCISE 2A*

State whether each of the following is a rational or irrational number.

**1** $\sqrt{7}$,  **2** $\sqrt{9}$,  **3** $\sqrt{\dfrac{5}{16}}$,  **4** $\sqrt{\dfrac{50}{72}}$,  **5** $\sqrt[3]{64}$,

**6** $\sqrt[3]{\dfrac{8}{27}}$,  **7** $2 - \sqrt[3]{6}$,  **8** $3 + 2^{\frac{1}{5}}$,  **9** $7 + \sqrt{4}$,  **10** $\pi^2$,

Sometimes, you will be required to give answers to problems in surd form since these answers are **exact**. If you use your calculator to get a decimal form, it can only give the answer to a certain number of decimal places and so can only be an approximation.

For example, $\sqrt{3}$ is exact, whereas $1.732050808$ is the full calculator display, but is still only an approximation to $\sqrt{3}$.

### Order of a surd

The **order** of a surd is determined by the root symbol. For example:

$\quad \sqrt{3}$ is a surd of order 2 (sometimes called a quadratic surd)
$\quad \sqrt[3]{5}$ is a surd of order 3
$\quad \sqrt[n]{x}$ is a surd of order $n$.

A rational quantity may be expressed in the form of a root of any required order. For example, $3 = \sqrt{9} = \sqrt[3]{27} = \sqrt[4]{81}$, etc.

A surd of any order may be transformed to a surd of a different order. For example, $\sqrt[5]{3} = 3^{\frac{1}{5}} = 3^{\frac{2}{10}} = \sqrt[10]{3^2} = \sqrt[10]{9}$

Notice the link between indices in the last chapter and surds.

## Worked example 2.1

Write the following surds in ascending size: $\sqrt[4]{9}$, $\sqrt[3]{5}$, $\sqrt[6]{26}$.

### Solution

It is difficult to see which is the biggest at a glance since they are all of a different order.

We can make the surds have the same order as follows:

Firstly, the lowest common multiple (LCM) of 4, 6 and 3 is 12 so we can change them all into surds of order 12.

$$\sqrt[4]{9} = 9^{\frac{1}{4}} = 9^{\frac{3}{12}} = \sqrt[12]{9^3} = \sqrt[12]{729}$$
$$\sqrt[3]{5} = 5^{\frac{1}{3}} = 5^{\frac{4}{12}} = \sqrt[12]{5^4} = \sqrt[12]{625}$$
$$\sqrt[6]{26} = 26^{\frac{1}{6}} = 26^{\frac{2}{12}} = \sqrt[12]{26^2} = \sqrt[12]{676}$$

We can now rearrange the surds, starting with the smallest:

$$\sqrt[3]{5}, \ \sqrt[6]{26}, \ \sqrt[4]{9}$$

In general, we shall be mostly concerned with surds of order 2.

> You could always cheat by typing the numbers into your calculator – but wait until the end and do this only as a check.

> An alternative approach is to let $a = \sqrt[4]{9}$, $b = \sqrt[3]{5}$, $c = \sqrt[6]{26}$.
> $$a^{12} = 9^3 = 729$$
> Then $b^{12} = 5^4 = 625$
> $$c^{12} = 26^2 = 676$$

## 2.3 Simplest form of surds

When simplifying surds, we try to make the number under the root sign as small as possible.

## Worked example 2.2

Simplify the following as far as possible.

**1** $\sqrt{18}$,         **2** $\sqrt[3]{48}$,         **3** $\sqrt{216}$.

> **Hint.** Look for a square number that divides exactly into the number under the square root sign (or a perfect cube if the surd is of order 3, etc.)

### Solution

**1** $\sqrt{18}$

> 9 is a square number that is also a factor of 18.

$$\sqrt{18} = \sqrt{9 \times 2} = \sqrt{9} \times \sqrt{2} = 3\sqrt{2}$$
$$\Rightarrow \quad \sqrt{18} = 3\sqrt{2}$$

> 8 is a perfect cube which is also a factor of 48.

**2** $\sqrt[3]{48}$

$$\sqrt[3]{48} = \sqrt[3]{8 \times 6} = \sqrt[3]{8} \times \sqrt[3]{6} = 2\sqrt[3]{6}$$
$$\Rightarrow \quad \sqrt[3]{48} = 2\sqrt[3]{6}$$

> **Note.** We could have used indices to obtain the same result $(18)^{\frac{1}{2}} = (9 \times 2)^{\frac{1}{2}} = 9^{\frac{1}{2}} \times 2^{\frac{1}{2}} = 3 \times 2^{\frac{1}{2}}$ but the square root sign is more compact.

**3** $\sqrt{216}$

$$\sqrt{216} = \sqrt{4 \times 54} = 2\sqrt{54}$$
$$2\sqrt{54} = 2\sqrt{9 \times 6} = 2\sqrt{9} \times \sqrt{6} = 6\sqrt{6}$$
$$\Rightarrow \quad \sqrt{216} = 6\sqrt{6}$$

> but $\sqrt{54}$ can itself be simplified.

> 4 is a square number that is a factor of 216.

# 2.4 Manipulating square roots

There are some simple rules which apply to all positive numbers and they will help us when working with square roots. The first rule generalises the idea demonstrated in the last worked example.

> **Rules**
> 1 $\sqrt{ab} = \sqrt{a} \times \sqrt{b}$
>
> 2 $\sqrt{\dfrac{a}{b}} = \dfrac{\sqrt{a}}{\sqrt{b}}$

## *Worked example 2.3*

Simplify each of the following surd expressions

1 $\sqrt{112}$,  2 $\dfrac{\sqrt{63}}{3}$,  3 $\sqrt{\dfrac{25}{9}}$  4 $\sqrt{12} \times \sqrt{21}$.

## *Solution*

1 $\sqrt{112} = \sqrt{16 \times 7} = \sqrt{16} \times \sqrt{7} = 4\sqrt{7}$

2 $\dfrac{\sqrt{63}}{3} = \dfrac{\sqrt{9 \times 7}}{3} = \dfrac{3 \times \sqrt{7}}{3} = \sqrt{7}$

3 $\sqrt{\dfrac{25}{9}} = \dfrac{\sqrt{25}}{\sqrt{9}} = \dfrac{5}{3}$

4 $\sqrt{12} \times \sqrt{21} = \sqrt{3} \times \sqrt{4} \times \sqrt{3} \times \sqrt{7}$
$= \sqrt{4} \times (\sqrt{3} \times \sqrt{3}) \times \sqrt{7}$
$= 2 \times 3 \times \sqrt{7} = 6\sqrt{7}$

## *EXERCISE 2B*

Simplify each of the surd expressions **1–18**

1 $\sqrt{8}$,  2 $\sqrt{12}$,  3 $\sqrt{20}$,

4 $\sqrt{75}$,  5 $\sqrt{52}$,  6 $\sqrt{120}$,

7 $\sqrt{245}$,  8 $\sqrt{252}$,  9 $\sqrt{192}$,

10 $\sqrt{1000}$,  11 $\dfrac{\sqrt{27}}{3}$,  12 $\dfrac{\sqrt{32}}{4}$,

13 $\dfrac{\sqrt{125}}{\sqrt{5}}$,  14 $\dfrac{\sqrt{448}}{4}$,  15 $\sqrt{35} \times \sqrt{7}$,

16 $\sqrt{75} \times \sqrt{27}$,  17 $\sqrt{20} \times \sqrt{15} \times \sqrt{6}$,  18 $\dfrac{\sqrt{48} \times \sqrt{14}}{\sqrt{56} \times \sqrt{18}}$.

**19** Express each of the following in the form $\sqrt[k]{p}$ where $k$ is an integer and $p$ is a prime number.

   **(a)** $\sqrt{72} - \sqrt{8}$,

   **(b)** $5\sqrt{28} - \sqrt{63}$,

   **(c)** $2\sqrt{147} - 5\sqrt{48} + \sqrt{75}$.

**20** Arrange the following surds in ascending size.

$$\sqrt[5]{13}, \quad \sqrt[6]{17}, \quad \sqrt[3]{5}, \quad \sqrt[10]{170}.$$

## 2.5 Use in geometry

One of the main areas in which you will need to use surds is in the use of Pythagoras' theorem in geometry. Often you need the exact value of a particular length.

### Worked example 2.4 _____

The hypotenuse of a right-angled triangle has length 18 cm and one of the other sides has length 6 cm. Find the length of the remaining side.

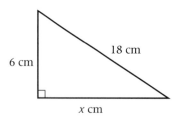

### Solution

Let the remaining side have length $x$ cm. By Pythagoras' theorem

$$x^2 + 6^2 = 18^2 \text{ so that } x^2 = 324 - 36 = 288$$

$$\Rightarrow \quad x = \sqrt{144} \times \sqrt{2} = 12\sqrt{2}$$

so the remaining side has length $12\sqrt{2}$ cm.

> $288 = 144 \times 2$

## 2.6 Like and unlike surds

Like surds have the same irrational factor.
For example $3\sqrt{5}, -6\sqrt{5}, 13\sqrt{5}$ are like surds since they have the same number under the root sign.

Unlike surds have different irrational factors.
For instance, $7\sqrt{3}, 2\sqrt{6}, -4\sqrt{11}$ are unlike surds since they have different numbers under the root sign.

**Student health warning**

It is well worth noting that:

$$\sqrt{a+b} \neq \sqrt{a} + \sqrt{b} \quad \text{and} \quad \sqrt{a-b} \neq \sqrt{a} - \sqrt{b}$$

For example, consider

$$\sqrt{9+16} = \sqrt{25} = 5 \quad ✓$$

However

$$\sqrt{9} + \sqrt{16} = 3 + 4 = 7. \quad ✗$$

This, of course, is not the same and demonstrates that we cannot split up $\sqrt{9+16}$ *as* $\sqrt{9} + \sqrt{16}$. This is a common mistake and must be guarded against.

# 2.7 Adding and subtracting surds

We can add or subtract surds as long as they are 'like' surds.

> Like surds can be 'collected'.
> Unlike surds cannot be 'collected'.

## Worked example 2.5

Simplify each of the following as much as possible.

**(a)** $14\sqrt{5} - 6\sqrt{5}$      **(b)** $\sqrt{75} + 2\sqrt{27} - 5\sqrt{108}$

**(c)** $4\sqrt{3} + 9\sqrt{6}$      **(d)** $5\sqrt{5} + 4\sqrt{3} - 2\sqrt{5} + 7\sqrt{3}$

## Solution

**(a)** $14\sqrt{5} - 6\sqrt{5} = 8\sqrt{5}$

> There are 14 lots of $\sqrt{5}$ minus 6 lots of $\sqrt{5}$ giving 8 lots of $\sqrt{5}$.

**(b)** $\sqrt{75} + 2\sqrt{27} - 5\sqrt{108}$

We first need to simplify these surds as far as possible.
$$= (\sqrt{25} \times \sqrt{3}) + (2 \times \sqrt{9} \times \sqrt{3}) - (5 \times \sqrt{36} \times \sqrt{3})$$
$$= 5\sqrt{3} + 2 \times 3\sqrt{3} - 5 \times 6\sqrt{3}$$
$$= 5\sqrt{3} + 6\sqrt{3} - 30\sqrt{3}$$

These are all like surds and, therefore, can be collected.

**(c)** $4\sqrt{3} + 9\sqrt{6}$

> $\sqrt{3}$ and $\sqrt{6}$ are 'unlike' surds and, therefore, cannot be collected so this expression cannot be simplified any further.

**(d)** $5\sqrt{5} + 4\sqrt{3} - 2\sqrt{5} + 7\sqrt{3}$

We can collect all the terms with $\sqrt{5}$ and then separately collect the terms with $\sqrt{3}$
$$= 5\sqrt{5} - 2\sqrt{5} + 4\sqrt{3} + 7\sqrt{3}$$
$$= 3\sqrt{5} + 11\sqrt{3}$$

> Note that we cannot combine these any further since $\sqrt{5}$ and $\sqrt{3}$ are 'unlike' surds.

**EXERCISE 2C**

Simplify each of the expressions from 1 to 10 as far as possible.

**1** $\sqrt{7} - 3\sqrt{7}$,  **2** $\sqrt{12} + \sqrt{3}$,

**3** $\sqrt{20} - 3\sqrt{5}$,  **4** $\sqrt{72} + \sqrt{12}$,

**5** $\sqrt{8} + \sqrt{18}$,  **6** $\sqrt{12} + \sqrt{108} - \sqrt{27}$,

**7** $\sqrt{20} - \sqrt{245} + 3\sqrt{5}$,  **8** $4\sqrt{6} - 3\sqrt{24} + \sqrt{150}$,

**9** $15\sqrt{45} - 3\sqrt{20} - \sqrt{180}$,  **10** $3\sqrt{175} + 6\sqrt{18} - 3\sqrt{28} + 4\sqrt{72}$.

**11** The two shorter sides of a right-angled triangle have lengths 3 m and 6 m. Find the length of the hypotenuse in the form $a\sqrt{b}$ metres, where $a$ and $b$ are prime numbers.

**12** The hypotenuse of a right-angled triangle has length 24 cm and another one of the sides has length 18 cm. Find the exact length of the third side.

**13** Find the length of the remaining side in each of the right-angled triangles below, giving your answers as simply as possible in surd form.

**(a)**
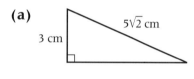

**(b)**
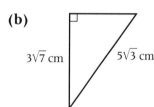

# 2.8 Multiplying surds

We multiply the rational factors then the irrational factors and then simplify (if possible).

## Worked example 2.6

Simplify each of the following:

**1** $3\sqrt{2} \times 5\sqrt{3}$,  **2** $2\sqrt{3} \times 3\sqrt{3}$,  **3** $5\sqrt{6} \times 3\sqrt{3}$.

## Solution

**1** $3\sqrt{2} \times 5\sqrt{3} = 3 \times 5 \times \sqrt{2} \times \sqrt{3} = 15\sqrt{6}$

**2** $2\sqrt{3} \times 3\sqrt{3} = 6\sqrt{9} = 6 \times 3 = 18$

**3** $5\sqrt{6} \times 3\sqrt{3} = 15\sqrt{18}$
$$= 15 \times \sqrt{9} \times \sqrt{2}$$
$$= 45\sqrt{2}$$

> You should be able to recognise that $\sqrt{3} \times \sqrt{3} = 3$ and in general $\sqrt{n} \times \sqrt{n} = n$.

An expression such as $\sqrt{3} + \sqrt{5}$ is called a **compound surd**.

To multiply compound surds, we use the same idea as multiplying out brackets in algebra.

> **Recall that**
> $$(a + b)(c + d) = ac + bc + bd + ad$$

**2**

## Worked example 2.7

Simplify each of the following.

**1** $(\sqrt{3} + \sqrt{5})(\sqrt{2} + \sqrt{3})$,  **2** $(3 + \sqrt{2})(5 - \sqrt{7})$,

**3** $(4\sqrt{2} - 3\sqrt{5})(3\sqrt{2} - 2\sqrt{5})$  **4** $(3 + \sqrt{5})^2$.

## Solution

**1** $(\sqrt{3} + \sqrt{5})(\sqrt{2} + \sqrt{3}) = \sqrt{6} + \sqrt{10} + \sqrt{9} + \sqrt{15}$
$$= \sqrt{6} + \sqrt{10} + 3 + \sqrt{15}$$

**2** $(3 + \sqrt{2})(5 - \sqrt{7}) = 15 - 3\sqrt{7} + 5\sqrt{2} - \sqrt{14}$

**3** $(4\sqrt{2} - 3\sqrt{5})(3\sqrt{2} - 2\sqrt{5}) = 12\sqrt{4} - 8\sqrt{10} - 9\sqrt{10} + 6\sqrt{25}$
$$= 24 - 8\sqrt{10} - 9\sqrt{10} + 30$$
$$= 54 - 17\sqrt{10}$$

**4** $(3 + \sqrt{5})^2 = (3 + \sqrt{5})(3 + \sqrt{5})$
$$= 9 + 3\sqrt{5} + 3\sqrt{5} + 5$$
$$= 14 + 6\sqrt{5}$$

## EXERCISE 2D

Multiply out the following and simplify the answers as far as possible.

**1** $5\sqrt{3} \times 2\sqrt{6}$,

**2** $6\sqrt{10} \times 5\sqrt{2}$,

**3** $\sqrt{5}(\sqrt{6} - 2)$

**4** $\sqrt{8}(\sqrt{2} + \sqrt{8})$,

**5** $2\sqrt{5}(3 + 6\sqrt{5})$,

**6** $(3 + \sqrt{2})(7 - \sqrt{3})$,

**7** $(\sqrt{5} - \sqrt{3})(\sqrt{5} + \sqrt{3})$,

**8** $(3\sqrt{6} - \sqrt{7})(\sqrt{6} + 2\sqrt{7})$,

**9** $(\sqrt{10} - 2)(\sqrt{10} + 2)$,

**10** $(4\sqrt{11} - 2\sqrt{3})(3\sqrt{11} + 2)$.

# 2.9 Rationalising the denominator

Whenever we have a fraction in which the denominator is a surd, we can rewrite the fraction so that the denominator no longer contains a surd.

This is done by multiplying the top and bottom of the fraction by the same number so that the final answer has a **rational number in the denominator**.

Since $(2 + \sqrt{3})(2 - \sqrt{3}) = 2^2 - (\sqrt{3})^2 = 1$, we could simplify $\dfrac{4}{2 + \sqrt{3}}$ by writing $\dfrac{4}{2 + \sqrt{3}} \times \dfrac{2 - \sqrt{3}}{2 - \sqrt{3}} = 4(2 - \sqrt{3})$.

This process is called '**rationalising the denominator**'.
The method is as follows.

> If the denominator is of the form $\sqrt{a}$ then multiply the top and bottom by $\sqrt{a}$.
>
> If the denominator is of the form $a + \sqrt{b}$ then multiply top and bottom by $a - \sqrt{b}$.
>
> If the denominator is of the form $a - \sqrt{b}$ then multiply top and bottom by $a + \sqrt{b}$.

Since $\sqrt{3} \times \sqrt{3} = 3$, we could simplify $\dfrac{2}{\sqrt{3}}$ by writing

$$\frac{2}{\sqrt{3}} = \frac{2}{\sqrt{3}} \times \frac{\sqrt{3}}{\sqrt{3}} = \frac{2\sqrt{3}}{3}$$

Since $(p - q)(p + q) = p^2 - q^2$

## *Worked example 2.8*

Rationalise the denominators of the following:

**1** $\dfrac{4}{\sqrt{7}}$,    **2** $\dfrac{3}{3 - \sqrt{6}}$,    **3** $\dfrac{1}{\sqrt{11} + \sqrt{7}}$    **4** $\dfrac{\sqrt{6} + 3\sqrt{2}}{\sqrt{5} + 2\sqrt{3}}$.

## *Solution*

**1** $\dfrac{4}{\sqrt{7}}$.

Multiply the top and bottom by $\sqrt{7}$.

$$\frac{4}{\sqrt{7}} \times \left(\frac{\sqrt{7}}{\sqrt{7}}\right) = \frac{4\sqrt{7}}{\sqrt{49}} = \frac{4\sqrt{7}}{7}$$

$$\Rightarrow \quad \frac{4}{\sqrt{7}} = \frac{4\sqrt{7}}{7}$$

We now have a rational number in the denominator.

**2** $\dfrac{3}{3 - \sqrt{6}}$.

$$\frac{3}{(3 - \sqrt{6})} \times \frac{(3 + \sqrt{6})}{(3 + \sqrt{6})} = \frac{3(3 + \sqrt{6})}{9 - 6} = \frac{3(3 + \sqrt{6})}{3} = 3 + \sqrt{6}$$

$$\Rightarrow \quad \frac{3}{3 - \sqrt{6}} = 3 + \sqrt{6}$$

Multiply the top and bottom by $(3 + \sqrt{6})$.

**3** $\dfrac{1}{\sqrt{11} + \sqrt{7}}$.

Multiply the top and bottom by $(\sqrt{11} - \sqrt{7})$.

$$\frac{1}{(\sqrt{11} + \sqrt{7})} \times \frac{(\sqrt{11} - \sqrt{7})}{(\sqrt{11} - \sqrt{7})} = \frac{\sqrt{11} - \sqrt{7}}{\sqrt{121} - \sqrt{49}} = \frac{\sqrt{11} - \sqrt{7}}{4}$$

$$\Rightarrow \quad \frac{1}{\sqrt{11} + \sqrt{7}} = \frac{\sqrt{11} - \sqrt{7}}{4}$$

> **Note**. The number that we multiply the top and bottom by in order to rationalise the denominator is sometimes called the **conjugate**.
>
> The conjugate of $\sqrt{11} + \sqrt{7}$ is $\sqrt{11} - \sqrt{7}$.
>
> The conjugate of $8 - 3\sqrt{5}$ is $8 + 3\sqrt{5}$.

**4** $\dfrac{\sqrt{6} + 3\sqrt{2}}{\sqrt{5} + 2\sqrt{3}}$.

$$\frac{(\sqrt{6} + 3\sqrt{2})}{(\sqrt{5} + 2\sqrt{3})} \times \frac{(\sqrt{5} - 2\sqrt{3})}{(\sqrt{5} - 2\sqrt{3})} = \frac{\sqrt{30} - 2\sqrt{18} + 3\sqrt{10} - 6\sqrt{6}}{\sqrt{25} - 4\sqrt{9}}$$

$$= \frac{\sqrt{30} - 6\sqrt{2} + 3\sqrt{10} - 6\sqrt{6}}{-7}$$

> Multiply top and bottom by the conjugate $(\sqrt{5} - 2\sqrt{3})$.

$$\Rightarrow \quad \frac{\sqrt{6} + 3\sqrt{2}}{\sqrt{5} + 2\sqrt{3}} = \frac{\sqrt{30} - 6\sqrt{2} + 3\sqrt{10} - 6\sqrt{6}}{-7}$$

$$= \frac{6\sqrt{2} + 6\sqrt{6} - \sqrt{30} - 3\sqrt{10}}{7}$$

> Although this answer is perfectly correct, it is customary to try to leave a positive denominator, where possible.

## EXERCISE 2E

Rationalise the denominators of the following:

**1** $\dfrac{1}{\sqrt{10}}$,

**2** $\dfrac{3}{\sqrt{2}}$,

**3** $\dfrac{\sqrt{7}}{2\sqrt{5}}$,

**4** $\dfrac{1}{\sqrt{2} - 1}$,

**5** $\dfrac{3}{\sqrt{21} - 3}$,

**6** $\dfrac{2}{\sqrt{5} - \sqrt{2}}$,

**7** $\dfrac{5}{\sqrt{14} + 2}$,

**8** $\dfrac{\sqrt{6}}{\sqrt{6} + \sqrt{3}}$,

**9** $\dfrac{\sqrt{7} + 5}{\sqrt{7} + \sqrt{3}}$,

**10** $\dfrac{2\sqrt{3} + \sqrt{7}}{5\sqrt{3} + \sqrt{7}}$,

**11** $\dfrac{\sqrt{13} + \sqrt{5}}{\sqrt{13} - \sqrt{5}}$,

**12** $\dfrac{10\sqrt{5}}{2\sqrt{15} - \sqrt{5}}$,

**13** $\dfrac{4\sqrt{2} + \sqrt{5}}{4\sqrt{2} - \sqrt{5}}$,

**14** $\dfrac{2\sqrt{2} + 4\sqrt{7}}{5\sqrt{2} - 3\sqrt{7}}$.

## Worked examination question

Express $\dfrac{4 + 5\sqrt{3}}{2 + 7\sqrt{3}}$ in the form $p + q\sqrt{3}$ where $p$ and $q$ are rational numbers.

## Solution

$$\frac{4 + 5\sqrt{3}}{2 + 7\sqrt{3}} \times \frac{2 - 7\sqrt{3}}{2 - 7\sqrt{3}}$$

$$= \frac{8 - 28\sqrt{3} + 10\sqrt{3} - 35(3)^2}{4 - 49(\sqrt{3})^2}$$

$$= \frac{8 - 105 - 18\sqrt{3}}{4 - 147}$$

$$= \frac{-97 - 18\sqrt{3}}{-143}$$

$$= \frac{97}{143} + \frac{18\sqrt{3}}{143}$$

which is in the given form $p = \dfrac{97}{143}$ and $q = \dfrac{18}{143}$.

> We need to rationalise the denominator and do this by multiplying top and bottom by $2 - 7\sqrt{3}$.

> A common mistake is to think that $(\sqrt{3})^2$ is 9.

> This would now score full marks, but it is good to state the actual values of $p$ and $q$.

## MIXED EXERCISE

**1** Simplify the following as far as possible:

  (a) $\sqrt{75}$,

  (b) $\sqrt{300}$,

  (c) $\sqrt{128}$,

  (d) $\sqrt{28} - \sqrt{175} + \sqrt{63}$,

  (e) $\sqrt{128} + \sqrt{98} - \sqrt{32}$,

  (f) $\sqrt{24} - \sqrt{216} + \sqrt{150}$.

**2** Expand the following and simplify where possible.

  (a) $\sqrt{3}(5 - 2\sqrt{3})$,

  (b) $\sqrt{5}(3 + \sqrt{45})$,

  (c) $\sqrt{2}(\sqrt{50} - \sqrt{18})$,

  (d) $(\sqrt{3} - 2)(\sqrt{3} + 7)$,

  (e) $(\sqrt{5} - 7)(3\sqrt{5} + 4)$,

  (f) $(3 + 2\sqrt{3})^2$.

**3** Rationalise the denominator, simplifying where possible:

  (a) $\dfrac{7\sqrt{3}}{\sqrt{5}}$,

  (b) $\dfrac{1}{\sqrt{3} - 1}$,

  (c) $\dfrac{\sqrt{5} + 1}{\sqrt{5} - 1}$,

  (d) $\dfrac{1}{\sqrt{13} - \sqrt{11}}$,

  (e) $\dfrac{11}{3\sqrt{3} + 7}$,

  (f) $\dfrac{5\sqrt{3} - 1}{3 + 2\sqrt{3}}$,

  (g) $\dfrac{5 - 3\sqrt{2}}{2\sqrt{2} + 3}$,

  (h) $\dfrac{\sqrt{7}}{\sqrt{2}(\sqrt{14} - \sqrt{7})}$.

**4** Express each of the following in the form $p + q\sqrt{2}$ where $p$ and $q$ are rational.

(a) $(3 - \sqrt{2})^2$,  (b) $\dfrac{1}{(3 - \sqrt{2})^2}$. [A]

**5 (a)** Write down:
  (i) a rational number which lies between 4 and 5.
  (ii) an irrational number which lies between 4 and 5.

(b) A student says: 'When you multiply two irrational numbers together the answer is always an irrational number'.

Simplify $(2 + \sqrt{3})(2 - \sqrt{3})$ and comment on the student's statement. [A]

**6** Express each of the following in the form $p + q\sqrt{7}$ where $p$ and $q$ are rational numbers.

(a) $(2 + 3\sqrt{7})(5 - 2\sqrt{7})$,  (b) $\dfrac{(5 + \sqrt{7})}{(3 - \sqrt{7})}$. [A]

## Key point summary

**1** A rational number is one which can be written in the form $\dfrac{a}{b}$, where $a$ and $b$ are integers. *p14*

**2** A real number that is not rational is called irrational. Its decimal representation neither terminates nor has a recurring pattern of digits. *p14*

**3** A surd is an irrational number containing a root sign. *p15*

**4** $\sqrt{ab} = \sqrt{a} \times \sqrt{b}$. *p17*

**5** $\sqrt{\dfrac{a}{b}} = \dfrac{\sqrt{a}}{\sqrt{b}}$. *p17*

**6** Like surds can be 'collected'. Unlike surds cannot be 'collected'. *p19*

**7** To rationalise the denominator of the form $\sqrt{a}$, multiply top and bottom by $\sqrt{a}$. *p22*

**8** To rationalise the denominator of the form $a + \sqrt{b}$, multiply top and bottom by $a - \sqrt{b}$. *p22*

**9** To rationalise the denominator of the form $a - \sqrt{b}$, multiply top and bottom by $a + \sqrt{b}$. *p22*

| Test yourself | What to review |
|---|---|
| **1** State whether each of the following is rational or irrational: | *Section 2.1* |
|     **(a)** $\sqrt[3]{8}$,     **(b)** $\dfrac{1}{\sqrt{3}}$,     **(c)** $\dfrac{2 + \sqrt{3}}{5}$,     **(d)** $\dfrac{\sqrt{12}}{\sqrt{3}}$. | |
| **2** Simplify each of the surd expressions below: | *Sections 2.3 and 2.4* |
|     **(a)** $\sqrt{27} \times \sqrt{6}$,     **(b)** $\dfrac{\sqrt{90}}{\sqrt{15}}$,     **(c)** $\dfrac{\sqrt{3} \times \sqrt{15}}{6}$. | |
| **3** Simplify each of the following surd expressions as far as possible. | *Section 2.7* |
|     **(a)** $\sqrt{27} - 2\sqrt{3}$,     **(b)** $\sqrt{20} + \sqrt{45}$,     **(c)** $\dfrac{\sqrt{13} - \sqrt{7}}{2}$. | |
| **4** Find the length of the hypotenuse of a right-angled triangle if the two smaller sides have lengths $3\sqrt{3}$ cm and $3\sqrt{5}$ cm. | *Section 2.5* |
| **5** Rationalise the denominator of the expression: $$\dfrac{9\sqrt{6} - 8}{\sqrt{6} - 1}.$$ | *Section 2.9* |

**Test yourself** ANSWERS

**5** $\dfrac{46 + \sqrt{6}}{5}$.

**4** $6\sqrt{2}$ cm.

**3 (a)** $\sqrt{3}$,     **(b)** $5\sqrt{5}$,     **(c)** cannot simplify.

**2 (a)** $9\sqrt{2}$,     **(b)** $\sqrt{6}$,     **(c)** $\dfrac{\sqrt{5}}{2}$.

**1 (a)** rational,     **(b)** irrational,     **(c)** irrational,     **(d)** rational.

# CHAPTER 3
# Linear equations and inequalities

## Learning objectives

After studying this chapter, you should be able to:
- solve simple linear equations
- solve linear equations involving surds and indices
- solve simultaneous linear equations
- solve linear inequalities.

## 3.1 Solving linear equations

> An equation of the form $ax + b = 0$, where $a$ and $b$ are constants, is said to be a **linear equation** with **variable** $x$.

> The method of solving linear equations is to collect all the terms involving $x$ on to one side of the equation and everything else on to the other side.

### *Worked example 3.1*

Solve each of the following equations:

**1** $5x - 3 = 2x + 15$,

**2** $3x - 5 + 7x + 3 = 5x - 11 + 3x - 7$,

**3** $5(x + 3) + 4(2x - 3) = 2(2x + 15)$.

### *Solution*

**1** $5x - 3 = 2x + 15$
$\Rightarrow 5x - 2x = 15 + 3$
$\Rightarrow 3x = 18$
$\Rightarrow x = 6$

> Collect all the terms involving $x$ onto one side of the equation.

**2** $3x - 5 + 7x + 3 = 5x - 11 + 3x - 7$
$\Rightarrow 3x - 5x + 7x - 3x = 5 - 11 - 3 - 7$
$\Rightarrow 2x = -16$
$\Rightarrow x = -8$

**3** $5(x + 3) + 4(2x - 3) = 2(2x + 15)$

$\Rightarrow 5x + 15 + 8x - 12 = 4x + 30$

$\Rightarrow 5x + 8x - 4x = 30 - 15 + 12$

$\Rightarrow 9x = 27$

$\Rightarrow x = 3$

> You can check the answer is correct by substituting back into the original equation:
>
> right-hand side $= 2 \times 21 = 42$
> left-hand side $= 5 \times 6 + 4 \times 3 = 42$ ✓

**Note.** The logical proof symbol $\Rightarrow$ meaning 'implies' has been used at each step. Beware of using a 'trailing equal sign' as you proceed from one line to the next. In each of the solutions above, the argument is valid if you work back from the last line to the first, and so we could have used the symbol $\Leftrightarrow$ in place of $\Rightarrow$.

> Sometimes the linear equations are disguised because they involve fractions. A good strategy is to multiply every term by the lowest common multiple of the denominators.

## *Worked example 3.2*

Solve the equation $\dfrac{x - 5}{4} - \dfrac{4 - x}{3} = 5$

## *Solution*

$\dfrac{x - 5}{4} - \dfrac{4 - x}{3} = 5$

Multiply through by 12.

$\Rightarrow \dfrac{12(x - 5)}{4} - \dfrac{12(4 - x)}{3} = 12 \times 5$

$\Rightarrow 3(x - 5) - 4(4 - x) = 60$

$\Rightarrow 3x - 15 - 16 + 4x = 60$

$\Rightarrow 3x + 4x = 60 + 15 + 16$

$\Rightarrow 7x = 91$

$\Rightarrow x = 13$

> Notice the need to introduce brackets around the terms being multiplied. A common error is to leave these out and then the minus sign causes problems.

## An historical problem

The earliest book on algebra using a mathematical notation to represent equations was called *Arithmetica* and was written by the Greek Diophantus around 250 CE in Alexandria. An interesting problem posed in a collection called the *Greek Anthology* allows us to calculate the age he lived if we form and solve an algebraic equation.

## Worked example 3.3

'Diophantus passed one-sixth of his life as a boy, one-twelfth in youth, and one seventh as a bachelor. Five years after his marriage he was granted a son who died four years before his father, at half the measure of his father's life.' How long did Diophantus live?

## Solution

Let the age when Diophantus died be $x$ years.

$\dfrac{x}{6} + \dfrac{x}{12} + \dfrac{x}{7} + 5$ is the age when his son was born

so if we add the son's age when he died, namely $\dfrac{x}{2}$, this must give us the age of Diophantus at that time, which must be $x - 4$.

Hence, the equation to allow us to solve the problem is

$$\frac{x}{6} + \frac{x}{12} + \frac{x}{7} + 5 + \frac{x}{2} = x - 4$$

$\Rightarrow 14x + 7x + 12x + 420 + 42x = 84x - 336$

$\Rightarrow 75x + 756 = 84x$

$\Rightarrow 756 = 9x \qquad \Rightarrow x = 84$

So Diophantus lived to the age of 84.

> Multiply throughout by 84 to clear the fractions.

## Worked example 3.4

Solve the equation $\dfrac{7}{x + 1} = \dfrac{8}{x - 2}$

## Solution

$$\frac{7}{x + 1} = \frac{8}{x - 2}$$

Multiply through by $(x + 1)(x - 2)$

$\Rightarrow \dfrac{7(x + 1)(x - 2)}{(x + 1)} = \dfrac{8(x + 1)(x - 2)}{(x - 2)}$

$\Rightarrow 7(x - 2) = 8(x + 1)$

$\Rightarrow 7x - 14 = 8x + 8$

$\Rightarrow 7x - 8x = 8 + 14$

$\Rightarrow -x = 22$

$\Rightarrow x = -22$

> Notice that we can cancel the algebraic factors $(x + 1)$ and $(x - 2)$ but only when they are at the top and bottom of the same expression.

> You could have made use of the fact that
> $$\frac{a}{b} = \frac{c}{d} \Rightarrow a \times d = c \times b$$
> (sometimes known as cross-multiplication) and obtained this equation directly from the original equation.

## *EXERCISE 3A*

Solve each of the equations in questions **1–12**.

**1** $3x - 4 = 2(7 - x),$

**2** $4 - 3x + 7x - 8 = 3x + 5 - x,$

**3** $5x - 17 + 3x = 3(5 - 2x),$

**4** $15 - 3x + 7(x - 2) = 3(x - 4),$

**5** $\dfrac{7x - 1}{5} = \dfrac{3(5 + 2x)}{3},$

**6** $\dfrac{7x - 8}{3} = \dfrac{3x + 5}{2},$

**7** $\dfrac{3x - 1}{2} - \dfrac{2(4 + 3x)}{13} = 2,$

**8** $\dfrac{2x + 3}{5} - \dfrac{5x + 2}{8} + 1 = 0,$

**9** $\dfrac{5}{2x + 1} = \dfrac{4}{x + 2},$

**10** $\dfrac{3}{2x - 5} = \dfrac{7}{3 - 5x},$

**11** $\dfrac{10}{3x + 1} = \dfrac{1}{2x - 5},$

**12** $\dfrac{5}{3x - 7} = \dfrac{2}{4 - 3x}.$

**13** A quadrilateral has three of its sides of lengths $x$, $2x - 5$ and $3x + 8$ cm. The fourth side has a length equal to one-third of the sum of the other three sides. Find the value of $x$ if the total perimeter is 45 cm.

**14** I am thinking of my age. When I multiply it by 7, subtract 3 and divide by 8 and then take away one-third of my age I get an answer of 11. What is my age?

**15** I have a number of sweets in a bag. If I removed three of them and divided the number remaining by 4, I would have two fewer than if I removed 7 and divided the number remaining by 3. How many sweets do I have?

# 3.2 Solving simultaneous linear equations

We shall be concerned primarily with two equations in two variables such as $x$ and $y$, and this idea will be used extensively in the next chapter to find points of intersection of straight lines.

> In the equation $3x - 5y = 7$, the coefficient of $x$ is **3** and the coefficient of $y$ is $-5$.

> The first example of solving simultaneous linear equations demonstrates the method of **elimination** where the coefficients of one of the variables are made equal and then the two equations are added or subtracted in order to eliminate one of the variables.

## Worked example 3.5 ────────────────

Solve the simultaneous equations

$$2x + 3y = 13$$
$$7x - 5y = -1$$

## Solution

$$2x + 3y = 13 \qquad (A)$$
$$7x - 5y = -1 \qquad (B)$$

> We label the equations $A$ and $B$, say, so that we can refer to the equations in our working.

**3**

Make the coefficients of $y$ the same:   multiply $(A)$ by 5
                                                multiply $(B)$ by 3

$$10x + 15y = 65 \qquad (C)$$
$$21x - 15y = -3 \qquad (D)$$

Adding equations $(C) + (D)$ gives

$$31x = 62$$
$$\Rightarrow x = 2$$

> We could have chosen to multiply $(A)$ by 7 and $(B)$ by 2 and obtained
> $$14x + 21y = 91$$
> $$14x - 10y = -2$$
> We would then subtract the two equations to give $31y = 93$, and hence $y = 3$.

Substitute $x = 2$ into equation $(A)$

$$4 + 3y = 13$$
$$\Rightarrow y = 3.$$

The solution is $x = 2$, $y = 3$.

> Another method of solving simultaneous linear equations involves rearranging one of the equations and substituting into the other. This technique is called the method of **substitution**.

## Worked example 3.6 ────────────────

Solve the simultaneous equations

$$7x + 2y = 11$$
$$4x - y = 7$$

## Solution

$$7x + 2y = 11 \qquad (A)$$
$$4x + y = 7 \qquad (B)$$

$$y = 7 - 4x$$

> Rearrange $(B)$ to make $y$ the subject.

Substitute $(7 - 4x)$ for $y$ in equation $(A)$

$$\Rightarrow 7x + 2(7 - 4x) = 11$$
$$\Rightarrow 7x + 14 - 8x = 11$$
$$\Rightarrow x = 3. \quad \Rightarrow y = 7 - 4(3) = -5$$

The solution is $x = 3$, $y = -5$.

## EXERCISE 3B

Solve the following pairs of simultaneous equations.

**1** $5x + 2y = 11$, $4x + 3y = 13$,

**2** $3x - 2y = 8$, $7x + 3y = 11$,

**3** $4x - 7y = 13$, $3x - 5y = 9$,

**4** $x - 7y = -11$, $3x + 4y = -8$,

**5** $3x + 2y = 10$, $4x + 7y = 12$,

**6** $5x - 8y = -3$, $3x + 2y = 1$,

**7** $3x + 2y + 5 = 0$, $4x + 7y + 3 = 0$,

**8** $5x + 4y + 5 = 3x - 7y$, $4(x + 3y) + 3 = 5x$,

**9** $x + 4(y - 1) = 3(x - 3) + 2y$, $3(x - y) = 5(x - 1)$,

**10** $\dfrac{x + 2y}{x - 3} = 2$, $\dfrac{x - 7}{2y + 3} = 5$.

# 3.3 Equations involving indices and surds

This section reviews some of the techniques considered in the previous two chapters.

An equation may look more complicated because it involves indices or surds when a simple substitution shows it to be linear.

## *Worked example 3.7*

Solve the following equations

**1** $x^5 - 7 = 2(1 - x^5)$,   **2** $\sqrt[3]{2x} + 11 = 7 - \sqrt[3]{2x}$.

## *Solution*

**1** $x^5 - 7 = 2(1 - x^5)$

Let $y = x^5$

$\Rightarrow y - 7 = 2(1 - y)$

$\Rightarrow y - 7 = 2 - 2y$

$\Rightarrow 3y = 9 \Rightarrow y = 3$

so we have $x^5 = 3$

$\Rightarrow x = \sqrt[5]{3}$ *or* $x = 3^{\frac{1}{5}}$

> With a little experience you will not need to make this substitution and will work with $x^5$ as a single quantity – writing $3x^5 = 9 \Rightarrow x^5 = 3$, but initially the substitution might help you.

> Either answer is correct and you should see that they are equivalent.

**2**  $\sqrt[3]{2x} + 11 = 7 - \sqrt[3]{2x}$

Let $y = \sqrt[3]{2x}$

$\Rightarrow y + 11 = 7 - y$

$\Rightarrow 2y = -4 \Rightarrow y = -2$

$\Rightarrow \sqrt[3]{2x} = -2$  — Cubing both sides.

$\Rightarrow 2x = -8$

$\Rightarrow x = -4$

## Worked example 3.8

Solve the $\sqrt{5} + 3x = 2\sqrt{5}x - 7$

## Solution

$\sqrt{5} + 3x = 2\sqrt{5}x - 7$

$\Rightarrow \sqrt{5} + 7 = 2\sqrt{5}x - 3x = (2\sqrt{5} - 3)x$

$\Rightarrow \dfrac{\sqrt{5} + 7}{2\sqrt{5} - 3} = x$

$\Rightarrow x = \dfrac{\sqrt{5} + 7}{2\sqrt{5} - 3} \times \dfrac{2\sqrt{5} + 3}{2\sqrt{5} + 3}$

$\Rightarrow x = \dfrac{10 + 14\sqrt{5} + 3\sqrt{5} + 21}{20 - 9} = \dfrac{31 + 17\sqrt{5}}{11}$

> Although this answer is now correct it is better if we rationalise the denominator.

## EXERCISE 3C

Solve each of the following, where possible.

**1** $3x^3 - 5 = 7x^3 + 11,$

**2** $4x^5 + 3 = 5(x^5 + 1),$

**3** $5x^2 + 3(2x^2 + 1) = 7x^2 + 12,$

**4** $2x^2 + 13 = x^2 + 1,$

**5** $\dfrac{x^5 - 8}{4} = \dfrac{10 + x^5}{7},$

**6** $3\sqrt{x} + 17 = 32 - 2\sqrt{x},$

**7** $5x^{\frac{1}{3}} - 7 = 3(x^{\frac{1}{3}} - 5),$

**8** $\dfrac{3x^{-1} + 7}{4} = \dfrac{2 - x^{-1}}{5},$

**9** $7\sqrt{3} - 3x = 5\sqrt{3}x - 6,$

**10** $6\sqrt{7} - 2x = 5 + 3\sqrt{7}x.$

# 3.4 Linear inequalities

We solve linear inequalities in very much the same way as linear equations. However, instead of the $=$ sign, we use one of the following signs:

| | |
|---|---|
| $>$ greater than | $<$ less than |
| $\geq$ greater than or equal to | $\leq$ less than or equal to |

The solution, rather than having a single value, is in the form of an interval of values such as $x > 2$, for example.

> In a single inequality, it is customary to present the final result with the variable on the left-hand side so that a solution
>
> $$2 < x$$
>
> is usually rewritten as
>
> $$x > 2.$$

## Worked example 3.9

Solve the inequality $3(x + 2) > x - 1$.

## Solution

$3(x + 2) > x - 1$
$\Rightarrow 3x + 6 > x - 1$
$\Rightarrow 3x - x > -1 - 6$
$\Rightarrow \quad 2x > -7$
$\Rightarrow \quad\quad x > -3\frac{1}{2}$

> The answer means that any value of $x$ greater than $-3\frac{1}{2}$ is part of the solution interval.

It is always good to check that the solution is correct. Choose a value of $x$ greater than $-3\frac{1}{2}$, such as $-2$ for example, and test to see that it satisfies the original inequality.

Left-hand side $= 3(x + 2) = 3(-2 + 2) = 0$
Right-hand side $= x - 1 = -2 - 1 = -3$

Is $0 > -3$? Yes, so we have confidence in our solution.

> **Important difference between solving equations and inequalities**
>
> Whenever we multiply or divide an inequality by a **negative** number we must **reverse** the inequality sign.

So, for example, if we have $-3y > -6$ then $y < 2$.

> You can verify this with a value for y such as 1 since $-3 > -6$ and $1 < 2$.

## Worked example 3.10

Solve the inequality $2(3 - 4x) \leq 5 - 2(3x + 5)$

## Solution

$2(3 - 4x) \leq 5 - 2(3x + 5)$
$\Rightarrow \quad 6 - 8x \leq 5 - 6x - 10$
$\Rightarrow 6x - 8x \leq 5 - 6 - 10$
$\Rightarrow \quad -2x \leq -11$
$\Rightarrow \quad\quad x \geq 5\frac{1}{2}$

> Dividing by $-2$ so we need to reverse the inequality sign.

**Note.** On the third line of the solution we could have collected the terms involving $x$ on the right instead of the left-hand side and the solution would have been written as:

$$6 - 5 + 10 \leqslant 8x - 6x$$

$$\Rightarrow \qquad 11 \leqslant 2x$$

$$\Rightarrow \qquad 5\tfrac{1}{2} \leqslant x \Rightarrow x \geqslant 5\tfrac{1}{2}$$

## EXERCISE 3D

Solve the inequalities in questions **1–8**.

**1**   $3(x - 3) < 2x + 7,$          **2**   $2(3x - 5) \leqslant 8x - 3,$

**3**   $7x + 9 > 5x + 3(x - 1),$      **4**   $7(2x + 1) > -3 - 5x,$

**5**   $\dfrac{7x - 1}{5} > 2\dfrac{(5 + 2x)}{3},$       **6**   $\dfrac{7x - 8}{3} \geqslant \dfrac{3x + 5}{2},$

**7**   $\dfrac{4(x - 2)}{3} > \dfrac{5(3 - x)}{2},$      **8**   $\dfrac{3x - 1}{5} - \dfrac{x + 1}{2} \leqslant 3.$

**9**   A rectangular plot of land has dimensions $2x + 3$ metres by $5x - 4$ metres. Explain why $x > \dfrac{4}{5}$.

     Given that the perimeter is less than 40 metres, find another inequality satisfied by $x$.

**10**   A piece of string has length $x$ cm. A second piece needs to be double the length of the first plus an extra 5 cm. A third piece is obtained by doubling the length of the second piece and subtracting 20 cm. The total length of the three pieces must be less than 1 m. Find two inequalities satisfied by $x$.

## Key point summary

**1**   A linear equation is of the form $ax + b = 0$.      *p27*

**2**   To solve a linear equation, collect all the terms involving $x$ on to one side of the equation.      *p27*

**3**   If equations involve fractions try multiplying through by the LCM of the denominators.      *p28*

**4**   Simultaneous linear equations can be solved by elimination or by substitution.      *p30*

**5**   The method of substitution enables simultaneous linear equations to be solved by rearranging one of the equations and substituting into the other.      *p31*

**6** Inequalities can be handled like equations but      *p34*
remember to reverse the inequality sign whenever you
multiply or divide by a negative number.

| Test yourself | What to review |
|---|---|
| **1** Solve the equation $$3x - 2 = 5 - 2x$$ | *Section 3.1* |
| **2** Solve the simultaneous equations $$3x + 7y = 15$$ $$5x - 2y = -16$$ | *Section 3.1* |
| **3** Solve the equation $$x^{-1} + 7 = 5(5 - x^{-1})$$ | *Section 3.1* |
| **4** Solve the inequality $$5(2x - 1) > 3(1 + 5x)$$ | *Section 3.1* |

**Test yourself** ANSWERS

**4** $x > -\dfrac{8}{5}$.

**3** $x = \dfrac{1}{3}$.

**2** $x = -2, y = 3$.

**1** $x = \dfrac{7}{5}$.

# CHAPTER 4

# Coordinate geometry

---

## Learning objectives

After studying this chapter, you should be able to:
- use the language of coordinate geometry
- find the distance between two given points
- find the coordinates of the mid-point of a line segment joining two given points
- find, use and interpret the gradient of a line segment
- know the relationship between the gradients for parallel and for perpendicular lines
- find the equations of straight lines given (a) the gradient and $y$-intercept, (b) the gradient and a point, and (c) two points
- verify, given their coordinates, that points lie on a line
- find the coordinates of a point of intersection of two lines
- find the fourth vertex of a parallelogram given the other three.

---

Coordinate geometry is the use of algebraic methods to study the geometry of straight lines and curves.

## 4.1 Cartesian coordinates

In your GCSE course you plotted points in two dimensions. This section revises that work and builds up the terminology required.

> Named after René Descartes (1596–1650), the French mathematician.

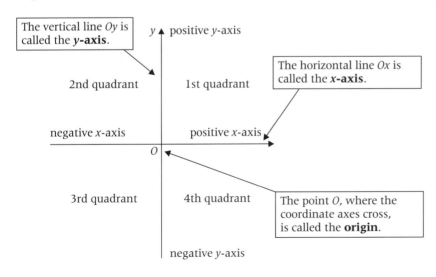

The vertical line $Oy$ is called the **y-axis**.

positive $y$-axis

The horizontal line $Ox$ is called the **x-axis**.

2nd quadrant

1st quadrant

negative $x$-axis

positive $x$-axis

3rd quadrant

4th quadrant

The point $O$, where the coordinate axes cross, is called the **origin**.

negative $y$-axis

> The plane is divided up into **four quadrants** by extending two perpendicular lines called the **coordinate axes** $Ox$ and $Oy$.

In the diagram below, the point P lies in the first quadrant.

Its distance from the y-axis is a.
Its distance from the x-axis is b.

We say that:

the **x-coordinate** of P is a
the **y-coordinate** of P is b.

We write 'P is the point (a, b)' or simply 'the point P(a, b)'.

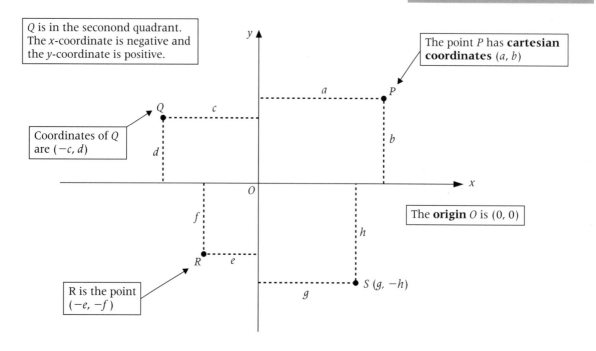

Q is in the seconond quadrant. The x-coordinate is negative and the y-coordinate is positive.

The point P has **cartesian coordinates** (a, b)

Coordinates of Q are (−c, d)

R is the point (−e, −f)

The **origin** O is (0, 0)

The diagram below shows part of the cartesian grid, where L is the point (−2, 3).

The x-coordinate of L is −2 and the y-coordinate of L is 3.

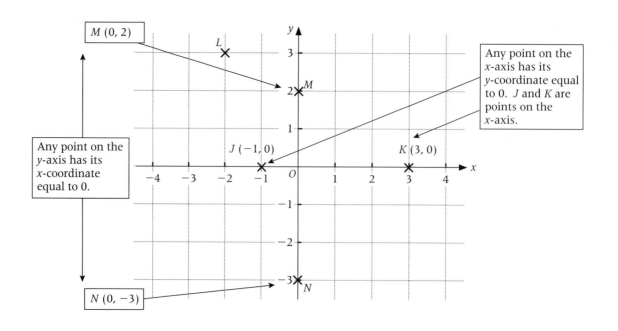

M (0, 2)

Any point on the x-axis has its y-coordinate equal to 0. J and K are points on the x-axis.

Any point on the y-axis has its x-coordinate equal to 0.

N (0, −3)

## *Worked example 4.1*

1 Draw coordinate axes $Ox$ and $Oy$ and plot the points
   $A(1, 2)$, $B(-3, 3)$, $C(1, -4)$ and $D(-2, -4)$

2 The line joining the points $C$ and $D$ crosses the $y$-axis at the point $E$. Write down the coordinates of $E$.

3 The line joining the points $A$ and $C$ crosses the $x$-axis at the point $F$. Write down the coordinates of $F$.

## *Solution*

1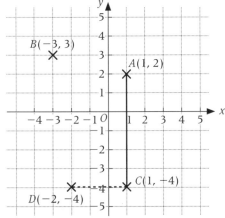

From the diagram in Worked example 4.1, you can see that the distance between the points $C(1, -4)$ and $D(-2, -4)$ is 3 units and the distance between the points $A(1, 2)$ and $C(1, -4)$ is 6 units, but how do you find the distance between points which do not lie on horizontal or vertical lines?

2 $E$ is on the $y$-axis so its $x$-coordinate is 0.   $E(0, -4)$.

3 $F$ is on the $x$-axis so its $y$-coordinate is 0.   $F(1, 0)$.

# 4.2 Distance between two points

The following example shows how you can use Pythagoras' theorem which you studied as part of your GCSE course in order to find the distance between two points.

## *Worked example 4.2*

Find the distance $AB$ where $A$ is the point $(1, 2)$ and $B$ is the point $(4, 4)$.

## *Solution*

First plot the points, join them with a line and make a right-angled triangle $ABC$.

The distance $AC = 4 - 1 = 3$.
The distance $BC = 4 - 2 = 2$.

Using Pythagoras' theorem   $AB^2 = 3^2 + 2^2$.
$$= 9 + 4 = 13$$
$$AB = \sqrt{13}$$

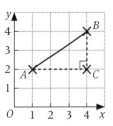

In order to get a numerical idea of this distance you could use your calculator and find that $AB \approx 3.61$ (to three significant figures).

We can generalise the method of the previous example to find a formula for the distance between the points $P(x_1, y_1)$ and $Q(x_2, y_2)$.

The distance $PR = x_2 - x_1$.
The distance $QR = y_2 - y_1$.

Using Pythagoras' theorem

$$PQ^2 = (x_2 - x_1)^2 + (y_2 - y_1)^2$$
$$PQ = \sqrt{[(x_2 - x_1)^2 + (y_2 - y_1)^2]}.$$

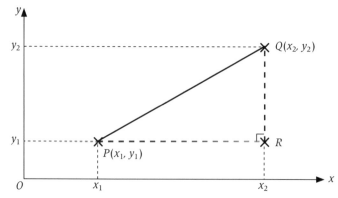

The distance between the points $(x_1, y_1)$ and $(x_2, y_2)$ is
$$\sqrt{(x_2 - x_1)^2 + (y_2 - y_1)^2}.$$

## Worked example 4.3

Find the distance $RS$ where $R$ is the point $(-1, 2)$ and $S$ is the point $(5, -6)$.

### Solution

The difference between the $x$-coordinates is $5 - (-1) = 6$.
The difference between the $y$-coordinates is $-6 - (2) = -8$.

$$RS = \sqrt{(6)^2 + (-8)^2} = \sqrt{36 + 64} = \sqrt{100} = 10$$

If you drew a diagram you would probably find yourself dealing with distances rather than the difference in coordinates in order to avoid negative numbers. This is not wrong.

Of course you could have considered the differences as $-1 - 5 = -6$ and $2 - (-6) = 8$ and obtained the same answer.

## Worked example 4.4

The distance $MN$ is 5, where $M$ is the point $(4, -2)$ and $N$ is the point $(a, 2a)$. Find the two possible values of the constant $a$.

You may prefer to draw a diagram but it is also good to learn to work algebraically.

### Solution

The difference between the $x$-coordinates is $a - 4$.
The difference between the $y$-coordinates is $2a - (-2) = 2a + 2$.

$$MN^2 = (a - 4)^2 + (2a + 2)^2$$
$$5^2 = (a - 4)^2 + (2a + 2)^2$$
$$25 = a^2 - 8a + 16 + 4a^2 + 8a + 4$$
$$25 = 5a^2 + 20$$
$$\Rightarrow a^2 = 1$$
$$\Rightarrow a = \pm 1.$$

Using $(x + y)^2 = x^2 + 2xy + y^2$.

Notice that this equation does have **two** solutions.

## EXERCISE 4A

1 Find the lengths of the line segments joining:

(a) $(0, 0)$ and $(3, 4)$,  (b) $(1, 2)$ and $(5, 3)$,

(c) $(0, 4)$ and $(5, 1)$,  (d) $(-3, 1)$ and $(-1, 6)$,

(e) $(4, -2)$ and $(3, 0)$,  (f) $(3, -2)$ and $(6, 1)$,

(g) $(-2, 7)$ and $(3, -1)$,  (h) $(-2, 0)$ and $(6, -3)$,

(i) $(-1.5, 0)$ and $(3.5, 0)$  (j) $(-3.5, 2)$ and $(4, -8)$

2 Calculate the lengths of the sides of the triangle $ABC$ and hence determine whether or not the triangle is right-angled.

(a) $A(0, 0)$, $B(0, 6)$, $C(4, 3)$

(b) $A(3, 0)$, $B(1, 8)$, $C(-7, 6)$

(c) $A(1, 2)$, $B(3, 4)$, $C(0, 7)$.

> From Question 2 onwards you are advised to draw a diagram.
> In longer questions, the results found in one part often help in the next part.

**4**

3 The distance between the two points $A(6, 2p)$ and $B(p, -3)$ is $5\sqrt{5}$. Find the possible values of $p$.

4 The vertices of a triangle are $P(1, 3)$, $Q(-2, 0)$ and $R(4, 0)$.

(a) Find the lengths of the sides of triangle $PQR$.

(b) Show that angle $QPR = 90°$.

(c) The line of symmetry of triangle $PQR$ meets the $x$-axis at point $S$. Write down the coordinates of $S$.

(d) The point $T$ is such that $PQTR$ is a square. Find the coordinates of $T$.

# 4.3 Coordinates of the mid-point of a line segment joining two known points

From the diagram you can see that the mid-point of the line segment joining $(0, 0)$ to $(6, 0)$ is $(3, 0)$ or

$$\left(\frac{0 + 6}{2}, 0\right)$$

the mid-point of the line segment joining $(0, 0)$ to $(0, -4)$ is $(0, -2)$

$$\text{or } \left(0, \frac{0 + (-4)}{2}\right)$$

the mid-point of the line segment joining $(0, -4)$ to $(6, 0)$ is $(3, -2)$

$$\text{or } \left(\frac{0 + 6}{2}, \frac{(-4) + 0}{2}\right)$$

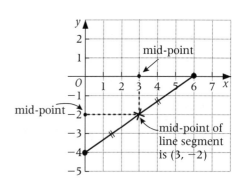

Going from $P(1, 2)$ to $Q(5, 8)$ you move 4 units horizontally and then 6 vertically.

If $M$ is the mid-point of $PQ$ then the journey is halved so to go from $P(1, 2)$ to $M$ you move 2 (half of 4) horizontally and then 3 (half of 6) vertically.

So $M$ is the point $(1 + 2, 2 + 3)$ or $M(3, 5)$ or $M\left(\dfrac{1+5}{2}, \dfrac{2+8}{2}\right)$.

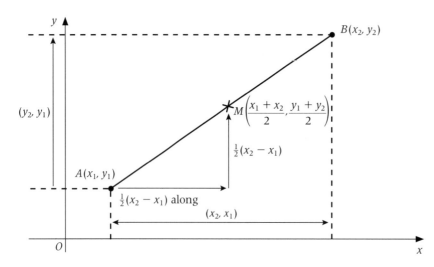

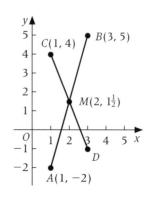

Check that $M$ to $Q$ is also 2 along and then 3 up.

Note that $x_1 + \frac{1}{2}(x_2 - x_1) = \frac{1}{2}(x_1 + x_2)$ which is the $x$-coordinate of $M$.

> In general, the coordinates of the mid-point of the line segment joining $(x_1, y_1)$ and $(x_2, y_2)$ are
> $$\left(\frac{x_1 + x_2}{2}, \frac{y_1 + y_2}{2}\right).$$

## Worked example 4.5

$M$ is the mid-point of the line segment joining $A(1, -2)$ and $B(3, 5)$.

**1** Find the coordinates of $M$.

**2** $M$ is also the mid-point of the line segment $CD$ where $C(1, 4)$. Find the coordinates of $D$.

## Solution

**1** Using $\left(\dfrac{x_1 + x_2}{2}, \dfrac{y_1 + y_2}{2}\right)$, $M$ is the point $\left(\dfrac{1+3}{2}, \dfrac{-2+5}{2}\right)$
so $M(2, 1\frac{1}{2})$.

**2** Let $D$ be the point $(a, b)$ then the mid-point of $CD$ is

$$\left(\frac{a+1}{2}, \frac{b+4}{2}\right) = (2, 1\tfrac{1}{2}) \quad \boxed{\text{coordinates of } M}$$

For this to be true $\dfrac{a+1}{2} = 2$ and $\dfrac{b+4}{2} = \dfrac{3}{2} \Rightarrow a = 3$ and $b = -1$.

The coordinates of $D$ are $(3, 1)$.

> Or, using the idea of 'journeys': $C$ to $M$ is 1 across and $2\tfrac{1}{2}$ down. So $M$ to $D$ is also 1 across and $2\tfrac{1}{2}$ down giving $D(2 + 1, 1\tfrac{1}{2} - 2\tfrac{1}{2})$ or $D(3, -1)$.

## EXERCISE 4B

**1** Find coordinates of the mid-point of the line segments joining:

**(a)** $(3, 2)$ and $(7, 2)$,

**(b)** $(1, -2)$ and $(1, 3)$,

**(c)** $(0, 3)$ and $(6, 1)$,

**(d)** $(-3, 3)$ and $(-1, 6)$,

**(e)** $(4, -2)$ and $(3, 6)$,

**(f)** $(-3, -2)$ and $(-6, 1)$,

**(g)** $(-2, 5)$ and $(2, -1)$,

**(h)** $(-2, 5)$ and $(6, -3)$,

**(i)** $(-1.5, 6)$ and $(3.5, 0)$

**(j)** $(-3.5, 2)$ and $(4, -1)$

**2** $M$ is the mid-point of the straight line segment $PQ$. Find the coordinates of $Q$ for each of the cases:

**(a)** $P(2, 2)$, $M(3, 4)$,  **(b)** $P(2, 1)$, $M(3, 3)$,

**(c)** $P(2, 3)$, $M(1, 5)$,  **(d)** $P(-2, -5)$, $M(3, 0)$,

**(e)** $P(-2, 4)$, $M(1, 2\tfrac{1}{2})$,  **(f)** $P(-1, -3)$, $M(2\tfrac{1}{2}, -4\tfrac{1}{2})$.

**3** The mid-point of $AB$, where $A(3, -1)$ and $B(4, 5)$, is also the mid-point of $CD$, where $C(0, 1)$.

**(a)** Find the coordinates of $D$.

**(b)** Show that $AC = BD$.

**4** The mid-point of the line segment joining $A(-1, 3)$ and $B(5, -1)$ is $D$. The point $C$ has coordinates $(4, 4)$. Show that $CD$ is perpendicular to $AB$.

# 4.4 The gradient of a straight line joining two known points

The gradient of a straight line is a measure of how steep it is.

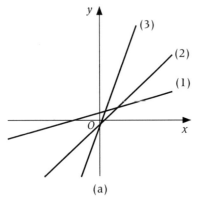

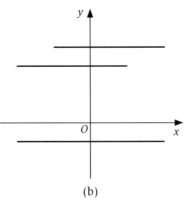

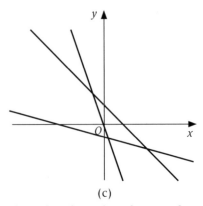

(a)

(b)

(c)

These three lines slope upwards from left to right. They have gradients which are positive. Line (2) is steeper than line (1) so the gradient of (2) is greater than the gradient of (1).

These three lines are all parallel to the *x*-axis. They are not sloping. Horizontal lines have gradient = 0.

These three lines slope downwards from left to right. They have gradients which are negative.

The gradient of the line joining two points $= \dfrac{\text{change in } y\text{-coordinate}}{\text{change in } x\text{-coordinate}}$

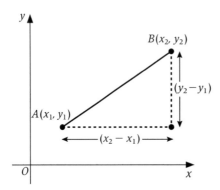

The gradient of the line joining the two points $A(x_1, y_1)$ and $B(x_2, y_2)$ is

$$\frac{y_2 - y_1}{x_2 - x_1}$$

Lines which are equally steep are parallel.

Parallel lines have equal gradients.

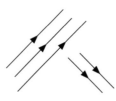

## Worked example 4.6

$O(0, 0)$, $P(3, 6)$, $Q(0, 5)$ and $R(-2, 1)$ are four points.

**1** Find the gradient of the line segment  **(a)** $OP$,  **(b)** $RQ$,

**2** Find the gradient of the line segment  **(a)** $OR$,  **(b)** $PQ$,

**3** What can you deduce from your answers?

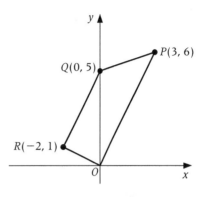

## Solution

**1 (a)** Gradient of $OP = \dfrac{6 - 0}{3 - 0} = 2$;

**(b)** Gradient of $RQ = \dfrac{1 - 5}{-2 - 0} = 2$

**2 (a)** Gradient of $OR = \dfrac{1 - 0}{-2 - 0} = -\dfrac{1}{2}$;

**(b)** Gradient of $PQ = \dfrac{5 - 6}{0 - 3} = \dfrac{1}{3}$

> A diagram is very helpful. You should try to position the points roughly in the correct place without plotting the points on graph paper then you might see properties such as parallel lines and possible right angles.

**3** The lines $OP$ and $RQ$ have gradients which are equal so they are parallel. Lines $OR$ and $PQ$ are not parallel since their gradients are not equal.

So we can deduce that the quadrilateral $OPQR$ is a trapezium.

### EXERCISE 4C

**1** By finding the gradients of the lines $AB$ and $CD$ determine if the lines are parallel.

**(a)** $A(2, 3)$,  $B(3, 5)$,  $C(0, 1)$,  $D(1, 3)$

**(b)** $A(3, 2)$,  $B(5, 1)$,  $C(-4, -3)$,  $D(-2, -2)$

**(c)** $A(-4, 5)$,  $B(4, 5)$,  $C(-1, -2)$,  $D(0, -2)$

**(d)** $A(-6, -3)$,  $B(1, -2)$,  $C(3\frac{1}{2}, 0)$,  $D(7, \frac{1}{2})$.

**2** By finding the gradients of the lines $AB$ and $BC$ show that $A(-2, 3)$, $B(2, 2)$ and $C(6, 1)$ are collinear points.

> 'Collinear' means 'in a straight line'.

**3** $A(1, -3)$, $B(4, -2)$ and $C(6\frac{1}{2}, 0)$ are the vertices of triangle $ABC$.

**(a)** Find the gradient of each side of the triangle.

**(b)** Which side of the triangle is parallel to $OP$ where $O$ is the origin and $P$ is the point $(-11, -6)$?

# 4.5 The gradients of perpendicular lines

(a)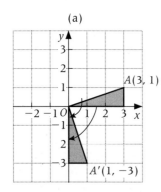

(b)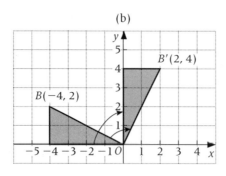

Rotate the shaded triangles clockwise through 90° as shown, keeping $O$ fixed.

Line $OA \rightarrow$ line $OA'$

$A(3, 1) \rightarrow A'(1, -3)$

Gradient of $OA = \dfrac{1}{3}$

Gradient of $OA' = \dfrac{-3}{1}$

$OA$ is perpendicular to $OA'$

Gradient of $OA \times$ Gradient $OA'$

$$= \dfrac{1}{3} \times \dfrac{-3}{1} = -1$$

Line $OB \rightarrow$ line $OB'$

$B(-4, 1) \rightarrow B'(2, 4)$

Gradient of $OB = -\dfrac{2}{4}$

Gradient of $OB' = \dfrac{4}{2}$

$OB$ is perpendicular to $OB'$

Gradient of $OB \times$ Gradient $OB'$

$$= -\dfrac{2}{4} \times \dfrac{4}{2} = -1$$

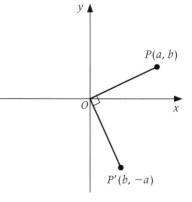

In general

$$\text{gradient of } OP = \dfrac{b}{a}, \qquad \text{gradient of } OP' = -\dfrac{a}{b}$$

**Lines are perpendicular if the product of their gradients is $-1$.**

> Lines with gradients $m_1$ and $m_2$
> – are parallel if $m_1 = m_2$,
> – are perpendicular if $m_1 \times m_2 = -1$.

## Worked example 4.7

Find the gradient of a line which is perpendicular to the line joining $A(1, 3)$ and $B(4, 5)$.

## Solution

Gradient of $AB = \dfrac{5-3}{4-1} = \dfrac{2}{3}$.

Let $m_2$ be the gradient of any line perpendicular to $AB$ then

$\dfrac{2}{3} \times m_2 = -1 \Rightarrow m_2 = -\dfrac{3}{2}$.

The gradient of any line perpendicular to $AB$ is $-\dfrac{3}{2}$.

### EXERCISE 4D

**4**

**1** Write down the gradient of lines perpendicular to a line with gradient:

    **(a)** $\dfrac{2}{5}$,    **(b)** $\dfrac{-1}{3}$,    **(c)** $4$,    **(d)** $-3\frac{1}{2}$,    **(e)** $2\frac{1}{4}$.

**2** Two vertices of a rectangle $ABCD$ are $A(-2, 3)$ and $B(4, 1)$.

    **(a)** Find the gradient of $DC$.

    **(b)** Find the gradient of $BC$.

**3** $A(1, 2)$, $B(3, 6)$ and $C(7, 4)$ are the three vertices of a triangle.

    **(a)** Show that $ABC$ is a right-angled isosceles triangle.

    **(b)** $D$ is the point $(5, 0)$. Show that $BD$ is perpendicular to $AC$.

    **(c)** Explain why $ABCD$ is a square.

    **(d)** Find the area of $ABCD$.

## 4.6 $y = mx + c$ form of the equation of a straight line

Consider any straight line which crosses the $y$-axis at the point $A(0, c)$. We say that $c$ **is the $y$-intercept**.
Let $P(x, y)$ be any other point on the line.
If the gradient of the line is $m$ then

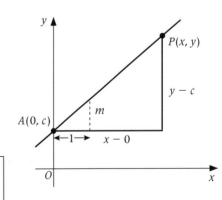

$$\dfrac{y - c}{x - 0} = m$$

so $y - c = mx$ or $y = mx + c$.

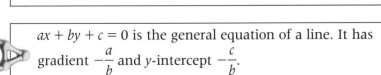

$y = mx + c$ is the equation of a straight line with gradient $m$ and $y$-intercept $c$.

$ax + by + c = 0$ is the general equation of a line. It has gradient $-\dfrac{a}{b}$ and $y$-intercept $-\dfrac{c}{b}$.

## Worked example 4.8

A straight line has gradient 2 and crosses the $y$-axis at the point $(0, -4)$. Write down the equation of the line.

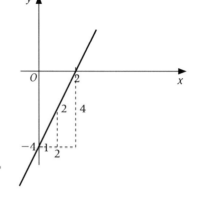

### Solution

The line crosses the $y$-axis at $(0, -4)$ so the $y$-intercept is $-4$, so $c = -4$. The gradient of the line is 2, so $m = 2$.
Using $y = mx + c$ you get $y = 2x + (-4)$.
The equation of the line is $y = 2x - 4$.

## Worked example 4.9

The general equation of a straight line is $Ax + By + C = 0$.
Find the gradient of the line, and the $y$-intercept.

### Solution

You need to rearrange the equation $Ax + By + C = 0$ into the form $y = mx + c$.

You can write $Ax + By + C = 0$ as $By = -Ax - C$

$$\text{or } y = -\frac{A}{B}x - \frac{C}{B}.$$

Compare with $$y = mx + c,$$

you see that $$m = -\frac{A}{B} \text{ and } c = -\frac{C}{B}.$$

so $Ax + By + C = 0$ is the equation of a line

with gradient $-\dfrac{A}{B}$ and $y$-intercept $-\dfrac{C}{B}$.

### EXERCISE 4E

**1** Find, in the form $ax + by + c = 0$, the equation of the line which has:

  **(a)** gradient 2 and $y$-intercept $-3$,

  **(b)** gradient $-\dfrac{2}{3}$ and $y$-intercept 2,

  **(c)** gradient $-\dfrac{1}{2}$ and $y$-intercept $-3$.

**2** Find the gradient and $y$-intercept for the line with equation:

  **(a)** $y = 2 + 3x$,         **(b)** $2y = 4x - 5$,

  **(c)** $4y - 7 = 2x$,       **(d)** $2x + 3y = 8$,

  **(e)** $8 - 5x + 4y = 0$,    **(f)** $0.5y = 4x - 3$,

  **(g)** $5y - 3x = -2$,      **(h)** $4 - 3x = 2y$,

  **(i)** $-2.5y + 5x = 3$,    **(j)** $2y = 4$.

# 4.7 $y - y_1 = m(x - x_1)$ form of the equation of a straight line

Consider any line which passes through the known point $A(x_1, y_1)$ and let $P(x, y)$ be any other point on the line.

If $m$ is the gradient of the line $AP$ then $\dfrac{y - y_1}{x - x_1} = m$

or $y - y_1 = m(x - x_1)$.

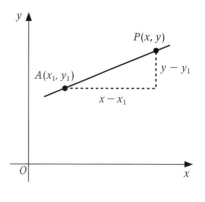

> The equation of the straight line which passes through the point $(x_1, y_1)$ and has gradient $m$ is
>
> $$y - y_1 = m(x - x_1).$$

**4**

## Worked example 4.10

Find the equation of the straight line which is parallel to the line $y = 4x - 1$ and passes through the point $(3, 2)$.

## Solution

The gradient of the line $y = 4x - 1$ is 4

so the gradient of any line parallel to $y = 4x - 1$ is also 4.

We need the line with gradient 4 and through the point $(3, 3)$

so its equation is, using $y - y_1 = m(x - x_1)$,
$$y - 2 = 4(x - 3)$$
$$or \ y = 4x - 10.$$

> Compare   $y = 4x - 1$
>           $\uparrow$
> with          $y = mx + c$

> Parallel lines have equal gradients

## Worked example 4.11

(a) Find a cartesian equation for the perpendicular bisector of the line joining $A(2, 1)$ and $B(4, -5)$.

(b) This perpendicular bisector cuts the coordinate axes at $C$ and $D$. Show that $CD = 1.5 \times AB$.

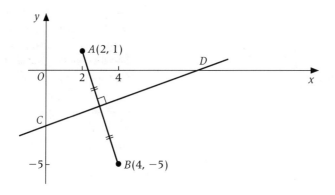

## Solution

First, we draw a rough sketch

**(a)** The gradient of $AB = \dfrac{-5-1}{4-2} = -3$.

so the gradient of the perpendicular is $\dfrac{1}{3}$.

$m_1 \times m_2 = -1$

The mid-point of $AB$ is $\left(\dfrac{2+4}{2}, \dfrac{1+(-5)}{2}\right) = (3, -2)$.

Using $\left(\dfrac{x_1 + x_2}{2}, \dfrac{y_1 + y_2}{2}\right)$.

The perpendicular bisector is a straight line which passes through the point $(3, -2)$ and has gradient $\dfrac{1}{3}$, so its equation is

$$y - (-2) = \frac{1}{3}(x - 3) \ \text{ or } \ y = \frac{1}{3}x - 3.$$

Using $y - y_1 = m(x - x_1)$

**(b)** Let $C$ be the point where the line $y = \dfrac{1}{3}x - 3$ cuts the $y$-axis.

When $x = 0$, $y = \dfrac{1}{3} \times 0 - 3 = -3$, so we have $C(0, -3)$.

Any point on the y-axis has x-coordinate = 0.

Let $D$ be the point where the line $y = \dfrac{1}{3}x - 3$ cuts the $x$-axis.

When $y = 0$, $0 = \dfrac{1}{3} \times x - 3$

Any point on the x-axis has y-coordinate = 0.

$\Rightarrow x = 9$, so we have $D(9, 0)$

Distance $CD = \sqrt{(9-0)^2 + (0-(-3))^2} = \sqrt{81 + 9} = \sqrt{90}$

Using $\sqrt{(x_2 - x_1)^2 + (y_2 - y_1)^2}$.

Distance $AB = \sqrt{(4-2)^2 + (-5-1)^2} = \sqrt{4 + 36} = \sqrt{40}$

$\dfrac{CD}{AB} = \dfrac{\sqrt{90}}{\sqrt{40}} = \sqrt{\dfrac{90}{40}} = \sqrt{\dfrac{9}{4}} = \dfrac{\sqrt{9}}{\sqrt{4}} = \dfrac{3}{2} = 1.5$

so $CD = 1.5 \times AB$.

### EXERCISE 4F

**1** Find an equation for the straight line with gradient 2 and which passes through the point $(1, 6)$.

Because a straight line equation can be arranged in a variety of ways you are usually asked to find *an* equation rather than *the* equation.

**2** Find a cartesian equation for the straight line which has gradient $-\dfrac{1}{3}$ and that passes through $(6, 0)$.

All correct equivalents would score full marks unless you have been asked specifically for a particular form of the equation.

**3** Find an equation of the straight line passing through $(-1, 2)$ that is parallel to the line with equation $2y = x + 4$

**4** Find an equation of the straight line that is parallel to $3x - 2y - 4 = 0$ and that passes through $(1, 3)$.

**5** Find a cartesian equation for the perpendicular bisector of the line joining $A(2, 3)$ and $B(0, 6)$.

**6** Given the points $A(0, 3)$, $B(5, 4)$, $C(4, -1)$ and $E(2, 1)$;

    **(a)** show that $BE$ is the perpendicular bisector of $AC$,

    **(b)** find the coordinates of the point $D$ so that $ABCD$ is a rhombus,

    **(c)** find an equation for the straight line through $D$ and $A$.

> **Hint for part (b).** The diagonals of a rhombus are perpendicular and bisect each other.

**7** The perpendicular bisector of the line joining $A(0, 1)$ and $C(4, -7)$ intersects the $x$-axis at $B$ and the $y$-axis at $D$. Find the area of the quadrilateral $ABCD$.

**8** Show that the equation of any line parallel to $ax + by + c = 0$ is of the form $ax + by + k = 0$.

# 4.8 The equation of a straight line passing through two given points

> The equation of the straight line which passes through the points $(x_1, y_1)$ and $(x_2, y_2)$ is
> $$\frac{y - y_1}{y_2 - y_1} = \frac{x - x_1}{x_2 - x_1}$$

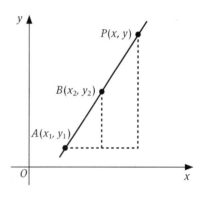

> The derivation of this equation is similar to previous ones and is left as an exercise to the reader.

## Worked example 4.12

Find a cartesian equation of the straight line which passes through the points $(2, 3)$ and $(-1, 0)$.

## Solution

If you take $(x_1, y_1) = (2, 3)$ and $(x_2, y_2) = (-1, 0)$ and substitute into the general equation

$$\frac{y - y_1}{y_2 - y_1} = \frac{x - x_1}{x_2 - x_1}.$$

you get

$$\frac{y - 3}{0 - 3} = \frac{x - 2}{-1 - 2}.$$

or    $y - 3 = x - 2$ which leads to $y = x + 1$.

> **Note.** You can check that your line passes through the points $(2, 3)$ and $(-1, 0)$ by seeing if the points satisfy the equation $y = x + 1$.
>
> $y = x + 1$
>
> Checking for $(2, 3)$
>
>     LHS $= 3$    RHS $= 2 + 1 = 3$ ✓
>
> Checking for $(-1, 0)$
>
>     LHS $= 0$    RHS $= -1 + 1 = 0$ ✓

# 4.9 Coordinates of the point of intersection of two lines

In this section you will need to solve simultaneous equations. If you need further practice, see Section 3.2 of Chapter 3.

> A point lies on a line if the coordinates of the point satisfy the equation of the line.

When two lines intersect, the point of intersection lies on both lines. The coordinates of the point of intersection must satisfy the equations of both lines. The equations of the lines must be satisfied simultaneously.

> To find the coordinates of the point of intersection of the two lines with equations $ax + by + c = 0$ and $Ax + By + C = 0$, you solve the two linear equations simultaneously.

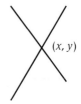

## Worked example 4.13

Find the coordinates of the point of intersection of the straight lines with equations $y = x + 2$ and $y = 4x - 1$.

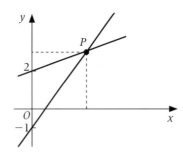

## Solution

At the point of intersection $P$, $y = x + 2$ and $y = 4x - 1$.
so eliminating $y$ gives $\quad 4x - 1 = x + 2$
rearranging gives $\qquad 4x - x = 2 + 1$
$$\Rightarrow 3x = 3 \Rightarrow x = 1.$$

The $x$-coordinate of $P$ is 1.

To find the $y$-coordinate of $P$, put $x = 1$ into $y = x + 2 \Rightarrow y = 3$
The point of intersection is $(1, 3)$.

Checking that $(1, 3)$ lies on the line $y = x + 2$;
$\quad$ LHS = 3 $\quad$ RHS = $1 + 2 = 3$ ✓

Checking that $(1, 3)$ lies on the line $y = 4x - 1$;
$\quad$ LHS = 3 $\quad$ RHS = $4 - 1 = 3$ ✓

## Worked example 4.14

The straight lines with equations $5x + 3y = 7$ and $3x - 7y = 13$ intersect at the point $R$. Find the coordinates of $R$.

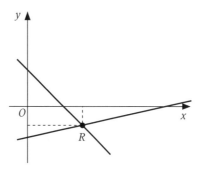

## Solution

To find the point of intersection $R$, you need to solve the simultaneous equations

$$5x + 3y = 7 \qquad (A)$$
$$3x - 7y = 13 \qquad (B)$$

$$35x + 21y = 49 \qquad (C)$$
$$9x - 21y = 39 \qquad (D)$$

$$44x + 0 = 88$$
$$\Rightarrow x = 2.$$

Multiply equation ($A$) by 7 and equation ($B$) by 3.

Adding ($C$) + ($D$).

Substituting $x = 2$ in ($A$) gives $10 + 3y = 7$
$$\Rightarrow 3y = -3. \qquad \Rightarrow y = -1.$$

The coordinates of the point $R$ are $(2, -1)$.

Checking in ($A$)
$$\text{LHS} = 10 + (-3) = 7 = \text{RHS} \quad \checkmark;$$
and in ($B$)
$$\text{LHS} = 6 - 7(-1) = 13 \quad \checkmark$$

**Hint.** Checking that the coordinates satisfy each line equation is advisable, especially if the result is being used in later parts of an examination question.
It can usually be done in your head rather than on paper.

## EXERCISE 4G

**1** Verify that $(2, 5)$ lies on the line with equation $y = 3x - 1$.

**2** Show that the point $(-4, 8)$ lies on the line passing through the points $(1, 3)$ and $(7, -3)$.

**3** **(a)** Find the equation of the line $AB$ where $A(-3, 7)$ and $B(5, -1)$.
   **(b)** The point $(k, 3)$ lies on the line $AB$. Find the value of the constant $k$.

**4** $A(-5, 2)$, $B(-2, 3)$, $C(-2, -1)$ and $D(-4, -2)$ are the vertices of the quadrilateral $ABCD$.
   **(a)** Find the equation of the diagonal $BD$.
   **(b)** Determine whether or not the mid-point of $AC$ lies on the diagonal $BD$.

**5** Find the coordinates of the point of intersection of these pairs of straight lines:

(a) $y = 2x + 7$ and $y = x + 1$,

(b) $3y + x = 7$ and $2y - x = 3$,

(c) $5x + 2y = 16$ and $3x + 2y = 8$,

(d) $y = 8x$ and $y = 40 + 3x$,

(e) $y = -7$ and $5y = -x - 1$,

(f) $y - 3x = 3$ and $2y - 5x = 9$,

(g) $4y + 9x = 8$ and $5y + 6x = 3$,

(h) $8y = 3x - 11$ and $2x - 5y = 6$.

## Worked example question

*ABCD* is a parallelogram in which the coordinates of *A*, *B* and *C* are $(1, 2)$, $(7, -1)$ and $(-1, -2)$, respectively.

(a) Find the equations of *AD* and *CD*.

(b) Find the coordinates of *D*.

(c) Prove that angle $BAC = 90°$.

(d) Calculate the area of the parallelogram.

(e) Find the length of the perpendicular from *A* to *BC*, leaving your answer in surd form.

## Solution

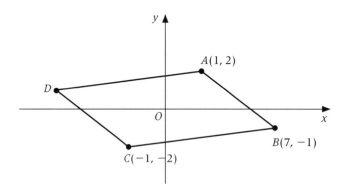

> Always start with a good sketch; this helps to spot obvious errors like wrong signs for gradients or wrong quadrants for points. Note that when it says the parallelogram *ABCD* the points must be connected in that order and so determines where *C* must be.

(a) *AD* is parallel to *BC* and *CD* is parallel to *BA*.

> Opposite sides of a parallelogram are equal and parallel.

Gradient of $BC = \dfrac{-1 - (-2)}{7 - (-1)} = \dfrac{1}{8} \Rightarrow$ gradient of AD $= \dfrac{1}{8}$

> $\dfrac{y_2 - y_1}{x_2 - x_1}$

*AD* is a line through $(1, 2)$ and has gradient $\dfrac{1}{8}$ so its

equation is $y - 2 = \dfrac{1}{8}(x - 1)$ or $\underline{8y - x = 15}$.

> Using $y - y_1 = m(x - x_1)$

Gradient of $BA = \dfrac{-1-2}{7-1} = -\dfrac{3}{6} = -\dfrac{1}{2}$

$\Rightarrow$ gradient of $CD = -\dfrac{1}{2}$.

CD is a line through $(-1, -2)$ and has gradient $-\dfrac{1}{2}$ so its equation is $y - (-2) = \dfrac{-1}{2}[x - (-1)]$ or $\underline{2y + x = -5}$.

> You could check the signs of the two gradients using your sketch.

**(b)** $D$ is the point of intersection of $AD$ and $CD$.

Solving $8y - x = 15$

and $\quad 2y + x = -5$ simultaneously,

adding gives $10y + 0 = 10 \Rightarrow y = 1$.

Substitution in the second equation gives $2(1) + x = -5$
$\Rightarrow x = -7$, i.e. $D(-7, 1)$

> Alternatively: since BA is equal and parallel to CD, the journey from B → A (6 left then 3 up) is the same as from C to D.
> $D(-1 - 6, -2 + 3)$ or $D(-7, 1)$.

> From the sketch you know D is in the 2nd quadrant. Checking in both equations $8 - (-7) = 15$ ✓
> $2 + (-7) = -5$ ✓

**(c)** Gradient of $AC = \dfrac{2 - (-2)}{1 - (-1)} = \dfrac{4}{2} = 2$

From earlier work, gradient of $BA = -\dfrac{1}{2}$.

Gradient of $AC \times$ gradient of $BA = 2 \times -\dfrac{1}{2} = -1$,

so $AC$ is perpendicular to $BA$ and angle $BAC = 90°$.

> Angle BAC = 90° if AC and BA are perpendicular.
> Aim to show that $m_1 \times m_2 = -1$.

> **Hint.** In exam questions look for possible links between the parts.

**(d)** Since angle $BAC = 90°$ you can use

Area of parallelogram $ABCD \quad = $ base $\times$ height
$\qquad\qquad\qquad\qquad\qquad\quad = AB \times AC$.

$AB = \sqrt{(7-1)^2 + (-1-2)^2} = \sqrt{36 + 9} = \sqrt{45}$

$AC = \sqrt{(-1-1)^2 + (-2-2)^2} = \sqrt{4 + 16} = \sqrt{20}$.

so area of parallelogram $ABCD = \sqrt{45} \times \sqrt{20} = \sqrt{900}$
$\qquad\qquad\qquad\qquad\qquad\qquad = 30$ sq units.

> $\sqrt{(x_2 - x_1)^2 + (y_2 - y_1)^2}$
> Keep your answers in surd form.

> **Hint.** In exam questions look for links between the parts: Length of perpendicular from A to BC is required. We have just found the area of the parallelogram ABCD. Can the two be linked?

**(e)** Using the base of the parallelogram as $CB$ and letting $h = $ length of the perpendicular from $A$ to $BC$,

$\Rightarrow$ area of parallelogram $ABCD = CB \times h$,

$30 = \sqrt{(7 - (-1))^2 + (-1 - (-2))^2} \times h$,

$30 = \sqrt{64 + 1} \times h, \quad \Rightarrow h = \dfrac{30}{\sqrt{65}}$.

> Since we were told to leave the answer in surd form we should not get a calculator approximation.

## MIXED EXERCISE

1 *ABCD* is a rectangle in which the coordinates of *A* and *C* are $(0, 4)$ and $(11, 1)$ respectively and the gradient of the side *AB* is $-5$.

   **(a)** Find the equations of the sides *AB* and *BC*.

   **(b)** Show that the coordinates of *B* are $(1, -1)$.

   **(c)** Calculate the area of the rectangle.

   **(d)** Find the coordinates of the point on the *y*-axis which is equidistant from *A* and *D*.          [A]

2 A rhombus *ABCD* is such that the coordinates of *A* and *C* are $(0, 4)$ and $(8, 0)$ respectively.

   **(a)** Show that the equation of the diagonal *BD* is $y = 2x - 6$.

   **(b)** The side *AB* has gradient -2. Find the coordinates of *B* and the coordinates of *D*.

   **(c)** Show that the area of the rhombus is 30 square units.  [A]

3 The points *A*, *B* and *C* have coordinates $(6, 3)$, $(5, 8)$ and $(-2, 4)$, respectively.

   **(a)** Prove that the triangle *ABC* is isosceles.

   **(b)** Find the equation of the straight line which passes through the points *A* and *B*.

   **(c)** Show that the shortest distance from *C* to the side *AB* of the triangle can be written as $k\sqrt{(26)}$, where k is a rational number whose value should be stated.          [A]

4 The straight line *l* with equation $12x - 5y + 10 = 0$ cuts the *x*-axis at *A* and the *y*-axis at *B*. The origin is at *O*.

   **(a)** Calculate the area of the triangle *OAB*.

   **(b)** Find the equation of the straight line which passes through *O* and which is perpendicular to the line *l*.

   **(c)** Find the length of *AB* and hence, or otherwise, calculate the shortest distance from *O* to the line *l*.          [A]

5 In the triangle *ABC* the point *A* has coordinates $(7, 8)$. The mid-point of *BC* is $M(4, 2)$ and the perpendicular bisector of *BC* meets *AB* at $N(3, 4)$.

   **(a)** Find a cartesian equation of the line passing through *A*, *B* and *N*.

   **(b)** Calculate the coordinates of *B*.

   **(c)** Prove that angle *BAC* is a right angle.          [A]

**6** In a triangle $ABC$, the coordinates of $A$ and $B$ are $(1, -3)$ and $(9, 3)$ respectively. The equation of $AC$ is $y = 2x - 5$ and the equation of $BC$ is $2y = 15 - x$.

 **(a)** Show that angle $ACB = 90°$.

 **(b)** Calculate the area of triangle $ABC$.

 **(c)** Calculate the coordinates of
  **(i)** $P$, the foot of the perpendicular from the origin $O$ to $BC$ produced.
  **(ii)** $Q$, the foot of the perpendicular from the origin $O$ to $AC$.

 **(d)** Given that $R(1.8, -2.4)$ is the foot of the perpendicular from $O$ to $AB$, show that $P$, $Q$ and $R$ lie on a straight line. [A]

**7** The points $A(-5, 8)$, $B(3, -4)$ and $C(7, 3)$ are three of the vertices of a trapezium $ABCD$ in which $BA$ is parallel to $CD$ and $CD = \frac{1}{4}BA$.

 **(a)** Find the coordinates of the point $D$.

 **(b)** Show that the equation of the side $AD$ is $5y + x = 35$.

 **(c)** Show that the line joining $D$ to the mid-point of $BA$ is perpendicular to $BA$.

 **(d)** Calculate the exact value of the area of the trapezium.

 **(e)** Show that angle $DAB = 45°$. [A]

**8 (a)** Calculate the coordinates of the point $P$ in which the perpendicular from the origin to the straight line $9x + 12y = 25$ meets this straight line.

 **(b)** From any point $Q(h, k)$ on the line $9x + 12y = 25$, perpendiculars $QA$ and $QB$ are drawn to the $x$-axis and $y$-axis respectively. Find the gradients of the lines $AP$ and $BP$ and show that these lines are at right angles.

 **(c)** Show also that the mid-point of $AB$ is equidistant from the origin and the point $P$. [A]

**9** The points $A(-1, 2)$ and $C(5, 1)$ are opposite vertices of a parallelogram $ABCD$; the vertex $B$ lies on the line $2x + y = 5$; the side $AB$ is parallel to the line $3x + 4y = 8$.
Find:

 **(a)** the coordinates of $B$,

 **(b)** the equations of the sides $AC$ and $CD$,

 **(c)** the coordinates of $D$,

 **(d)** the area of the parallelogram $ABCD$. [A]

**10** The line whose equation is $7y = 3x - 6$ meets the $x$-axis at $A$ and the line whose equation is $3y = 18 - x$ meets the $y$-axis at $C$. The two lines intersect at the point $B$ and $O$ is the origin of coordinates.

(a) Calculate the coordinates of $A$, $C$ and $B$.

(b) Show that $OB$ is perpendicular to $AC$.

(c) (i) Calculate the area of triangle $OBC$.

   (ii) Hence, given that $D$ is the point of intersection of $OB$ and $AC$, show that $DC = \dfrac{9\sqrt{10}}{5}$.

(d) Find the coordinates of the point $P$ such that $ABPC$ is a parallelogram. [A]

---

## Key point summary

**1** The distance between the points $(x_1, y_1)$ and $(x_2, y_2)$ is $\sqrt{(x_2 - x_1)^2 + (y_2 - y_1)^2}$.     *p40*

**2** The coordinates of the mid-point of the line segment joining $(x_1, y_1)$ and $(x_2, y_2)$ are $\left( \dfrac{x_1 + x_2}{2}, \dfrac{y_1 + y_2}{2} \right)$.     *p42*

**3** The gradient of a line joining the two points $A(x_1, y_1)$ and $B(x_2, y_2) = \dfrac{y_2 - y_1}{x_2 - x_1}$.     *p44*

**4** Lines with gradients $m_1$ and $m_2$:     *p46*
 – are parallel if $m_1 = m_2$,
 – are perpendicular if $m_1 \times m_2 = -1$.

**5** $y = mx + c$ is the equation of a straight line with gradient $m$ and $y$-intercept $c$.     *p47*

**6** $ax + by + c = 0$ is the general equation of a line.     *p47*
 It has gradient $-\dfrac{a}{b}$ and $y$-intercept $-\dfrac{c}{b}$.

**7** The equation of the straight line which passes through the point $(x_1, y_1)$ and has gradient $m$ is     *p49*

$$y - y_1 = m(x - x_1).$$

**8** The equation of the straight line which passes through the points $(x_1, y_1)$ and $(x_2, y_2)$ is     *p51*

$$\frac{y - y_1}{y_2 - y_1} = \frac{x - x_1}{x_2 - x_1}.$$

**9** A point lies on a line if the coordinates of the point   *p52*
satisfy the equation of the line.

**10** To find the coordinates of the point of intersection of   *p52*
the two lines with equations $ax + by + c = 0$ and
$Ax + By + C = 0$, you solve the two equations
simultaneously.

| Test yourself | What to review |
|---|---|
| **1** Calculate the distance between the points $(2, -3)$ and $(7, 9)$. | *Section 4.2* |
| **2** State the coordinates of the mid-point of the line segment $PQ$ where $P(3, -2)$ and $Q(7, 1)$. | *Section 4.3* |
| **3** Find the gradient of the line joining the points $A$ and $B$ where $A$ is the point $(-3, -2)$ and $B$ is the point $(-5, 4)$. | *Section 4.4* |
| **4** The lines $CD$ and $EF$ are perpendicular where $C(1, 2)$, $D(3, -4)$, $E(-2, 5)$ and $F(k, 4)$. Find the value of the constant $k$. | *Section 4.5* |
| **5** Find a cartesian equation of the line perpendicular to the line $5y + 3x = 7$ and which passes through the point $(-2, 1)$. | *Sections 4.5 and 4.7* |
| **6** Find the point of intersection of the lines with equations $3x - 5y = 11$ and $y = 4x - 9$. | *Section 4.9* |

**Test yourself   ANSWERS**

**6** $(2, -1)$.

**5** $3y = 5x + 13$.

**4** $k = -5$.

**3** $-3$.

**2** $(5, -\frac{1}{2})$.

**1** $13$.

# CHAPTER 5

# Functions and graphs

## Learning objectives

After studying this chapter, you should be able to:
- be familiar with the terms one–one and many–one mappings
- understand the terms domain and range for a mapping
- understand the term function
- to find the range of a function
- understand the terms odd function and even function
- form composite functions
- realize when an inverse function exists.

> In this chapter you will need to use a graphic calculator or graph plotting software on a computer.

## 5.1 Mapping

Suppose you input a number into a black box that performs various operations on the number before giving a single value as output. Imagine that each number in the set $\{-2,0,1,3,4\}$ is input in turn to the box. The corresponding values of output could be represented as a **mapping diagram** shown below.

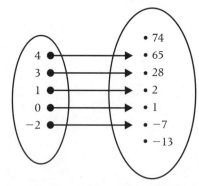

Because each element of the first set is mapped to exactly one element of the second set, we say the mapping is **one–one**.

The set of input values is called the **domain**. So for this mapping the domain is the set $\{-2,0,1,3,4\}$.

If you map from the domain using arrows, the set of values where the arrows map onto is called the **range**.

Here, the range is the set $\{-7, 1, 2, 28, 65\}$.

> It doesn't matter that no elements are mapped onto 74 and $-13$.

> The larger set on the right that contains the range is called the codomain so that, in this example, the codomain is the set $\{-13,-7, 1, 2, 28, 65, 74\}$.

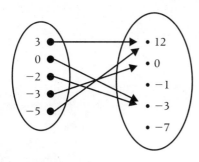

This time the domain is the set $\{-5, -3, -2, 0, 3\}$ and the range is the set $\{-3, 0, 12\}$.

If the operation being performed by the black box is now changed you might produce the mapping diagram shown above. In this case more than one element of the domain maps onto the same element in the range. The mapping is **many–one**.

 When a mapping is *one–one* or *many–one* it is called a **function**. It is usually represented by a single letter such as f, g, or h, etc.

 The set of numbers for which a function is defined is called the domain.

 The set of values the function can take for a given domain is called the range.

If a general element in the domain is denoted by $x$, the mapping for diagram 1 in function notation can be written as:

In mapping diagram 1, did you recognize what the black box was actually doing?

Each number was cubed and then one was added to the result.

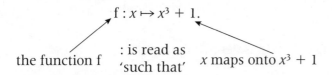

$$f : x \mapsto x^3 + 1.$$

the function f

: is read as 'such that'

$x$ maps onto $x^3 + 1$

## Worked example 5.1

The black box to produce mapping diagram 2 used the sequence of operations 'add 1', 'square the result', 'subtract 4'. Express the mapping in function notation representing it by g.

## Solution

$$g : x \mapsto (x + 1)^2 - 4$$

You read this as the function g such that $x$ is mapped onto $(x + 1)^2 - 4$.

# 5.2 Other notatation

An alternative to writing $f : x \mapsto x^3 + 1$ is to write $f(x) = x^3 + 1$.

> You read this as 'f of x equals...'

The expression $f(x)$ is called the **image of x**.

> The form $f(x) = \ldots$ is a much more convenient notation when you want to evaluate a function for different values of $x$.

## Worked example 5.2

The function h has domain $\{-2, -1, 0, 3, 7\}$ and is defined by:

$$h : x \mapsto (x - 3)^2 + 2.$$

Find the range of h.

## Solution

$h(-2) = (-2 - 3)^2 + 2 = 25 + 2 = 27$
$h(-1) = (-1 - 3)^2 + 2 = 16 + 2 = 18$
$h(0) = (0 - 3)^2 + 2 = 9 + 2 = 11$
$h(3) = (3 - 3)^2 + 2 = 0 + 2 = 2$
$h(7) = (7 - 3)2 + 2 = 16 + 2 = 18$

The range of h is $\{2, 11, 18, 27\}$

> Because $h(-1)$ and $h(7)$ give the same value, we only write the value 18 once in the range.

### EXERCISE 5A

1  The function f has domain $\{-2, -1, 0, 1, 2, 3\}$ and is defined by

$$f : x \mapsto x^2 + 2.$$

Find the range of f.

2  The function g has domain $\{-2, -1, 0, 1, 2\}$ and is defined by
$$g : x \mapsto (2x - 1)^3 - 7.$$
Find the range of g.

3  The function h has domain $\{-2, -1, 1, 2, 3\}$ and is defined by
$$h : x \mapsto x^{-2} + 1.$$
Find the range of h.

4  Given that $f(x) = x^3 - 3x^2 + 2x - 1$, evaluate
   **(a)** $f(0)$,   **(b)** $f(1)$,   **(c)** $f(2)$,   **(d)** $f(-1)$,   **(e)** $f(-2)$.

5  Given that $g(x) = (x + 3)^{-3}$, evaluate
   **(a)** $g(0)$,      **(b)** $g(1)$,      **(c)** $g(2)$,
   **(d)** $g(-1)$,     **(e)** $g(-2)$,     **(f)** $g(-4)$,
   **(g)** $g(-2.99)$,  **(h)** $g(b)$,      **(i)** $g(a - 3)$.

6  Given that $f(x) = \sqrt{(2x + 5)}$, find the exact values of
   **(a)** $f(0)$,   **(b)** $f(1)$,   **(c)** $f(2)$,   **(d)** $f(-1)$,   **(e)** $f(-2)$.

# 5.3 Functions and graphs

The function f is defined by $f : x \mapsto 3x + 2$ with domain equal to $\{-2, 0, 1, 3\}$. After finding the image of each element, namely, $\{-4, 2, 5, 11\}$ the pairs of values $(-2, -4)$, $(0, 2)$, $(1, 5)$, $(3, 11)$ can be plotted as points in the cartesian plane.

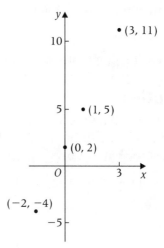

> The values of $x$ are the values in the domain.
>
> The values of $y$ are the values in the range.

The graph shows the values of $y = f(x)$, which in this case consists of four isolated points.

Suppose you now change the domain so that it consists of all real numbers from $-2$ to $3$ inclusive. The function now has a continuous graph with equation $y = 3x + 2$, which you should recognise as the equation of a straight line.

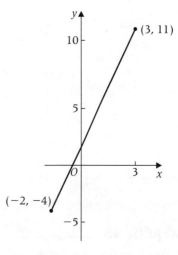

> The domain is $-2 \leqslant x < 3$.
> The range can be written as $-4 \leqslant y < 11$ or $-4 \leqslant f(x) \leqslant 11$.

## Worked example 5.3

A function g with domain $-1 \leqslant x \leqslant 2$ is defined by

$$g : x \mapsto x^3 - 7.$$

Sketch the graph of g and find its range.

## Solution

Using a graphic calculator or computer software you can obtain a sketch similar to that on the right.

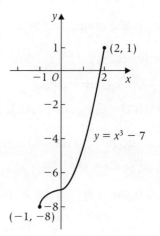

You need to find the smallest and greatest values of $y = g(x)$ from the graph.

$$g(-1) = (-1)3 - 7 = -1 - 7 = -8 \quad \boxed{\text{Least value of g(x).}}$$

$$g(2) = 2^3 - 7 = 8 - 7 = 1 \quad \boxed{\text{Greatest value of g(x).}}$$

The graph shows that the function g can take all values between $-8$ and $1$.

Hence, the range of g is given by

$$-8 \leqslant g(x) \leqslant 1.$$

## Worked example 5.4

A function p with domain $x > 1$ is defined by:

$$p(x) = 4 - x^2.$$

Sketch the graph of p and find its range.

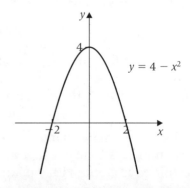

## Solution

It is likely that your first attempt to obtain a sketch has produced something like this. You need to restrict the set of values so that it draws a graph for $x > 1$.

The graph of p for $x > 1$ is shown below

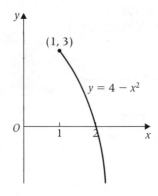

Although the value $x = 1$ is not actually in the domain we need to find $p(1) = 4 - 1^2 = 3$

As $x$ gets larger than 1 we can see that $p(x)$ decreases continuously from the value 3.

Notice the correct inequality sign is $<$ and not $\leqslant$.

The range is therefore given by $p(x) < 3$.

## EXERCISE 5B

**1** The function g with domain $-4 \leqslant x \leqslant 1$ is defined by

$$g : x \mapsto 7 - x.$$

Sketch the graph of g and find its range.

You are expected to have a graphic calculator or graph plotting facilities on a computer to help you with your sketches.

**2** The function f with domain $1 < x < 3$ is defined by

$$f : x \mapsto 1 + x^2.$$

Sketch the graph of f and find its range.

**3** The function q with domain $-1 \leqslant x \leqslant 2$ is defined by

$$q : x \mapsto 1 - x^3.$$

Sketch the graph of q and find its range.

**4** The function g with domain $x \leqslant 1$ is defined by

$$g : x \mapsto 3 - 5x.$$

Sketch the graph of g and find its range.

**5** The function f with domain $-4 \leqslant x < 1$ is defined by

$$f(x) = 3 + x^5.$$

Sketch the graph of f and find its range.

**6** The function h with domain $-2 < x \leqslant 3$ is defined by

$$h(x) = 2 - x^3.$$

Sketch the graph of h and find its range.

**7** The function f with domain $x \geqslant 1$ is defined by

$$f(x) = 3 + \frac{1}{x}.$$

Sketch the graph of f and find its range.

**8** The function g with domain $x > 3$ is defined by

$$g(x) = \frac{6}{x}.$$

Sketch the graph of g and find its range.

**9** The function f with domain $-3 \leqslant x \leqslant -1$ is defined by

$$f(x) = 1 - \frac{1}{x}.$$

Sketch the graph of f and find its range.

**10** The function h with domain $-2 < x < -1$ is defined by

$$h(x) = 3 + \frac{1}{x^2}.$$

Sketch the graph of h and find its range.

# 5.4 Greatest possible domain

A function is sometimes defined for all real values of $x$. We say the domain is the set of real numbers, $\mathbb{R}$, or $x \in \mathbb{R}$. When this is the case, the domain is sometimes omitted and implicitly understood to be the set of real numbers.

Sometimes restrictions on the domain are necessary.

For instance $f(x) = 3 + \dfrac{1}{x}$ cannot be defined for $x = 0$.

Its greatest possible domain is therefore $x \in \mathbb{R}, x \neq 0$.

Since we cannot find square roots of negative quantities, the function g, where $g : x \mapsto \sqrt{x - 3}$, does not exist for $x < 3$.

The greatest possible domain for g is $x \geqslant 3$.

$x$ 'belongs to' $\mathbb{R}$

For instance $f(x) = x^2 + 3x - 2$ (*with no mention of a domain*) implies that $x$ can take all real values.

If you try to find f(0) on your calculator you will get an error message.

## EXERCISE 5C

Determine the greatest possible domain for each of the following functions.

**1** $f : x \mapsto \dfrac{1}{(x - 1)},$  **2** $f : x \mapsto \sqrt{3 + x},$  **3** $f : x \mapsto \dfrac{1 + x}{2 - x},$

**4** $f : x \mapsto \dfrac{3 - x}{(1 + x)^2},$  **5** $f : x \mapsto \dfrac{4 + x}{1 + x^2},$  **6** $f : x \mapsto \dfrac{1}{\sqrt{x - 2}},$

**7** $f : x \mapsto \dfrac{(x + 4)}{(x - 1)(x - 2)},$  **8** $f : x \mapsto \dfrac{3}{x\sqrt{4 - x}}.$

# 5.5 Graphs that represent functions

Consider the two graphs on the right.

In graph (a), for each value of $x$ you can draw a vertical line and see that it gives a unique $y$ value. Any horizontal line for a particular value of $y$ also corresponds to a unique value of $x$. Graph (a) represents a **one–one** function.

Repeating the procedure for graph (b). Any vertical line gives one value of $y$ and so the graph represents a function. This time, however, some of the horizontal lines pass through more than one point on the curve and would indicate that more than one value of $x$ maps onto a particular value of $y$.

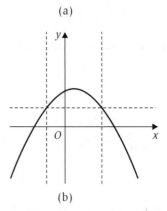

(a)

(b)

The function represented by graph (b) is **many–one**.

# 5.6 Graphs that do not represent functions

Contrast the graphs shown below with those in the previous section.

For certain values of $x$ you can draw a vertical line and see that it does not correspond to a unique value of $y$. These graphs do **not** represent functions.

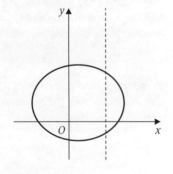

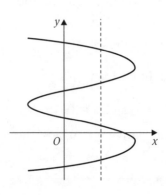

*EXERCISE 5D*

For each of the following graphs, state whether it represents a function or not. For the functions, identify them as one–one or many–one.

**1**
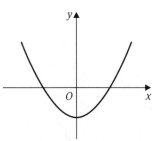

**2**
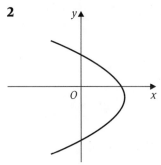

**3**
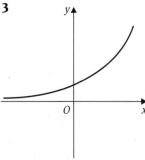

**4**
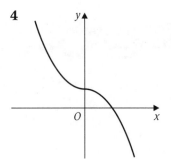

**5**
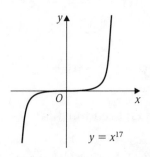

**6**
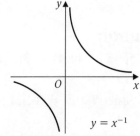

# 5.7 Odd and even functions

If you were to sketch the graphs of $y = x^n$ for different integer values of $n$, you would notice that their symmetry properties depend on whether $n$ is odd or even.

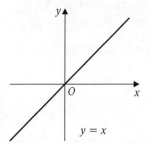
$y = x$

$y = x^5$

$y = x^{17}$

$y = x^{-1}$

Each of these graphs is unchanged after rotation through 180° about the origin. They have rotational symmetry of order 2. Functions, such as $f(x) = x^n$ ($n$ odd), whose graphs have this property are called **odd functions**.
This can be expressed algebraically

Consider $f(x) = x^5$.
$f(-a) = (-a)^5 = -a^5$
$f(a) = a^5$
So $f(-a) = -f(a)$ and therefore f is an odd function.

When $f(-a) = -f(a)$ for all values of $a$, we say that f is an **odd** function.

Similarly for graphs of even powers.

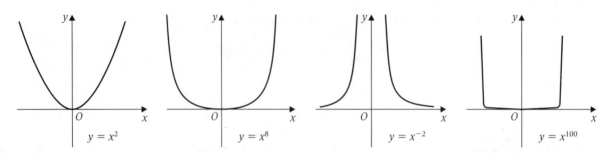

Each of these graphs is unchanged after reflection in the *y*-axis.
They have reflective symmetry.
Functions, such as $f(x) = x^n$ (*n* even) whose graphs have this
property are called **even functions**.

This can be expressed algebraically

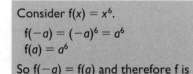

Consider $f(x) = x^6$.

$$f(-a) = (-a)^6 = a^6$$
$$f(a) = a^6$$

So $f(-a) = f(a)$ and therefore f is
an even function.

> When $f(-a) = f(a)$ for all values of *a*, we say that f is an
> **even** function.

## Worked example 5.5 _____

Determine whether the following functions are odd, even, or
neither:

**(a)** $f(x) = x^4 - 3x^2$,    **(b)** $g(x) = \dfrac{x^4 + 2}{x}$,    **(c)** $h(x) = 2x^3 + x^2$.

You may wish to draw the
graphs on a graphic calculator in
order to check for rotational or
reflective symmetry but you
need to prove the result
algebraically.

### Solution

**(a)** $f(-a) = (-a)^4 - 3(-a)^2 = a^4 - 3a^2$

$f(a) = a^4 - 3a^2$

Since $f(-a) = f(a)$, f is an even function.

**(b)** $g(-a) = \dfrac{(-a)^4 + 2}{(-a)} = \dfrac{a^4 + 2}{-a} = -\left(\dfrac{a^4 + 2}{a}\right)$

$g(a) = \dfrac{a^4 + 2}{a}$

Hence $g(-a) = -g(a) \Rightarrow$ g is an odd function.

Notice how important it is to
use brackets to avoid sign errors.

**(c)** $h(-a) = 2(-a)^3 + (-a)^2 = -2a^3 + a^2$

But since $h(a) = 2a^3 + a^2$, there is no simple relationship
between $h(-a)$ and $h(a)$ and so h is neither odd nor even.

## *EXERCISE 5E*

Determine whether the following functions are odd, even or neither.

**1** $f : x \mapsto x^2 + 2,$

**2** $g : x \mapsto x^3 + 2,$

**3** $h : x \mapsto \dfrac{x^2 + 2}{x},$

**4** $p : x \mapsto \dfrac{x^2 - x + 1}{x},$

**5** $q : x \mapsto (x^2 + 1)^3,$

**6** $r : x \mapsto (x^3 + 1)^2,$

**7** $f(x) = x^8 + \dfrac{5}{x^2},$

**8** $g(x) = \dfrac{x^4}{x^2 - 3},$

**9** $h(x) = 2 + x^{-5},$

**10** $f : x \mapsto \dfrac{x^2 + 2}{x + x^3}.$

## 5.8 Composite functions

The term composition is used when one operation is performed after another operation. For instance:

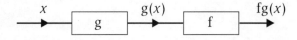

This function can be written as $h : x \mapsto 5(x + 3).$

Sometimes you have two given functions such as f and g and need to perform one function after another.

Suppose $f : x \mapsto x^2$ and $g : x \mapsto 2 + 3x, x \in \mathbb{R}.$
What is $f[g(x)]$?

$$g(x) = 2 + 3x$$
$$f[g(x)] = f(2 + 3x) = (2+3x)^2.$$

You could try with a number
$$g(2) = 2 + 6 = 8$$
$$f[g(2)] = f(8) = 8^2 = 64$$

> The expression $f[g(x)]$ is usually written without the extra brackets as $fg(x)$ and fg is said to be a **composite function**.
>
> $$x \xrightarrow{\quad} \boxed{g} \xrightarrow{g(x)} \boxed{f} \xrightarrow{fg(x)}$$

Although we write $fg(x)$ the function g operates first on $x$ because it is closest to $x$.

The function gf can be found in a similar way.

$$f(x) = x^2$$

so that $gf(x) = g[f(x)] = g(x^2) = 2 + 3\,(x^2) = 2 + 3x^2$

The composite function gf is

$$gf : x \mapsto 2 + 3x^2$$

## Worked example 5.6

Given that $f : x \mapsto x^3 + 5$ and $g : x \mapsto 3 - 2x$, $x \in \mathbb{R}$, find the composite functions fg and gf in a similar form.

## Solution

$g(x) = 3 - 2x$

$\Rightarrow f[g(x)] = f[3 - 2x] = (3 - 2x)^3 + 5$

The composite function fg is given by

$fg : x \mapsto (3 - 2x)^3 + 5.$

$f(x) = x^3 + 5$
$g(f(x)) = g(x^3 + 5) = 3 - 2(x^3 + 5)$

So gf is given by

$gf : x \mapsto 3 - 2(x^3 + 5)$

> Note that fg is not the same as gf. Although we could multiply out the brackets, it is best to leave the functions in this more compact form

## EXERCISE 5F

Assume that the domain of the functions in this exercise is $\mathbb{R}$.

1  Find the composite function fg for each of these functions:

   **(a)** $f : x \mapsto x - 1$ and $g : x \mapsto 5 - 2x$,

   **(b)** $f : x \mapsto x^2 - 3$ and $g : x \mapsto 2 + x$,

   **(c)** $f : x \mapsto x^3 + 1$ and $g : x \mapsto 3x - 1$,

   **(d)** $f : x \mapsto x^4 - 2$ and $g : x \mapsto (x + 1)^2$.

2  Find the composite function gf for each pair of functions in question **1**.

3  Given that $f(x) = x^2 - 2x + 1$ and $g(x) = 1 - 3x$, find:

   **(a)** $fg(x)$,      **(b)** $gf(x)$, simplifying your answers.

4  Given that $f(x) = 2x - 3$, find **(a)** $ff(2)$,    **(b)** $ff(a)$.
   Solve the equation $ff(a) = a$.

5  Given that $f(x) = kx - 2$ and $g(x) = 4 - 3x$, find in terms of $k$ and $x$:

   **(a)** $fg(x)$,      **(b)** $gf(x)$.

   State the value of $k$ for which $fg(x) = gf(x)$.

6  Given that $f(x) = x^2$ and $g(x) = 5 + x$, find $fg(x)$ and $gf(x)$.
   Show that there is a single value of $x$ for which $fg(x) = gf(x)$
   and find this value of $x$.

# 5.9 Domains of composite functions

In the examples of composite functions considered so far the domains have been the real numbers, but sometimes the domains need more careful consideration.

Consider the composite function fg

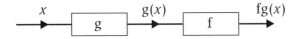

The whole of the range of g must be included in the domain of f, otherwise the domain of g needs restricting.

## Worked example 5.7

Given the functions f and g such that

$$f : x \mapsto \sqrt{x + 1}, \ x > 0, \text{ and } g : x \mapsto 5 - x, \ x \in \mathbb{R},$$

find the maximum possible domain of fg.

## Solution

It is necessary to solve the inequality $g(x) > 0$ so that the range of g consists only of positive numbers.

$$5 - x > 0 \implies x < 5.$$

The maximum domain of fg is therefore $x < 5$.

> Initially it might seem that any real number can be part of the domain of fg since the domain of g is $\mathbb{R}$.
>
> However $g(7) = -2$, for example, and this is not acceptable to be fed into f (see the diagram above).

# 5.10 Inverse functions

The function f defined for all real values of $x$ by $f : x \mapsto 3x - 4$ can be thought of as a sequence of operations.

If you reverse the operations and the flow,

The new function, g say, can be written as $g : x \mapsto \dfrac{x + 4}{3}$.

> Notice that $f(3) = 5$ and $g(5) = 3$. Similarly $f(-1) = -7$ and $g(-7) = -1$, etc.

In general $fg(x) = f\left(\dfrac{x + 4}{3}\right) = 3 \times \left(\dfrac{x + 4}{3}\right) - 4 = x$

Also $gf(x) = g(3x - 4) = \dfrac{(3x - 4) + 4}{3} = \dfrac{3x}{x} = x$.

A function g such that $fg(x) = x$ and $gf(x) = x$ is said to be the **inverse function** of f and is denoted by $f^{-1}$.

$f^{-1}$ is purely a symbol and should not be thought of as a reciprocal.

In this case, $f^{-1} : x \mapsto \dfrac{x + 4}{3}$.

## Worked example 5.8

Find: **(a)** $f^{-1}(x)$ and **(b)** $g^{-1}(x)$, where

$$f : x \mapsto x^3 + 5, \; x \in \mathbb{R} \text{ and}$$

$$g : x \mapsto \frac{x + 1}{x - 2}, \; x \in \mathbb{R}, \; x \neq 2.$$

The reverse flow diagram method can be used to find inverse functions in simple cases when $x$ occurs only once in f(x). This worked example gives a more general method for finding inverse functions.

## Solution

**(a)** $f(x) = x^3 + 5$ so let $y = x^3 + 5$

Rearrange to make $x$ the subject of the equation

$$y - 5 = x^3 \Rightarrow x = \sqrt[3]{y - 5}$$

Now interchange $x$ and $y$

$$\Rightarrow y = \sqrt[3]{x - 5}$$

Hence $f^{-1}(x) = \sqrt[3]{x - 5}$.

The forward flow diagram has the boxes 'cube' then 'add 5'.

The reverse flow diagram would be 'subtract 5' then 'take the cube root' – giving the same answer for the inverse function.

**(b)** $g(x) = \dfrac{x + 1}{x - 2}$ so let $y = \dfrac{x + 1}{x - 2}$

$$\Rightarrow (x - 2)y = x + 1$$

Multiply up by $(x - 2)$.

$$\Rightarrow xy - 2y = x + 1$$

$$\Rightarrow xy - x = 2y + 1$$

Collect all the terms involving $x$ onto one side.

$$\Rightarrow x(y - 1) = 2y + 1$$

$$\Rightarrow y = \frac{2y + 1}{(y - 1)}$$

Make $x$ the subject of the formula.

Now interchange $x$ and $y$

$$\Rightarrow y = \frac{2x + 1}{(x - 1)}$$

Essentially we are interchanging the domain and range to produce an inverse function.

Hence

$$g^{-1}(x) = \frac{2x + 1}{(x - 1)}$$

The domain for $g^{-1}$ is $x \in \mathbb{R}$, $x \neq 1$.

# 5.11 Condition for inverse function to exist

In order for $f^{-1}$ to exist, the function f must be one–one.

This is because the domain and range are interchanged when you perform an inverse mapping. If a function were many–one, the inverse mapping would be one–many and, as you have seen in Section 5.6, this could not be a function.

You can easily draw the graph of $f^{-1}$ when it exists.

The graph of $f^{-1}$ is obtained from the graph of f by reflection in the line $y = x$ provided you have equal scales on the $x - 1$ and $y$-axes.

**5**

## Worked example 5.9

The function f is defined by

$$f : x \mapsto (x - 2)^3, \ x \geqslant 0.$$

and is sketched with equal scales on the axes.

(a) Find the range of f.

(b) State why the inverse function $f^{-1}$ exists.

(c) Find $f^{-1}(x)$ and sketch the graph of $f^{-1}$.

(d) State the domain and range of $f^{-1}$.

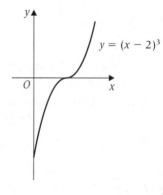

## Solution

(a) $f(0) = -8$ and the graph shows that the values of $f(x)$ increase as $x$ increases.

$$\Rightarrow \text{Range is } f(x) > -8.$$

(b) For each value of $f(x)$, there is a unique value of $x$. The function f is one–one.

(c) $f(x) = (x - 2)^3$ so let $y = (x - 2)^3$

Rearranging to make $x$ the new subject.

$$\Rightarrow \sqrt[3]{y} = (x - 2) \Rightarrow x = 2 + \sqrt[3]{y}$$

Graph of $f^{-1}$ obtained by reflection of graph of f in line $y = x$.

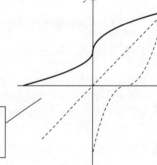

Interchanging $x$ and $y$.

$$y = 2 + \sqrt[3]{x} \Rightarrow f^{-1}(x) = 2 + \sqrt[3]{x}$$

(d) The domain of $f^{-1}$ is $x \geqslant -8$ (since the range of f is $f(x) \geqslant -8$)
The range of $f^{-1}$ is $f^{-1}(x) \geqslant 0$ (since the domain of f is $x \geqslant 0$)

# 5.12 Self-inverse functions

Consider the function g given by $g : x \mapsto 2 - x,\ x \in \mathbb{R}$.
If the inverse of g is $g^{-1}$, then $g\,g^{-1}(x) = x$ and $g^{-1}\,g(x) = x$

But $gg(x) = g(2 - x) = 2 - (2 - x) = 2 - 2 + x = x$

This proves that the inverse of g is itself g.

We call g a **self-inverse function**.

Alternatively $g(x) = 2 - x$
so let $y = 2 - x$
$\Rightarrow x + y = 2 \Rightarrow x = 2 - y$
Interchange $x$ and $y$.
$y = 2 - x$
$g^{-1} : x \mapsto 2 - x,\ x \in \mathbb{R}$

## EXERCISE 5G

**1** Find the inverse of each of the following functions with domain $\mathbb{R}$ by means of a reverse flow diagram:

**(a)** $f : x \mapsto 5x + 7$,

**(b)** $f : x \mapsto (x + 2)^3$,

**(c)** $f : x \mapsto \dfrac{(2x + 1)}{6}$,

**(d)** $f : x \mapsto (2x - 1)^{\frac{1}{3}}$,

**(e)** $f : x \mapsto \dfrac{(-2)x + 3}{5}$,

**(f)** $f : x \mapsto \dfrac{7 - 3x}{4}$.

**2** For each of the following functions:
**(i)** find its range,
**(ii)** find the inverse function, stating its domain,
**(iii)** state the range of the inverse function.

**(a)** $f : x \mapsto (3x - 1)^3,\ x \geqslant -1$,

**(b)** $g : x \mapsto 1 - \dfrac{2}{x},\ x \geqslant 1$,

**(c)** $h : x \mapsto (2x + 3)^5,\ x > 0$,

**(d)** $q : x \mapsto 1 + \dfrac{5}{x},\ x < -5$,

**(e)** $r : x \mapsto \dfrac{4}{3 - x},\ x \geqslant 5$.

Use a graphic calculator if you need to.

**3 (a)** Sketch the graph of the function:
$$f : x \mapsto x^2 + 3,\ x \in \mathbb{R}.$$
Explain why f does not have an inverse function.

**(b)** Sketch the graph of the function:
$$g : x \mapsto x^2 + 3,\ x \geqslant 1.$$
Explain why g has an inverse and find $g^{-1}(x)$.
State the domain and range of $g^{-1}$.

**4** The function h has domain $x < 0$ and is defined by:
$$h(x) = x^2 - 3$$

**(a)** Explain by means of a sketch why h has an inverse.

**(b)** Find $h^{-1}(x)$ and state the domain and range of $h^{-1}$.

## Worked exam question

The function f is defined for $x \geqslant 0$ by

$$f : x \mapsto \frac{3x - 2}{x + 1}.$$

**(a)** Express f$(x)$ in the form $a + \dfrac{b}{x + 1}$, where $a$ and $b$ are constants.

**(b)** Determine the range of f.

**(c)** The inverse of function f is f$^{-1}$. Find f$^{-1}(x)$, and state the domain of f$^{-1}$. [A]

## Solution

**(a)** $3x - 2 = 3(x + 1) - 5$

$$\Rightarrow \frac{3x - 2}{x + 1} = \frac{3(x + 1) - 5}{x + 1} = \frac{3(x + 1)}{x + 1} - \frac{5}{x + 1} = 3 - \frac{5}{x + 1}$$

which is of the required form with $a = 3$ and $b = -5$.

> We could use the original expression or the one found in part **(a)**. Because the answers are identical, it gives us confidence that the answer to part **(a)** is correct.

**5**

**(b)** $f(0) = -2$

As you substitute larger numbers into $\dfrac{5}{x + 1}$, the answer gets smaller and smaller. Since you are subtracting this number from 3, the value of f$(x)$ never quite reaches the value 3.

This suggests that the range is greater than or equal to $-2$ but also strictly less than 3.

The range is $-2 \leqslant f(x) < 3$.

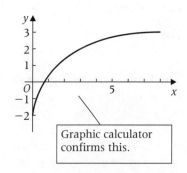

Graphic calculator confirms this.

**(c)** Let $y = \dfrac{3x - 2}{x + 1} \Rightarrow y(x + 1) = 3x - 2$

$\Rightarrow xy + y = 3x - 2$
$\Rightarrow 2 + y = 3x - xy$
$\Rightarrow 2 + y = x(3 - y) \Rightarrow x = \dfrac{2 + y}{3 - y}$

Interchange $x$ and $y$: $\Rightarrow y = \dfrac{2 + x}{3 - x}$

so f$^{-1}(x) = \dfrac{2 + x}{3 - x}$.

Domain of f$^{-1}$ is $-2 \leqslant x < 3$.

> Multiply throughout by $(x + 1)$.

> Make $x$ the subject of the formula.

> Using the result from part **(b)**.

## MIXED EXERCISE

1 The function f has domain $x > 5$ and is defined by

$$f : x \mapsto \frac{3}{4 - x}.$$

(a) Find the range of f.

(b) The inverse of f is $f^{-1}$. Find $f^{-1}(x)$.　　　　[A]

2 The functions f and g are defined by

$$f : x \mapsto 3x + 4 \quad x \in \mathbb{R},$$

$$g : x \mapsto \frac{1}{x^2} \quad x \in \mathbb{R}, \quad x \neq 0$$

Write down, in a similar form:

(a) the composite function fg,

(b) the inverse function $f^{-1}$.　　　　[A]

3 The function f has domain $x \geqslant 2$ and is defined by

$$f(x) = \frac{2x - 3}{x}.$$

(a) Determine the range of f.

(b) The inverse of f is $f^{-1}$. Find $f^{-1}(x)$.　　　　[A]

4 The functions f and g are defined with their respective domains by

$$f : x \mapsto \frac{3}{2x - 1} \quad x \in \mathbb{R}, \quad x \neq \tfrac{1}{2},$$

$$g : x \mapsto x^2 + 1 \quad x \in \mathbb{R}.$$

(a) Find the range of g.

(b) The domain of the composite function fg is $\mathbb{R}$.
　　Find $fg(x)$ and state the range of fg.　　　　[A]

5 The function f with domain $x > 2$ is defined by

$$f : x \mapsto \frac{1}{\sqrt{x - 2}}.$$

(a) Sketch the graph of f.

(b) Explain briefly why f has an inverse function, state the
　　domain of $f^{-1}$, and express $f^{-1}(x)$ in terms of x.　　[A]

> In the P1 examination, you would not be expected to sketch graphs as difficult as the ones in this exercise. If you needed to use such a graph, the sketch would be given.
>
> In this exercise, you are encouraged to use your graphic calculator to obtain a sketch to enable you to find the range.

**6** The function f with domain $\{x : x \geq 0\}$ is defined by

$$f(x) = \frac{8}{x+2}.$$

  **(a)** Sketch the graph of f and state the range of f.

  **(b)** Find $f^{-1}(x)$, where $f^{-1}$ denotes the inverse of f.

  **(c)** Calculate the value of $x$ for which $f(x) = f^{-1}(x)$.    [A]

**7** The function f with domain $\{x : x \geq 2\}$ is defined by

$$f(x) = 1 - \frac{2}{x}.$$

  **(a)** Sketch the graph of f and state the range of f.

  **(b)** Explain why the inverse function $f^{-1}$ exists and state its domain. Find an expression for $f^{-1}(x)$.    [A]

---

## Key point summary

**1** A function is a one–one or a many–one mapping.    *p61*

**2** The set of numbers for which a function is defined is called the domain.    *p61*

**3** The set of values the function can take for a given domain is called the range.    *p61*

**4** An odd function satisfies $f(-a) = -f(-a)$ for all values $a$ in the domain of f.    *p67*

An odd function has 180° rotational symmetry about the origin.

**5** An even function satisfies $f(-a) = f(-a)$ for all values $a$ in the domain of f.    *p68*

An even function has reflective symmetry about the y-axis.

**6** The composite function fg means first g then f, since:    *p69*

$$fg(x) = f[g(x)].$$

**7** A function f has an inverse only when f is one–one.    *p73*
Its graph is obtained by reflecting the graph of f in the line $y = x$.

| Test yourself | What to review |
|---|---|
| **1** Given that $f(x) = x^3 - 3x + 2$ find $f(-2)$. | *Section 5.2* |
| **2** Find the range of the function f with domain $x > 3$, where $f : x \mapsto x^3 - 1$. | *Section 5.3* |
| **3** State the maximum possible domain for the function $g : x \mapsto \sqrt{4 - x}$. | *Section 5.4* |
| **4** Determine whether the function $h : x \mapsto \dfrac{x^3 - x}{x^2 + 2}$ is an odd function, an even function or neither of these. | *Section 5.7* |
| **5** Given that $f : x \mapsto x^2 + 5$ and $g : x \mapsto 7 - x$, and each has domain $\mathbb{R}$, find the composite function gf in its simplest form. | *Section 5.8* |
| **6** Given that $f : x \mapsto 2x^3 + 7$, with domain $x < 1$, find the inverse function $f^{-1}$ and state its domain. | *Section 5.10* |

**Test yourself** ANSWERS

**1** 0,    **2** $f(x) > 26$,    **3** $x \leqslant 4$,    **4** odd,

**5** $gf : x \mapsto 2 - x^2$,    **6** $f^{-1} : x \mapsto \sqrt[3]{\dfrac{x - 7}{2}}$,   $x < 9$.

# CHAPTER 6

# Introduction to differentiation

---

## Learning objectives

After studying this chapter, you should be able to:

■ understand the terms 'chord' and 'tangent' to a curve and how they are related
■ understand the term 'derivative' and how you can find gradients of curves from first principles
■ use differentiation to find the gradient function of simple curves
■ find the gradient of a curve at any desired point on the curve.

---

## 6.1  Introduction

6

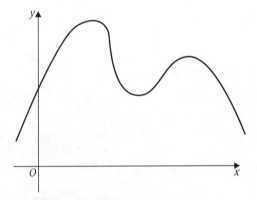

Imagine that the curve above represents part of a roller coaster track and that a pole extends out in front of the car which indicates the direction of motion. Clearly, as you are riding the roller coaster, the direction of the pole will change: at times you may be climbing and the pole will be pointing upwards, it may be momentarily horizontal at the top of a curve or the pole will be pointing downwards as you plunge towards the ground.

All of this tells you that the direction of the curve is constantly changing which, in turn, means that the gradient of the curve is always changing.

How do you find the gradient of a curve if it is different at each point on the curve ?

The aim of this chapter is to develop a systematic way of finding the gradient of a curve at any point you choose.

# 6.2 Gradients of chords

**A straight line that joins two points on a curve is called a chord.**

Since the chord is a straight line you can use:

$$\text{gradient of chord} = \frac{\text{difference in } ys}{\text{difference in } xs} = \frac{y_2 - y_1}{x_2 - x_1}$$

See Section 4.4 of chapter 4.

Using the definitions :

$\delta x$ is the 'increase in $x$'      $\delta y$ is the 'increase in $y$'

The Greek letter $\delta$ (delta) [or the capital letter $\Delta$] is used as an abbreviation for difference.

The word difference can be a little confusing since it does not take into account the sign of the result.

Gradient of chord $= \dfrac{\delta y}{\delta x}$

## Worked example 6.1

The diagram shows part of the curve $y = x^3$.
Find the gradient of the chord joining the two points $A$, where $x = 1$, and $B$, where $x = 3$.

## Solution

First, you need to find the $y$-coordinates of the points $A$ and $B$.

at $A$, $x = 1 \Rightarrow y = 1^3 = 1$
at $B$, $x = 3 \Rightarrow y = 3^3 = 27$

So $A$ is the point $(1, 1)$ and $B$ is the point $(3, 27)$.

For the chord joining $A(1, 1)$ to $B(3, 27)$ we have

$\delta x = 3 - 1 = 2$   and   $\delta y = 27 - 1 = 26$

The gradient of the chord $AB = \dfrac{\delta y}{\delta x} = \dfrac{26}{2} = 13$.

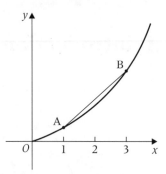

Since the curve has equation $y = x^3$.

**Note.** To find the 'increase' you take the second value and subtract the first value.

## Worked example 6.2

A curve has equation $y = 13 - x^2$. Find the gradient of the chord joining the points on the curve with $x$-coordinates 2 and 3.

## Solution

The coordinates of the points are $(2, 9)$ and $(3, 4)$.

Hence $\delta x = 3 - 2 = 1$ and $\delta y = 4 - 9 = -5$

The gradient of the chord $\dfrac{\delta y}{\delta x} = \dfrac{-5}{1} = -5$.

when $x = 2$,   $y = 13 - 2^2 = 9$
when $x = 3$,   $y = 13 - 3^2 = 4$

Notice that this is a negative answer since the $y$-value has actually decreased.

## EXERCISE 6A

**1** A curve has equation $y = x^2$. Find the gradient of the chord joining the points on the curve with $x$-coordinates 3 and 4.

**2** Find the gradient of the chord joining the points $(1, 5)$ and $(3, 45)$ on the curve $y = 5x^2$.

**3** A curve is given by the equation $y = 6 - x^2$. Find the gradient of the chord joining the points with $x$-coordinates 2 and 4.

**4** Find the gradient of the chord through the points with $x$-coordinates $-1$ and 2 on the curve $y = 3x^2 + 2$.

**Hint.** Watch out for double negatives.

**5** A curve has equation $y = 7 - x^3$. Find the gradient of the chord through the points with $x$-coordinates 1 and 1.5.

## 6.3 Tangent to a curve at a point

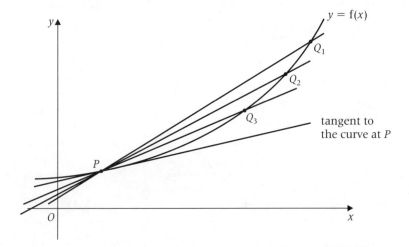

Consider a point $P$ on the curve with equation $y = f(x)$.

The position of $P$ is fixed but a second point $Q$ moves along the curve so that it gets closer and closer to $P$.
Assume that $Q$ starts at position $Q_1$ then moves to position $Q_2$ then to $Q_3$, etc. Clearly, the directions of the chords $PQ_1$, $PQ_2$, $PQ_3$, ... are different.
You can continue this process of moving $Q$ closer to $P$ until they become infinitely close together.
When the two points are infinitely close together, the resulting chord is called the **tangent to the curve at $P$**.

> The tangent to a curve at any point $P$ is the straight line which just touches the curve at the point $P$.

This idea of making the two points on the curve get closer and closer to each other will be essential in developing a systematic method of finding the gradient of a curve at any point.

In fact, the gradient of the tangent to the curve is used in order to define the gradient of the curve itself.

> The gradient of a curve at any point $P$ is equal to the gradient of the tangent to the curve at $P$.

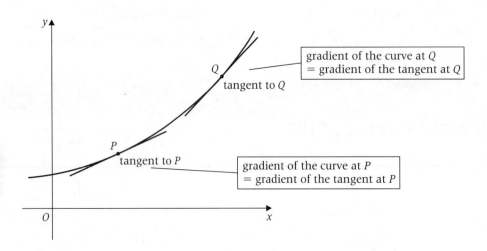

This definition forms the basis of a method for finding the gradient of a curve at any point.

## Worked example 6.3

A curve has equation $y = 4x^2$.

Find the gradient of the chord joining the following points:

**(a)** $x = 1$ and $x = 1.1$,

**(b)** $x = 1$ and $x = 1.01$,

**(c)** $x = 1$ and $x = 1.001$.

Use your answers to **(a)**, **(b)** and **(c)** to suggest what the gradient of the curve is when $x = 1$.

### Solution

**(a)** $(1, 4)$ and $(1.1, 4.84)$

Hence $\delta x = 1.1 - 1 = 0.1$ and $\delta y = 4.84 - 4 = 0.84$

the gradient of the chord $= \dfrac{\delta y}{\delta x} = \dfrac{0.84}{0.1} = 8.4$

> You need the $y$-coordinates of each of the points:
> when $x = 1$,  $y = 4(1)^2 = 4$
> when $x = 1.1$,  $y = 4(1.1)^2 = 4.84$
> when $x = 1.01$,  $y = 4(1.01)^2 = 4.0804$
> when $x = 1.001$,  $y = 4(1.001)^2 = 4.008004$

**(b)** (1, 4) and (1.01, 4.0804)

$\delta x = 1.01 - 1 = 0.01$ and $\delta y = 4.0804 - 4 = 0.0804$

the gradient of the chord $= \dfrac{\delta y}{\delta x} = \dfrac{0.0804}{0.01} = 8.04$

**(c)** (1, 4) and (1.001, 4.008004)

$\delta x = 1.001 - 1 = 0.001$ and $\delta y = 4.008004 - 4 = 0.008004$

the gradient of the chord $= \dfrac{\delta y}{\delta x} = \dfrac{0.008004}{0.001} = 8.004$

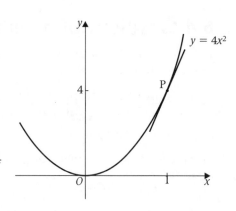

You are taking two points on the curve and making the second point get closer and closer to (1, 4).

This process eventually gives the gradient of the tangent at (1, 4) and, therefore, the gradient of the curve at (1, 4). Consider the sequence formed by the gradients of the chords:

8.4, 8.04, 8.004, …

It seems sensible to suggest that the sequence is converging to 8.

In other words, this process suggests that the gradient of the curve $y = 4x^2$ at the point (1, 4) is 8.

> We say that the **limit** of the sequence is 8.

> While this offers strong evidence that the gradient is 8, it cannot be considered as a proof.
> A more general method which can prove this result is considered later.

**6**

## EXERCISE 6B

**1** Find the gradient of the chord joining the points with $x$-coordinates 2 and 2.1 on the curve $y = 4x^2 - 5$.

**2** Find the gradient of the chord joining the points with $x$-coordinates 1 and 1.1 on the curve $y = x^4$.

**3** A curve has equation $y = x^5$.

Find the gradients of the chords joining the following pairs of points on the curve.

**(a)** $x = 1$ and $x = 1.1$

**(b)** $x = 1$ and $x = 1.01$

**(c)** $x = 1$ and $x = 1.001$ .

Using your answers to **(a)**, **(b)** and **(c)**, make a guess at what you think the gradient of the curve is at the point where $x = 1$?

**4** Use a similar approach to question **3** to find the gradient of the curve $y = 2x^3$ at the point $P$ where $x = 2$.

> You need to consider two points on the curve: *P* and another point close to it and let the second point get closer to *P*.

# 6.4 Gradient of a curve at a given point

There are two problems with the method above using a sequence of numerical values:

**(i)** it only offers strong evidence that the gradient has a particular value ( it does not prove the result),

**(ii)** it is time consuming.

The method can be generalized by using $h$ to represent a small increase in $x$.

> $h$ is used for the 'increase in $x$' instead of $\delta x$. This is because the notation becomes easier later on: writing $h^2$ instead of $(\delta x)^2$, etc. looks a little less cumbersome.

## Worked example 6.4

A curve has equation $y = x^2$ and the points $P$ and $Q$ have coordinates $(2, 4)$ and $(2 + h, (2 + h)^2)$ respectively. Show that the gradient of $PQ$ is $4 + h$ and deduce the gradient of the curve at $P$.

## Solution

The diagram illustrates the situation.

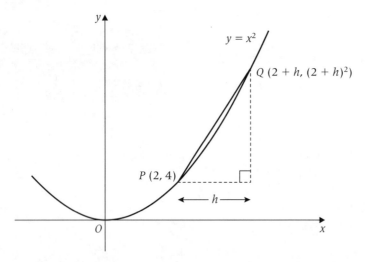

> The coordinates of $P$ are $(2, 4)$ and the coordinates of $Q$ are $(2 + h, (2 + h)^2)$ since both points lie on the curve $y = x^2$.

$\Rightarrow$ Gradient of chord $PQ = \dfrac{(2 + h)^2 - 4}{(2 + h) - 2}$

$= \dfrac{(4 + 4h + h^2) - 4}{(2 + h) - 2}$

> Note how the bracket in the numerator has been expanded.

$= \dfrac{4h + h^2}{h}$

$= \dfrac{h(4 + h)}{h}$

> $h$ is a common factor in the numerator.

$= 4 + h$

$\Rightarrow$ Gradient of $PQ = 4 + h$

> $h$ has been cancelled in the top and bottom.

To find the **gradient of the curve at** *P*, you must find the **gradient of the tangent at** *P*.

To do this we use the basic idea of moving point *Q* closer and closer to *P*.
In doing this, it is important to realise that the value of *h* gets smaller and smaller.

It is not difficult to see that as *h* **tends to zero**, the gradient gets closer and closer to 4

'tends to'

gradient of the curve at $P$ = gradient of $PQ$ as $h \to 0$

gradient of the curve at $P = \lim_{h \to 0} (4 + h)$

limit as *h* tends to 0

Therefore, the gradient of the curve at P $= 4 + 0 = 4$.

The very same method can be used to generate the gradient of a curve at **any point** where $x = a$.

## Worked example 6.5

6

The points *P* and *Q* lie on the curve $y = 3x^2$ and have *x*-coordinates $x = a$ and $x = a+h$, respectively.

Show that the gradient of the chord *PQ* is $6a + 3h$. Hence find the gradient of the curve at the point P.

## Solution

coordinates of *P* are $(a, 3a^2)$

coordinates of *Q* are $(a + h, 3(a + h)^2)$

Gradient of $PQ = \dfrac{3(a + h)^2 - 3a^2}{(a + h) - a}$

$$= \dfrac{3a^2 + 6ah + 3h^2 - 3a^2}{h}$$

$$= \dfrac{6ah + 3h^2}{h} = 6a + 3h$$

To find the gradient of the curve, let $h \to 0$

i.e. let *Q* get closer to *P*

$\Rightarrow$ gradient $= 6a + 3(0) = 6a$

## EXERCISE 6C

**1** A curve has equation $y = 5x^2$. The points *P* and *Q* have coordinates $(1, 5)$ and $(1+h, 5(1+h)^2)$, respectively. Find the gradient of the chord *PQ* in as simplified a form as possible. Hence find the gradient of the curve at the point *P*.

**2** A curve has equation $y = 3 - 2x^2$. Find the gradient of the chord $PQ$ and deduce the gradient of the curve at the point $P$ in the following cases.

   **(a)** $P(1,1)$ and $Q(1 + h, 3 - 2(1 + h)^2)$,

   **(b)** $P(2, -5)$ and $Q(2 + h, 3 - 2(2 + h)^2)$,

   **(c)** $P(a, 3 - 2a^2)$ and $Q(a + h, 3 - 2(a + h)^2)$.

**3** A curve has equation $y = \dfrac{1}{3 + x}$ and the points $P$ and $Q$ have

the coordinates $\left(2, \dfrac{1}{5}\right)$ and $\left(2 + h, \dfrac{1}{5 + h}\right)$, respectively, where

$h$ is small. Show that the gradient of the chord $PQ$ can be

written as $\dfrac{-1}{5(5 + h)}$.

By considering the limit as $h$ tends to zero, deduce the value
of the gradient at $P$.         [A]

**4** A curve has equation $y = x^3 - 5x^2$. The point $P$ has coordinates $(2, -12)$ and the point $Q$ has $x$-coordinate $2 + h$.

   **(a)** Find the $y$-coordinate of $Q$ as a cubic polynomial in $h$.

   **(b)** Show that the gradient of the chord $PQ$ is given
by $h^2 + h - 8$.

   **(c)** Use the result in part **(b)** to deduce the gradient of the
tangent to the curve at $P$.         [A]

# 6.5 The gradient function

Using the result from Worked example 6.5, the gradient of
the curve $y = 3x^2$ at the point where $x = a$ is $6a$.

It follows that the gradient of the curve at **any point** $P(x, y)$ is
actually $6x$. This is a very interesting result since the gradient of
the curve turns out to be a function of the variable $x$.

This function allows us to substitute different values of $x$ and
obtain the gradient of the curve at that point. For this reason,
the function is sometimes called the gradient function.
Since $P$ was any point on the curve, this gives a method for
finding the gradient of the curve $y = 3x^2$ at any point, e.g.

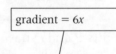

     at the point where $x = 3$,    the gradient $= 6(3) = 18$

     at the point where $x = -5$,  the gradient $= 6(-5) = -30$

This method can be used to generate gradient functions of other curves:

> If you need to find the gradient function of a curve
> $y = f(x)$ then take two points on the curve $P(x, f(x))$ and
> $Q(x + h, f(x + h))$ and let $Q$ become infinitely close to $P$.
>
> $$\text{gradient function} = \lim_{h \to 0} \left\{ \frac{f(x + h) - f(x)}{h} \right\}$$

## Worked example 6.6

Find the gradient function, by a suitable limiting process, for the curve with equation $y = x^3$.

Hence find the gradient at the points $(1, 1)$ and $(2, 8)$ on the curve.

## Solution

Consider the two points $P(x, f(x))$ and $Q(x + h, f(x + h))$ on the curve where $f(x) = x^3$

and 
$$\begin{aligned} f(x + h) &= (x + h)^3 = (x + h)(x + h)(x + h) \\ &= (x^2 + 2xh + h^2)(x + h) \\ &= x^3 + 3x^2h + 3xh^2 + h^3 \end{aligned}$$

So the gradient function is

$$= \lim_{h \to 0} \left\{ \frac{f(x + h) - f(x)}{h} \right\}$$

$$= \lim_{h \to 0} \frac{(x + h)^3 - x^3}{h}$$

$$= \lim_{h \to 0} \frac{(x^3 + 3x^2h + 3xh^2 + h^3) - x^3}{h}$$

$$= \lim_{h \to 0} \frac{3x^2h + 3xh^2 + h^3}{h}$$

$$= \lim_{h \to 0} (3x^2 + 3xh + h^2) \qquad \boxed{h \text{ has been cancelled in every term}}$$

$$= 3x^2 + 3x(0) + 0^2 \qquad \boxed{\text{Let } h \text{ tend to } 0}$$

$$\Rightarrow \text{gradient function} = 3x^2$$

The gradient at the point $(1,1)$ is obtained by substituting $x = 1$ into the gradient function.

Gradient $= 3$

Similarly at the point $(2, 8)$, the gradient $= 3 \times 2^2 = 12$

# 6.6 Differentiation from first principles

This method of finding gradient functions was invented by two mathematicians: *Sir Isaac Newton* and *Gottfried Wilhelm von Leibniz*. While they used different notation and were using the idea to solve very different problems they had in fact developed **differential calculus** at around the same time. It was Leibniz who published his calculus first in 1684 but it is generally thought that Newton had been using the idea earlier. A bitter argument erupted between the supporters of each mathematician as to which should be given credit for the technique. It raged for many years but over time both men have been credited equally for their development of one of the most powerful and significant advances in the history of mathematics.

> The process of finding gradient functions is called **differentiation**.

## Notation

> The gradient function is more commonly known as the **derivative or derived function**.

Recall that if $y = 3x^2$, then the gradient function $= 6x$,

We say:

$3x^2$ is **differentiated with respect to $x$** to give $6x$

or     $6x$ is the derivative of $3x^2$.

> Since the variable is $x$.

Rather than having to write the word derivative every time, various ways of denoting the derivative have been developed:

(i)  $\dfrac{dy}{dx}$ ——— This is read as 'dy by dx'

> This was the notation used by *Leibniz*.

For example

$$y = 3x^2 \implies \frac{dy}{dx} = 6x.$$

> Sometimes this may be seen as
> $$\frac{d}{dx}(3x^2) = 6x$$

(ii)  $f'(x)$ ——— This is read as 'f dashed x'

So that

$$f(x) = 3x^2 \implies f'(x) = 6x.$$

> Newton's 'fluxion' notation.

The method given previously for finding the derivative (gradient function) of a curve is called

**differentiation from first principles**.

The method of differentiation from first principles can be summarised by the following.

$$\text{If } y = f(x) \text{ then } \frac{dy}{dx} = \lim_{h \to 0} \left\{ \frac{f(x + h) - f(x)}{h} \right\}$$

## Worked example 6.7

Use differentiation from first principles to find the derivative of the function $y = 2x^2 + 5x$.

## Solution

Now $\quad f(x) = 2x^2 + 5x$

and $\quad f(x + h) = 2(x + h)^2 + 5(x + h)$

$$\Rightarrow \quad \frac{dy}{dx} = \lim_{h \to 0} \left\{ \frac{f(x + h) - f(x)}{h} \right\}$$

$$= \lim_{h \to 0} \frac{[2(x + h)^2 + 5(x + h)] - [2x^2 + 5x]}{h}$$

$$= \lim_{h \to 0} \frac{[2x^2 + 4xh + 2h^2 + 5x + 5h] - [2x^2 + 5x]}{h}$$

$$= \lim_{h \to 0} \frac{4xh + 2h^2 + 5h}{h}$$

$$= \lim_{h \to 0} (4x + 2h + 5)$$

$$= 4x + 0 + 5$$

$$\Rightarrow \quad \frac{dy}{dx} = 4x + 5$$

## EXERCISE 6D

1 Use differentiation from first principles to find the derivative of the following functions.

(a) $y = 8x$,

(b) $y = 5x^2$,

(c) $y = 4x^2 + 2x$,

(d) $y = x^2 - 6$,

(e) $y = 2x^3$,

(f) $y = 4x^3$,

(g) $y = x^3 - 3x$,

(h) $y = \dfrac{1}{x}$.

## 6.7 General rules for differentiation

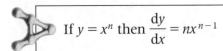

If $y = x^n$ then $\dfrac{dy}{dx} = nx^{n-1}$

> Having to use differentiation from first principles every time you need to find the gradient of a curve can become very time-consuming. Fortunately, shortcuts have been developed in the form of a simple strategy which allows you to differentiate functions very quickly and easily.

Suppose you need to differentiate $y = x^5$

$\dfrac{dy}{dx} = 5x^4$

Index has been reduced by 1

The 5 brought down in front.

If $y = cx^n$ then $\dfrac{dy}{dx} = cnx^{n-1}$ (where $c$ is a constant)

> Differentiate the function and multiply by the scaling factor, the constant $c$.

For example

The constant here is 7.

Differentiate $y = 7x^3$

$\dfrac{dy}{dx} = 7 \times 3x^2 = 21x^2$

Bring the power down in front and reduce the power of $x$ by 1, then multiply the answer by 7.

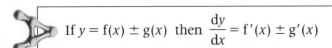

If $y = f(x) \pm g(x)$ then $\dfrac{dy}{dx} = f'(x) \pm g'(x)$

> If the function is made of of the sum or difference of two (or more) simpler functions, then differentiate term by term.

Differentiate $y = x^7 - x^4 + 5x^3$

$5(3x^2) = 15x^2$

$\dfrac{dy}{dx} = 7x^6 - 4x^3 + 15x^2$

Differentiate each term separately.

## *Worked example 6.8*

Differentiate the following with respect to $x$.

**(a)** $y = 6x^3$      **(b)** $y = -3x^5$    **(c)** $y = 9x$

**(d)** $y = 6$          **(e)** $y = 3x^5 - 4x^2 + 8x + 15$

## Solution

6 is the constant

**(a)** $\dfrac{dy}{dx} = 6(3x^2) = 18x^2$

**(b)** $\dfrac{dy}{dx} = -3(5x^4) = -15x^4$

**(c)** $\dfrac{dy}{dx} = 9(1x^0) = 9$ —— This is what you should expect since $y = 9x$ is the equation of a straight line with gradient 9.

$x^0 = 1$

In $y = 9x$ the power of $x$ is 1.

**(d)** There does not seem to be a power of $x$ here and so it looks like you cannot use the quick method of differentiating.

You must have $y = x^{\text{something}}$ in order to use this method.

This is not the case since you can re-write $y$ as

$$y = 6x^0 \quad (\text{since } x^0 = 1)$$

You now have a power of $x$.

$$\Rightarrow \quad \frac{dy}{dx} = 6(0x^{-1}) = 0$$

This is what you should expect since $y = 6$ is a horizontal line and therefore has a gradient of 0.

**Any line with the equation $y = $ constant has a gradient of 0.**

**(e)** $\dfrac{dy}{dx} = 3(5x^4) - 4(2x^1) + 8(1x^0) + 0$

$\qquad = 15x^4 - 8x + 8$

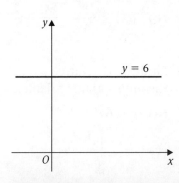

You are not restricted to differentiating with respect to $x$.

## Worked example 6.9

The constant is $\frac{1}{4}$

Differentiate $y = \dfrac{5t^3}{3} + \dfrac{t^2}{4} - 7t - 4$.

The constant is $\frac{5}{3}$

## Solution

Differentiate $y$ with respect to $t$.

Since the variable is $t$.

$$\frac{dy}{dt} = \frac{5}{3}(3t^2) + \frac{1}{4}(2t^1) - 7(1t^0) - 0$$

$$= \frac{15t^2}{3} + \frac{2t}{4} - 7$$

$$= 5t^2 + \frac{t}{2} - 7$$

## *EXERCISE 6E*

**1** Differentiate the following with respect to $x$.

(a) $y = 5$,

(b) $y = 3x^3 - 7x^2$,

(c) $y = x^6 - 4x^2 + 5x$,

(d) $y = x^6 + x^3$,

(e) $y = 3 - 2x + 5x^2$,

(f) $y = 7x^3 - 9$,

(g) $y = 1 + 4x^2 - 9x^3$,

(h) $y = 8x^{10} - 7x^6 + 42$,

(i) $y = 8x^2 + 4x - 3$,

(j) $y = 6x^2 - 4x + 11$,

(k) $y = x^7 - 3x^2 + 2x - 1$,

(l) $y = x^4 - 3x^3 - x - 5$.

**2** Find $f'(x)$ for each of these functions.

(a) $f(x) = \dfrac{x^3}{3}$,

(b) $f(x) = 6x^5 - 8x^2 + \dfrac{x^2}{6}$,

(c) $f(x) = 7x^2 - \dfrac{x}{5} + 2$,

(d) $f(x) = \dfrac{2}{3}x^6 - \dfrac{3}{4}x^8 + 9$,

(e) $f(x) = \dfrac{3x^5}{4} - \dfrac{5x^2}{9} + \dfrac{1}{2}$,

(f) $f(x) = \dfrac{2x^{12}}{3} - \dfrac{7x^3}{6} + \dfrac{5x}{4}$.

**3** Find the derivative of each of the following with respect to the appropriate variable.

(a) $p = 6q^3 - 7q$,

(b) $y = 3t^9 - 0.4t + 7$,

(c) $m = \dfrac{4n^2}{3} - \dfrac{4n}{7}$,

(d) $r = 7s^3 - \dfrac{s}{4} + 3$,

(e) $t = \dfrac{3w^2}{4} - \dfrac{4w^7}{7}$,

(f) $z = 5p^3 - \dfrac{p^8}{4} + 2p$.

# 6.8 Negative and fractional powers

The quick method of differentiation that you have been using still works if you have negative and/or fractional powers of $x$.

> The use of the laws of indices from Chapter 1 will be needed for these questions.

## *Worked example 6.10*

Differentiate the following functions with respect to $x$.

(a) $y = \dfrac{1}{x^3}$,

(b) $y = \dfrac{7}{x^6}$,

(c) $y = \dfrac{2}{3x^7}$,

(d) $y = \dfrac{5}{x^3} - \dfrac{4}{3x} + 8x^2$.

> The functions must be in the form $y = x^n$.

## Solution

**(a)** First you must re-write $y$ in an appropriate form.

$$y = \frac{1}{x^3} = x^{-3}$$

> Using the negative power rule.

You can now use the quick method for differentiating.

$$\frac{dy}{dx} = -3x^{-4}$$

> Bring the power to the front and reduce the power by 1.

This can be 'tidied-up' as

$$\frac{dy}{dx} = -\frac{3}{x^4}.$$

> Again, using the negative power rule.

**(b)** First you need to re-write it in an appropriate form.

$$y = 7x^{-6}$$

$$\Rightarrow \quad \frac{dy}{dx} = 7(-6x^{-7})$$

$$= -42x^{-7}$$

$$= -\frac{42}{x^7}$$

**(c)** Re-write $y$ using powers of $x$:

$$y = \frac{2}{3}x^{-7}$$

> Notice that the 3 is left on the bottom since the power only applied to $x$.

$$\Rightarrow \quad \frac{dy}{dx} = \frac{2}{3}(-7x^{-8})$$

$$= -\frac{14}{3}x^{-8}$$

$$= -\frac{14}{3x^8}$$

**(d)** Re-write $y$ using powers of $x$:

$$y = 5x^{-3} - \frac{4}{3}x^{-1} + 8x^2$$

> Notice the double negative.

$$\Rightarrow \quad \frac{dy}{dx} = 5(-3x^{-4}) - \frac{4}{3}(-1x^{-2}) + 8(2x^1)$$

$$= -15x^{-4} + \frac{4}{3}x^{-2} + 16x$$

$$= -\frac{15}{x^4} + \frac{4}{3x^2} + 16x$$

6

## Worked example 6.11

Differentiate the following with respect to $x$.

**(a)** $y = 2x^{\frac{1}{3}}$,　　　**(b)** $y = 7\sqrt{x}$,　　　**(c)** $y = \dfrac{4}{\sqrt{x}}$.

## Solution

**(a)**　　$\dfrac{dy}{dx} = 2\left(\dfrac{1}{3}x^{-\frac{2}{3}}\right)$

$\boxed{\dfrac{1}{3} - 1 = -\dfrac{2}{3}}$

$= \dfrac{2}{3}x^{-\frac{2}{3}} = \dfrac{2}{3x^{\frac{2}{3}}}$

**(b)**　Write $y$ using powers of $x$:

> Power of $\frac{1}{2}$ means square root.

$y = 7x^{\frac{1}{2}}$

$\Rightarrow\quad \dfrac{dy}{dx} = 7\left(\dfrac{1}{2}x^{-\frac{1}{2}}\right)$

$\boxed{\dfrac{1}{2} - 1 = -\dfrac{1}{2}}$

$= \dfrac{7}{2}x^{-\frac{1}{2}}$

$= \dfrac{7}{2x^{\frac{1}{2}}} = \dfrac{7}{2\sqrt{x}}$

**(c)**　Re-write $y$ using powers of $x$:

$y = 4x^{-\frac{1}{2}}$

$\Rightarrow\quad \dfrac{dy}{dx} = 4\left(-\dfrac{1}{2}x^{-\frac{3}{2}}\right)$

$= -\dfrac{4}{2}x^{-\frac{3}{2}} = -2x^{-\frac{3}{2}} = -\dfrac{2}{\sqrt{x^3}}$

## EXERCISE 6F

**1** Differentiate the following with respect to $x$.

**(a)** $y = 3x^3 - \dfrac{2}{x}$,　　　　　**(b)** $y = 5x - \dfrac{4}{3x^2} + 15$,

**(c)** $y = \dfrac{4}{7x} + \dfrac{3}{5x^2} - 8x^2$,　　　**(d)** $y = \dfrac{5}{x^7} + \dfrac{x^2}{5} - 27x$,

**(e)** $y = \dfrac{5}{x^5} + \dfrac{1}{x^6} - 7x$,　　　**(f)** $y = \dfrac{4}{5x^2} - \dfrac{2}{3x} + \dfrac{8x}{3}$,

**(g)** $y = \dfrac{3}{2x} + \dfrac{4}{3x^3} - 2x^3$,　　　**(h)** $y = \dfrac{10}{x^4} + \dfrac{x^7}{14} + 1$.

**2** Find the derivative of the following.

(a) $y = 5\sqrt{x} - 2$,
(b) $y = \sqrt[3]{x}$,
(c) $y = 3x^{\frac{1}{3}} + 2x^{\frac{1}{5}}$,
(d) $y = 7x^3 - \dfrac{1}{\sqrt{x}}$,
(e) $y = \dfrac{6}{5x^4} - \dfrac{x^3}{5}$,
(f) $y = 3x^{-\frac{1}{3}} - 10x^{-\frac{2}{5}}$,
(g) $y = 6x^2 - \sqrt{x^3} - \dfrac{2}{x^2}$,
(h) $y = \dfrac{4}{\sqrt[5]{x}} - 3\sqrt{x^3}$.

**3** Find the derived function, $f'(x)$, of the following.

(a) $f(x) = \dfrac{6}{5x^3} + 4x^3$,
(b) $f(x) = 6\sqrt{x} - 3x + 12$,
(c) $f(x) = 23 - 4x - \dfrac{3}{x^2}$,
(d) $f(x) = \dfrac{5}{x^2} + \dfrac{3}{x^5} - 3$,
(e) $f(x) = \sqrt[4]{x^3} + \sqrt[4]{x^5}$,
(f) $f(x) = 3x^4 - \dfrac{3}{\sqrt[5]{x}} + \dfrac{4}{5\sqrt{x^4}}$,
(g) $f(x) = 2 - 5\sqrt{x} - \dfrac{2}{x^2}$,
(h) $f(x) = \dfrac{6}{\sqrt[3]{x^2}} + 10\sqrt[5]{x} - 13$.

**4** Differentiate each of the following with respect to the appropriate variable.

(a) $z = 3x^2 - \dfrac{2}{x^4}$,
(b) $v = 3t - \dfrac{7}{2t^2} + 3\sqrt{t}$,
(c) $p = \dfrac{4}{b^3} + \dfrac{3}{4b^{12}} - 8b^7$,
(d) $y = \dfrac{5}{z^2} + \dfrac{z^{\frac{3}{5}}}{5} - 27z$,
(e) $s = \dfrac{12}{t^6} + \dfrac{1}{t^2} - 7$,
(f) $h = \dfrac{4}{5c^2} - \dfrac{2}{3\sqrt{c}} + \dfrac{8\sqrt{c}}{3}$.

## 6.9 Finding gradients at specific points on a curve

> In order to find the gradient at a particular point on the curve:
> (i) differentiate the equation of the curve.
> (ii) substitute into the derivative the $x$-coordinate of the point at which we need the gradient.

### Worked example 6.12

(a) Find the gradient of the curve $y = 3x - 8x^2$ at the point $P(3, -63)$.
(b) Find the gradient of the curve $y = 4x^3 + 20x^2$ at the point $P$ where $x = -2$.

## Solution

**(a)** $$\frac{dy}{dx} = 3 - 16x$$

> Differentiate to find the derivative

$\Rightarrow$ gradient at $P = 3 - 16(3) = -45$

> Substitute the $x$-coordinate of $P$ which is 3.

**(b)** $$\frac{dy}{dx} = 12x^2 + 40x$$

$\Rightarrow$ gradient at $P = 12(-2)^2 + 40(-2)$
$$= 48 - 80$$
$$= -32$$

> Substitute $x = -2$

> You may need to know the points where a curve has a particular gradient.

## Worked example 6.13 _____

**(a)** At what point(s) on the curve $y = \dfrac{9}{x} + 3x$ is the gradient equal to 2 ?

**(b)** Where is the tangent to the curve $y = 2x^2 - 3x + 4$ parallel to the line $y = 7x - 15$?

## Solution

**(a)** The expression needs to be converted into an appropriate form:

$$y = 9x^{-1} + 3x$$

$\Rightarrow$ $$\frac{dy}{dx} = -9x^{-2} + 3 = \frac{-9}{x^2} + 3$$

You need the point(s) where the gradient $= 2$

$$\frac{-9}{x^2} + 3 = 2$$

$\Rightarrow$ $$\frac{9}{x^2} = 1$$

$$x^2 = 9$$

$\Rightarrow$ $x = \pm 3$

> Multiply through by $x^2$.

So there are two points where the gradient equals 2.

when $x = 3$, $y = \dfrac{9}{3} + 3(3) = 12$

when $x = -3$, $y = \dfrac{9}{-3} + 3(-3) = -12$

> To find the corresponding $y$-coordinates, we substitute each $x$-coordinate into the original equation.

The points where the gradient is 2 are
$$(3, 12) \text{ and } (-3, -12)$$

**(b)** You can find the gradient of the curve:

$$y = 2x^2 - 3x + 4 \qquad \Rightarrow \qquad \frac{dy}{dx} = 4x - 3$$

Line $y = 7x - 15$ has gradient 7.

The two lines are parallel.

$$\Rightarrow \quad 4x - 3 = 7$$

$$\Rightarrow \quad x = 2.5$$

when $x = 2.5$, $y = 2(2.5)^2 - 3(2.5) + 4 = 9$

The tangent to the curve $y = 2x^2 - 3x + 4$ is parallel to $y = 7x - 15$ at the point (2.5, 9)

> Parallel lines have equal gradients.

> Substitute $x = 2.5$ in the equation of the curve to find the $y$-coordinate.

## MIXED EXERCISE

**1** Find the gradient of $y = 3x^3 - 5x^2 - 10$ when $x = 3$.

**2** What is the gradient of $y = 6x + \dfrac{5}{x}$ at the point (1, 11)?

**3** Find the gradient of:

    **(a)** $y = \dfrac{2}{x^2} - 3x^2$ at the point (1, −1),

    **(b)** $y = 2x^5 + 8x^2$ at the point (−2, −32),

    **(c)** $y = \dfrac{27}{x^2} - \dfrac{27}{x^3} + 5$ at the point (3, 7).

**4** The equation of a curve is $y = x^2 - 2x - 24$.
Find the gradient of the curve:

    **(a)** at the point where the curve crosses the $y$-axis

    **(b)** at each of the points where the curve crosses the $x$-axis.

**5** At what point is the gradient of $y = x^2 - 6x + 12$ equal to 8?

**6** Where is the tangent to the curve $y = 4x^2 - 4x - 15$ parallel to the line $y = 8 - 20x$?

**7** At what two points is the gradient of the curve
$y = \dfrac{x^3}{3} - \dfrac{x^2}{2} + 6x - 1$ equal to 12?

**8** Find the coordinates of the point(s) on the curve
$y = 3x^2 - 12x + 3$ at which:

    **(a)** the gradient equals 9,

    **(b)** the gradient equals 0.

**9** Find the gradient of the following curves at the given point.

    **(a)** $y = \dfrac{7}{x} - 12$,      where $x = 1$,

    **(b)** $y = 10\sqrt{x} + 10$,    where $x = 9$.

10 Find the coordinates of the points on the curve
$y = x^3 - 9x^2 + 24x - 3$ at which the tangent is parallel to the
$x$-axis.

11 A curve is given by the equation $y = x^2 - 8x + 10$. Find the
gradient of the curve at the point where $x = 4$.
What can you say about the tangent to the curve at this
point and what might the curve look like around this point ?

## Key point summary

1 Gradient of chord $= \dfrac{\delta y}{\delta x}$      *p80*

2 The tangent to a curve at any point $P$ is the straight    *p81*
line which just touches the curve at the point $P$.

3 The gradient of a curve $y = f(x)$ at a point $P$ is defined   *p82*
to be equal to the gradient of the tangent to the curve
at $P$.

4 If you need to find the gradient function of a curve    *p87*
$y = f(x)$ then take two points on the curve $P(x, f(x))$
and $Q(x + h, f(x + h))$ and let $Q$ become infinitely
close to $P$.
$$\text{gradient function} = \lim_{h \to 0} \left\{ \frac{f(x + h) - f(x)}{h} \right\}$$

5 The process of finding the gradient function is called    *p88*
differentiation.

6 The gradient function is also known as the derivative    *p88*
or derived function.
It is commonly denoted by $\dfrac{dy}{dx}$ or $f'(x)$.
$\dfrac{dy}{dx}$ is called the derivative of y with respect to x.
It is the rate of change of $y$ with respect to $x$.

7 $\dfrac{dy}{dx} = f'(x) = \lim_{h \to 0} \left( \dfrac{f(x + h) - f(x)}{h} \right)$    *p89*

8 When differentiating, you can use the following    *p90*
strategy:
  **(i)** if $y = x^n$ then $\dfrac{dy}{dx} = nx^{n-1}$.
  **(ii)** if $y = cx^n$ ($c$ is a constant) then $\dfrac{dy}{dx} = cnx^{n-1}$.
  **(iii)** if $y = f(x) \pm g(x)$ then $\dfrac{dy}{dx} = f'(x) \pm g'(x)$.

9 To find the gradient of a curve at a specific point,    *p95*
substitute the $x$-coordinate of the point into the
expression for the derivative.

| Test yourself | What to review |
|---|---|
| **1** Find the gradient of the chord joining the points with $x$-coordinates 2 and 3 on the curve with equation $y = 3x^2 - 7x - 2$. | *Section 6.1* |
| **2** A curve has equation $y = 2x^3 - 4x$. The point $P$ has coordinates $(2, 8)$ and the point $Q$ has $x$-coordinate $2 + h$ where $h$ is small.<br><br>**(a)** Show that the gradient of the chord $PQ$ can be written as $20 + 12h + 2h^2$.<br><br>**(b)** By considering the limit as $h$ tends to zero, deduce the value of the gradient at $P$. | *Section 6.3* |
| **3** Use differentiation from first principles to find the derivative of the function $y = 4x^2 + 9x$. | *Section 6.5* |
| **4** Differentiate the following functions with respect to $x$.<br><br>**(a)** $y = 8x^3 - 2x + \dfrac{3}{x} + 8$<br><br>**(b)** $y = 4\sqrt{x}$<br><br>**(c)** $y = 4x^5 + \dfrac{5}{\sqrt{x}}$<br><br>**(d)** $y = \dfrac{5}{x^2} - \dfrac{3}{x^3}$ | *Sections 6.6 and 6.7* |
| **5** Find the gradient of the curve $y = 6x^2 - 5x - 2$ at the point $(3, 37)$. | *Section 6.8* |

6

**Test yourself** **ANSWERS**

**1** 8.  **2** 20.  **3** $8x + 9$.

**4 (a)** $\dfrac{dy}{dx} = 24x^2 - 2 - \dfrac{3}{x^2}$

**(b)** $\dfrac{dy}{dx} = \dfrac{2}{\sqrt{x}}$

**(c)** $\dfrac{dy}{dx} = 20x^4 - \dfrac{5}{2x\sqrt{x}}$

**(d)** $\dfrac{dy}{dx} = \dfrac{9}{x^4} - \dfrac{10}{x^3}$

**5** 31.

CHAPTER 7

# Quadratics

## Learning objectives

After studying this chapter, you should be able to:
- solve quadratic equations
- complete the square of a quadratic expression
- understand the term discriminant
- solve simultaneous equations involving linear and quadratic equations.

## 7.1 Parabolas and quadratic functions

When you throw a ball, its path is part of a **parabola**. The cross-section of a satellite dish also has a parabolic shape. Special features of a parabola are its **vertex** (the highest or lowest point of the curve) and its **axis of symmetry**.

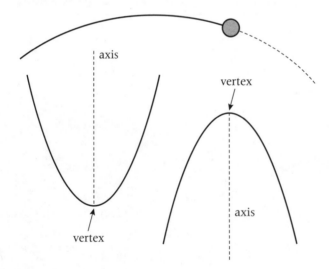

A general function for this type of curve is

$$f : x \mapsto ax^2 + bx + c,$$

where $a$ is called the coefficient of $x^2$, $b$ is the coefficient of $x$, and $c$ is a constant. It is called a **quadratic function**.

In chapter 4, you learned how to identify the features of a line of the form $y = mx + c$, related to the values of $m$ and $c$. In this chapter, you will learn how to sketch graphs of quadratic functions, dependent on the values of $a$, $b$ and $c$.

# 7.2 Factorising quadratics and sketching graphs

The expression $(2x + 3)(x - 4)$ can be multiplied out to give $2x^2 - 5x - 12$ and the reverse process is called factorisation.

Although you might need a graphic calculator to draw the graph of $y = 2x^2 - 5x - 12$, you should be able to sketch the graph of $y = (2x + 3)(x - 4)$ without one.

Where does the graph cross the $x$-axis?

You need to solve $(2x + 3)(x - 4) = 0$.

Either $(2x + 3) = 0 \Rightarrow x = -\dfrac{3}{2} = -1\tfrac{1}{2}$

or $(x - 4) = 0 \Rightarrow x = 4$

The values 4 and $-1\tfrac{1}{2}$ are called the **roots** of the equation and they are the values of $x$ where the curve crosses the $x$-axis.

You know that the curve is either like ∩ or like ∪.

By choosing another value of $x$, such as $x = 0$,
$\Rightarrow y = (2 \times 0 + 3)(0 - 4) = -12$, you know that the parabola also passes through $(0, -12)$.

Since you know a parabola is symmetrical about its axis, you can now sketch the graph of $y = (2x + 3)(x - 4)$.

> The graph of $y = ax^2 + bx + c$ is called a parabola.

> A quadratic equation that can be written in the form $(x - p)(x - q) = 0$ has roots $p$ and $q$.
> The graph of $(x - p)(x - q)$ crosses the $x$ axis at the points $(p, 0)$ and $(q, 0)$.

The equation $p \times q = 0$ implies that either $p = 0$ or $q = 0$.

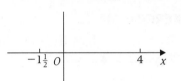

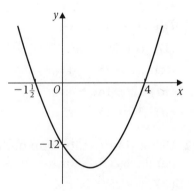

## *Worked example 7.1*

Factorise $10 - 13x - 3x^2$ and hence sketch the graph of $y = 10 - 13x - 3x^2$.

### *Solution*

| Two numbers which multiply to give 10. | These two terms multiply to give $-3x^2$. |

You need to form two brackets ( ) ( )

$$10 - 13x - 3x^2 = (5 + x)(2 - 3x)$$

Since $\begin{aligned} & 5 \times (-3x) + 2 \times x \\ & = -15x + 2x = -13x \end{aligned}$

**7**

Now find where the graph crosses the $x$-axis.

$$(5 + x)(2 - 3x) = 0$$

$$\Rightarrow (5 + x) = 0 \text{ or } (2 - 3x) = 0$$

$$\Rightarrow x = -5 \text{ or } x = \frac{2}{3}$$

You can check the factorisation is correct by substituting these values into the original quadratic:
$$10 - 13 \times (-5) - 3 \times (-5)^2$$
$$= 10 + 65 - 75 = 0 \checkmark$$

Check one other point such as when $x = 0$. $x = 0 \Rightarrow y = 10$.

**Note.** It is not always necessary to have equal axes on the scales in a sketch.

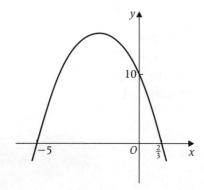

## EXERCISE 7A

**1** Factorise each of the following.

(a) $x^2 - 3x + 2$,  (b) $x^2 - 7x - 8$,

(c) $x^2 + 7x + 12$,  (d) $2x^2 - x - 3$,

(e) $3x^2 - 7x + 2$,  (f) $4x^2 + x - 3$.

(g) $7 - 13x - 2x^2$,  (h) $6x^2 + 5x - 6$,

(i) $6 + 5x - 4x^2$.  (j) $5x - 2x^2$,

(k) $21 + 25x - 4x^2$,  (l) $15 - 14x - 8x^2$,

(m) $12 + 16x - 3x^2$,  (n) $3x + 4x^2$,

(o) $54 - 15x - 25x^2$.

**2** Using your results from question **1**, find where the following parabolas cross the x-axis and sketch their graphs.

(a) $y = x^2 - 3x + 2$,  (b) $y = x^2 - 7x - 8$,

(c) $y = x^2 + 7x + 12$,  (d) $y = 2x^2 - x - 3$,

(e) $y = 3x^2 - 7x + 2$,  (f) $y = 4x^2 + x - 3$,

(g) $y = 7 - 13x - 2x^2$,  (h) $y = 6x^2 + 5x - 6$,

(i) $y = 6 + 5x - 4x^2$,  (j) $y = 5x - 2x^2$,

(k) $y = 21 + 25x - 4x^2$,  (l) $y = 15 - 14x - 8x^2$,

(m) $y = 12 + 16x - 3x^2$,  (n) $y = 3x + 4x^2$,

(o) $y = 54 - 15x - 25x^2$.

**3** By considering the graphs you have drawn in question **2**, comment on the shape of $y = ax^2 + bx + c$ in the cases:

(i) $a > 0$,    (ii) $a < 0$.

What is the shape of the graph when $a = 0$?

**4** When a parabola crosses the $x$-axis at the points $A$ and $B$, the axis of symmetry is the perpendicular bisector of the line joining the points $A$ and $B$. In worked example 1, since $A(-5, 0)$ and $B(\frac{2}{3}, 0)$, the equation of the line of symmetry is $x = -\dfrac{13}{6}$.

Find the equation of the line of symmetry for each of the parabolas in question **2**.

**5** A parabola passes through the three points given. Find their equations.

(a)  $(3, 0)$, $(5, 0)$, $(0, 15)$,

(b)  $(-2, 0)$, $(3, 0)$, $(0, -6)$,

(c)  $(4, 0)$, $(6, 0)$, $(0, 48)$,

(d)  $(1, 0)$, $(-1, 0)$, $(0, 1)$,

(e)  $(2, 0)$, $(3, 0)$, $(0, 3)$,

(f)  $(-2, 0)$, $(-5, 0)$, $(0, -30)$.

> **Hint.** Consider an equation of the form:
> $$y = k(x - a)(x - b).$$

# 7.3 Completing the square

The expression $x^2 + 14x$ is not quite a perfect square. However, by adding 49 it can be written as $(x + 7)^2$.

Hence, $x^2 + 14x = (x + 7)^2 - 49$

> Recall that
> $$(x + a)^2 = x^2 + 2ax + a^2.$$

> Writing a quadratic in this form is known as completing the square.

 $A(x + B)^2 + C$ is the completed square form.

## Worked example 7.2

Express the quadratics:

(a)  $x^2 + 10x + 31$,        (b)  $x^2 - 6x + 7$.

in the form $(x + p)^2 + q$, where $p$ and $q$ are constants.

## Solution

(a)  $(x + p)^2 + q = x^2 + 2px + p^2 + q$

Comparing this with $x^2 + 10x + 31$

$2p = 10$

$\Rightarrow p = 5$

Also $p^2 + q = 31$

$\Rightarrow 5^2 + q = 31 \Rightarrow q = 6$

Therefore $x^2 + 10x + 31 \equiv (x + 5)^2 + 6$

> Look at the coefficient of $x$ in each case.

> Comparing the constant term.

> The sign $\equiv$ means 'is identical to' and is used sometimes rather than $=$ to indicate that the expressions are identical for all values of $x$.

A more direct approach to completing the square is to start with $x^2 + 10x + 31$ and to ask yourself what number $p$ would make $(x + p)^2$ have the first two terms the same as those in $x^2 + 10x + 31$?

Since $(x + 5)^2 = x^2 + 10x + 25$, the value of $p$ is 5.

$$x^2 + 10x = (x + 5)^2 - 25$$
$$\Rightarrow x^2 + 10x + 31 = (x + 5)^2 - 25 + 31 = (x + 5)^2 + 6$$

Notice that 5 is half of 10 and so in general you need to add half the coefficient of $x$.

**(b)** This time you need to consider $(x - 3)^2$.

$$(x - 3)^2 = x^2 - 6x + 9$$
$$x^2 - 6x = (x - 3)^2 - 9$$
$$\Rightarrow x^2 - 6x + 7 = (x - 3)^2 - 9 + 7$$
$$\Rightarrow x^2 - 6x + 7 \equiv (x - 3)^2 - 2$$

Since $-3$ is half of $-6$.

This is of the given form with $p = -3$ and $q = -2$.

## Worked example 7.3

Express the quadratic $x^2 + 6x + 17$ in completed square form. Hence find the coordinates of the vertex and axis of symmetry of the parabola with equation $y = x^2 + 6x + 17$.

This technique can help you to find the equation of the line of symmetry and the coordinates of the vertex of any parabola.

## Solution

Since 3 is half of 6.

$$x^2 + 6x = (x + 3)^2 - 9$$
$$\Rightarrow x^2 + 6x + 17 = (x + 3)^2 - 9 + 17 = (x + 3)^2 + 8$$

This form of the quadratic which involves a perfect square is called the completed square form.

The equation of the parabola $y = x^2 + 6x + 17$ can be written as $y = (x + 3)^2 + 8$

Since the coefficient of $x^2$ is positive, the graph is $\cup$ shaped (see Question 3 of Exercise 7A)

Since $(x + 3)^2 \geqslant 0$, the least value of $x^2 + 6x + 17$ occurs when $x + 3 = 0 \Rightarrow x = -3$.

The corresponding $y$-coordinate is $y = 0 + 8 = 8$.

So the vertex of the parabola is at $(-3, 8)$.

The axis of symmetry has equation $x = -3$ and the parabola is sketched on the right.

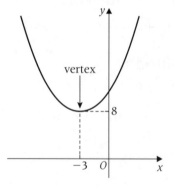

You will notice that this parabola does not cross the $x$-axis at all. A general condition for this to happen will be developed later.

## Worked example 7.4

Complete the square for the quadratic $x^2 - 8x + 1$. Hence find the exact roots of the quadratic equation

$$x^2 - 8x + 1 = 0.$$

To complete the square, you need to find a perfect square with first two terms identical to those of $x^2 - 8x + 1$.

## Solution

Consider $(x - 4)^2 = x^2 - 8x + 16$

$$x^2 - 8x + 1 = (x - 4)^2 - 16 + 1$$
$$= (x - 4)^2 - 15$$

To solve $x^2 - 8x + 1 = 0$, this is equivalent to solving:

$$(x - 4)^2 - 15 = 0.$$
$$\Rightarrow (x - 4)^2 = 15$$
$$\Rightarrow (x - 4) = \pm\sqrt{15}$$
$$\Rightarrow x = 4 \pm \sqrt{15}$$

> You choose $-4$ because this is half of the coefficient of $x$, then consider $(x - 4)^2$.

> When you have written the expression in this form, you have completed the square.

### EXERCISE 7B

**1** Express each of the following quadratics in the form $(x + p)^2 + q$, where $p$ and $q$ are constants (some of the values may be negative).

**(a)** $x^2 + 8x + 19$,  **(b)** $x^2 + 4x + 13$,

**(c)** $x^2 + 10x + 14$,  **(d)** $x^2 - 10x + 30$,

**(e)** $x^2 - 8x + 3$,  **(f)** $x^2 + 3x + 3$,

**(g)** $x^2 + x + 1$,  **(h)** $x^2 - 5x + 7$,

**(i)** $x^2 - x + 2$,  **(j)** $x^2 - 7x - 2$.

**2** Express each of the following equations in the completed square form. Hence find the coordinates of the vertex and an equation for the line of symmetry for each parabola.

**(a)** $y = x^2 + 4x + 12$,  **(b)** $y = x^2 + 12x + 40$,

**(c)** $y = x^2 - 6x + 2$,  **(d)** $y = x^2 + 8x + 5$,

**(e)** $y = x^2 - 2x - 3$,  **(f)** $y = x^2 - 14x + 32$,

**(g)** $y = x^2 + x + 3$,  **(h)** $y = x^2 - 3x + 2$,

**(i)** $y = x^2 - 5x + 1$,  **(j)** $y = x^2 - 9x + 15$.

**3** By completing the square, solve the following quadratic equations, giving your answers in surd form.

**(a)** $x^2 + 4x - 3 = 0$,  **(b)** $x^2 + 6x + 4 = 0$,

**(c)** $x^2 - 8x + 5 = 0$,  **(d)** $x^2 - 2x - 4 = 0$,

**(e)** $x^2 - 10x - 3 = 0$,  **(f)** $x^2 - 14x + 4 = 0$,

**(g)** $x^2 - x - 1 = 0$,  **(h)** $x^2 + 3x - 5 = 0$,

**(i)** $x^2 - 3x + 1 = 0$,  **(j)** $x^2 - 7x - 1 = 0$,

**(k)** $x^2 - 5x + 3 = 0$,  **(l)** $x^2 - x - 3 = 0$.

**7**

## Worked example 7.5

(a) Complete the square for each of the following quadratics.

    (i)   $3x^2 + 6x + 17$,        (ii)   $12x - 2x^2 + 11$.

(b) Hence determine:

    (i)   the least value of $3x^2 + 6x + 17$ and the value of $x$ at which this occurs.

    (ii)   the greatest value of $12x - 2x^2 + 11$ and the value of $x$ at which this occurs.

> So far, all the examples have involved quadratics where the coefficient of $x^2$ has been 1. You can extend the procedure for more general quadratics.

## Solution

(a)  (i)   $3x^2 + 6x + 17 = 3[x^2 + 2x] + 17$

           | Completing the square on $x^2 + 2x$ |

$$= 3[(x + 1)^2 - 1^2] + 17$$
$$= 3(x + 1)^2 - 3 \times 1 + 17$$
$$= 3(x + 1)^2 + 14$$

> Make the coefficient of $x^2$ equal to 1 by taking out the factor 3 from the first two terms.

> You can multiply this out and check it gives you the original expression.

    (ii)   $12x - 2x^2 + 11 = -2[x^2 - 6x] + 11$

           | Completing the square on $x^2 - 6x$ |

$$= -2[(x - 3)^2 - 9] + 11$$
$$= -2(x - 3)^2 + 18 + 11$$
$$= -2(x - 3)^2 + 29$$

> Taking factor of $-2$ out of first two terms.

(b)  (i)   The least value of $(x + 1)^2$ is zero and occurs when $x = -1$.

       Hence the least value of $3x^2 + 6x + 17 = 3(x + 1)^2 + 14$ is 14.

> This least value occurs when $x = -1$.

    (ii)   The least value of $(x - 3)^2$ is zero.

       Hence the **greatest** value of $12x - 2x^2 + 11$ $= 29 - 2(x - 3)^2$ is 29 and occurs when $x = 3$.

> Notice this is the greatest value of the expression since the squared term is being subtracted.

> This technique can be used to find the shortest distance from a point to a straight line.

## Worked example 7.6

The distance from the point $A(-4, 3)$ to a general point $P(x, y)$ on the straight line with equation $y = 3x - 5$ is $d$.
Find an expression for $d^2$, in terms of $x$ only.

By completing the square on the expression for $d^2$, find the closest point on the line $y = 3x - 5$ to the point $(-4, 3)$ and the shortest distance from the point to the line.

## Solution

Since $y = 3x - 5$, the point $P$ has coordinates $(x, 3x - 5)$

$$d^2 = AP^2 = (x + 4)^2 + ([3x - 5] - 3)^2$$
$$= (x + 4)^2 + (3x - 8)^2$$
$$= (x^2 + 8x + 16) + (9x^2 - 48x + 64)$$
$$= 10x^2 - 40x + 80$$

You need to complete the square on $10x^2 - 40x + 80$

$$10x^2 - 40x + 80 = 10(x^2 - 4x) + 80$$
$$= 10[(x - 2)^2 - 4] + 80$$
$$= 10(x - 2)^2 - 40 + 80$$
$$= 10(x - 2)^2 + 40$$

Least value of the expression for $d^2$ is 40.

Therefore the closest distance of the point to the line is $\sqrt{40} = 2\sqrt{10}$.

When $x = 2$, $y = 3x - 5 = 6 - 5 = 1$.
Closest point on the line to $A$ is the point $(2,1)$.

> See Chapter 4 Section 4.2
> $$d = \sqrt{(x_2 - x_1)^2 + (y_2 - y_1)^2}$$

> Since $A$ is the point $(-4, 3)$.

> The least value of $(x - 2)^2$ is 0 and occurs when $x = 2$.

## EXERCISE 7C

**1** Complete the square for each of the following

**(a)** $3x^2 + 6x - 2$   **(b)** $5x^2 + 40x + 7$,

**(c)** $2x^2 + 12x - 1$,   **(d)** $4x^2 + 8x - 11$,

**(e)** $5x^2 + 5x + 11$,   **(f)** $3x^2 + 9x - 8$,

**(g)** $2x^2 + 5x + 1$,   **(h)** $3x^2 + 4x + 7$,

**(i)** $4x^2 + 7x - 2$.

**2 (a)** Express $3x^2 - 12x + 5$ in the form $A(x - B)^2 - C$, where $A$, $B$ and $C$ are constants whose values should be stated.

**(b)** Find the minimum value of each of the following expressions

   **(i)** $3x^2 - 12x + 5$,

   **(ii)** $(3x^2 - 12x + 5)^2$.

**(c)** For each of the expressions in part **(b)**, state a value of $x$ which gives the minimum value.          [A]

**3 (a)** Determine the value of each of the constants $a$ and $b$ such that $a - (3x + b)^2 = 1 - 30x - 9x^2$.

**(b)** Hence, or otherwise, determine the greatest value of $f(x) = 1 - 30x - 9x^2$, and state the value of $x$ for which this greatest value occurs.          [A]

7

**4** A parabola has equation $y = ax^2 + bx + c$, where $a$, $b$ and $c$ are constants. Show that the axis of the parabola has equation $2ax + b = 0$, and find the coordinates of its vertex. Hence show that the vertex lies on the $x$-axis when $b^2 = 4ac$.

**5** The function f is defined for all real values of $x$ by

$$f(x) = x^3 + 6x^2 + 11x + k, \text{ where } k \text{ is a constant.}$$

**(a)** Given that $f(-1) = 3$, find the value of $k$.

**(b)** Show that $f'(x)$ can be expressed in the form $a(x + b)^2 + c$, and state the values of the constants $a$, $b$ and $c$.

**(c)** Use your result from part **(b)** to write down the least value of $f'(x)$ and the value of $x$ at which this least value occurs.

**6** Using the method of Worked example 5, find the shortest distance from the point $A$ to the given line in the cases

**(a)** $A(5, 4)$ from $y = 2x + 9$,

**(b)** $A(-1, 2)$ from $y = x + 5$,

**(c)** $A(5, 4)$ from $x + y = 7$.

**7** A piece of wire has length 20 cm and it is bent into a rectangle with one side equal to $x$ cm. Show that the area of the rectangle, $A$ cm$^2$, is given by $A = x(10 - x)$.

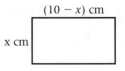

Complete the square on the expression for $A$ and hence find the greatest value of $A$ and the value of $x$ for which this occurs.

*(Was this value of x the value you expected?)*

**8** A farmer has 120 metres of fencing. By using an existing wall, he decides to make a rectangular pen by adding three sides, with two sides equal to $x$ metres as shown in the diagram. Show that the area enclosed, $A$ m$^2$, is given by $A = x(120 - 2x)$.

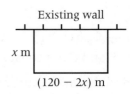

Complete the square on the expression for $A$ and hence find the greatest value of $A$ and the value of $x$ for which this occurs.

*(Was this value of x the value you expected?)*

**9** A pen is built onto an existing rectangular building (shaded) where $AF$ is 10 units and $FE$ is 5 units, as shown in the diagram. The perimeter $ABCDE$ is 65 units. Find a relationship between $x$ and $y$, where $AB = x$ and $DE = y$.

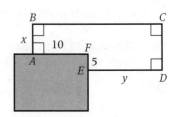

Show that the area enclosed by the pen is $125 + 30x - x^2$.

By completing the square, find the greatest possible area enclosed by the pen.

# 7.4 General quadratic equation formula

The general quadratic equation is $ax^2 + bx + c = 0$, $(a \neq 0)$.

$$\Rightarrow x^2 + \frac{b}{a}x + \frac{c}{a} = 0$$

> Divide throughout by $a$ since $a \neq 0$.

$$\Rightarrow \left(x + \frac{b}{2a}\right)^2 - \left(\frac{b}{2a}\right)^2 + \frac{c}{a} = 0$$

> Completing the square.

$$\Rightarrow \left(x + \frac{b}{2a}\right)^2 = \frac{b^2}{4a^2} - \frac{c}{a}$$

$$\Rightarrow \left(x + \frac{b}{2a}\right)^2 = \frac{b^2 - 4ac}{4a^2}$$

$$\Rightarrow x + \frac{b}{2a} = \frac{\pm \sqrt{b^2 - 4ac}}{\sqrt{4a^2}}$$

> Note the need for $\pm$ when you take square roots of both sides.

$$\Rightarrow x = \frac{-b}{2a} \pm \frac{\sqrt{b^2 - 4ac}}{2a}$$

$$\Rightarrow x = \frac{-b \pm \sqrt{b^2 - 4ac}}{2a}$$

> This is a formula which needs to be learned off by heart so you can use it to solve quadratic equations which do not factorise.

## *Worked example 7.7*

Find the exact solutions of the equation $3x^2 - 7x - 5 = 0$.

## *Solution*

Comparison with $ax^2 + bx + c = 0$ gives $a = 3$, $b = -7$, $c = -5$.

Using $x = \dfrac{-b \pm \sqrt{b^2 - 4ac}}{2a}$

$$x = \frac{-(-7) \pm \sqrt{(-7)^2 - 4(3)(-5)}}{2(3)} = \frac{7 \pm \sqrt{49 + 60}}{6} = \frac{7 \pm \sqrt{109}}{6}$$

> Answers should be left in this exact form since that was the request.

$$x = \frac{7 + \sqrt{109}}{6} \quad \text{or} \quad x = \frac{7 - \sqrt{109}}{6}$$

You can make a check on your calculator by taking one of the roots, e.g. $x = \dfrac{7 + \sqrt{109}}{6} \approx 2.9067$ and substituting into

$3x^2 - 7x - 5 \approx 3 \times 2.9067^2 - 7 \times 2.9067 - 5 \approx -1.85 \times 10^{-4}$.

> This is very close to zero and confirms that your answer is correct.

## EXERCISE 7D

1 Find the exact values of the roots of the following equations (in some cases there are no real roots and you should say so)

(a) $x^2 - 3x - 1 = 0$,      (b) $2x^2 + 7x - 1 = 0$,

(c) $5x^2 - 7x + 3 = 0$,      (d) $4x^2 - 5x - 2 = 0$,

(e) $7x^2 + 2x + 1 = 0$,      (f) $5x^2 + 3x - 1 = 0$,

(g) $2x^2 - 5x + 1 = 0$,      (h) $3x^2 + 2x + 1 = 0$,

(i) $4x^2 + 3x - 7 = 0$.

> When the final values are in surd form, you will find that the two answers are **conjugate pairs**, such as $-3 \pm 17$ whenever $a$, $b$ and $c$ are rational numbers.

2 Find the approximate solutions to the following equations, giving your answers correct to three significant figures

(a) $x^2 - 4x - 1 = 0$,      (b) $2x^2 + 5x - 6 = 0$,

(c) $4x^2 - 13x + 5 = 0$,      (d) $5x^2 - 3x - 3 = 0$,

(e) $4x^2 + 7x + 2 = 0$,      (f) $5x^2 + 7x - 1 = 0$,

(g) $2x^2 - 11x + 7 = 0$,      (h) $3x^2 + 5x + 1 = 0$,

(i) $4x^2 + 7x - 1 = 0$.

# 7.5 The discriminant

The expression $b^2 - 4ac$ that appears in the quadratic equation formula is known as the **discriminant**, because it discriminates between the types of solutions the quadratic equation can have.

> When $b^2 - 4ac$ is a perfect square, the solutions will be rational and it means that the original quadratic expression will factorise.

## Worked example 7.8

Use the quadratic equation formula to solve the equation

$$32x^2 + 12x - 27 = 0$$

and hence factorise the quadratic $32x^2 + 12x - 27$.

> Comparison with $ax^2 + bx + c = 0$ gives $a = 32$, $b = 12$, $c = -27$.

## Solution

> Using $x = \dfrac{-b \pm \sqrt{b^2 - 4ac}}{2a}$

$$x = \frac{-12 \pm \sqrt{12^2 - 4(32)(-27)}}{64} = \frac{-12 \pm \sqrt{3600}}{64}$$

> $3600 = 60^2$ (a perfect square)

$$\Rightarrow x = \frac{-12 + 60}{64} \text{ or } x = \frac{-12 - 60}{64}. \text{ Roots are } \frac{3}{4} \text{ and } \frac{-9}{8}.$$

> Sometimes when the numbers are rather large, it is easier to use the formula than to spend time looking for correct factors.

This suggests the factors to be $(4x - 3)$ and $(8x + 9)$ and in fact $32x^2 + 12x - 27 = (4x - 3)(8x + 9)$.

The number of real roots of the equation $ax^2 + bx + c = 0$ is determined by the discriminant.

$b^2 - 4ac > 0 \Rightarrow$ the equation has two real distinct roots

$b^2 - 4ac = 0 \Rightarrow$ the equation has one real (repeated) root

$b^2 - 4ac < 0 \Rightarrow$ the equation has no real roots

The graphical situation is illustrated below.

$b^2 - 4ac > 0$
Two points of intersection
with $x$-axis.

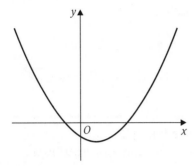 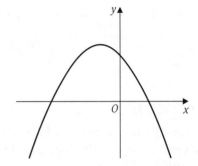

$b^2 - 4ac = 0$
Single point of intersection;
curve touches $x$-axis.

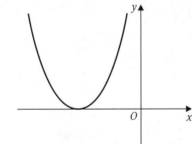 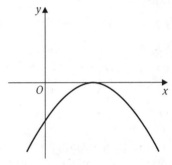

$b^2 - 4ac < 0$
No points of intersection
with $x$-axis,

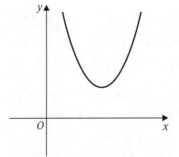 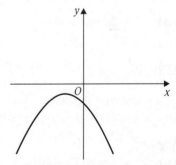

## Worked example 7.9

Find the values of $k$ for which the equation $kx^2 - 6x + (8 + k) = 0$ has equal roots.

This is another way of saying the equation has one (repeated) root.

## Solution

For equal roots $(-6)^2 - 4k(8 + k) = 0$

$\Rightarrow 36 - 4k(8 + k) = 0 \Rightarrow 9 - k(8 + k) = 0$

$\Rightarrow 9 - 8k - k^2 = 0$

$\Rightarrow (9 + k)(1 - k) = 0$

$\Rightarrow k = -9 \text{ or } k = 1$

Using $b^2 - 4ac = 0$.

## Worked example 7.10

Find the condition on $k$ for the equation $12x^2 - 8x + (5 + k) = 0$ to have two distinct real roots.

## Solution

For two distinct real roots $(-8)^2 - 4(12)(5 + k) > 0$

$\Rightarrow 64 - 48(5 + k) > 0$

$\Rightarrow 64 > 48(5 + k) \Rightarrow 4 > 3(5 + k)$

$\Rightarrow 4 > 15 + 3k \Rightarrow -11 > 3k$

$\Rightarrow -\dfrac{11}{3} > k \ \text{ or } \ k < -\dfrac{11}{3}.$

Using $b^2 - 4ac > 0$.

## EXERCISE 7E

**1** Find the discriminant of each of the following equations and hence state whether the equation has rational or irrational roots.

You need to check whether the discriminant is a perfect square, in which case the roots are rational.

   **(a)** $x^2 - 4x - 12 = 0,$     **(b)** $x^2 - 5x - 6 = 0,$

   **(c)** $x^2 - 3x - 7 = 0,$     **(d)** $x^2 - 7x + 8 = 0,$

   **(e)** $x^2 - 7x - 8 = 0,$     **(f)** $2x^2 - 5x + 3 = 0,$

   **(g)** $5x^2 - 7x + 2 = 0,$     **(h)** $2x^2 - 3x - 4 = 0,$

   **(i)** $24x^2 + 6x - 25 = 0.$

**2** Obtain an inequality satisfied by $k$ if the equations below have two distinct real roots:

   **(a)** $x^2 - 2x - k = 0,$     **(b)** $(3 + k)x^2 - 4x + 4 = 0,$

   **(c)** $x^2 - 5x - 6k = 0,$     **(d)** $(2 + k)x^2 - 7x - 8 = 0,$

   **(e)** $5x^2 - 7x + (2k - 3) = 0,$   **(f)** $(3k - 1)x^2 - 5x + 3 = 0.$

**3** The following equations have repeated roots. Find the value(s) of the constant $p$, leaving your answer(s) in exact form.

   **(a)** $px^2 - 5x + p = 0,$     **(b)** $(3 - p)x^2 - 6x + 9 = 0,$

   **(c)** $x^2 + 3px + 12 = 0,$     **(d)** $(2p - 5)x^2 - 8x + 16 = 0,$

   **(e)** $2x^2 - (p + 1)x + 8 = 0,$   **(f)** $(p - 1)x^2 + 6x + (p + 7) = 0.$

**4** Determine, by considering the discriminant, the number of points of intersection with the $x$-axis of the following parabolas.

   **(a)** $y = x^2 - 7x + 3,$     **(b)** $y = 3x^2 - 7x + 5,$

   **(c)** $y = 3x^2 + 12x + 12,$     **(d)** $y = 5x^2 - x - 5,$

   **(e)** $y = 9x^2 - 6x + 1,$     **(f)** $y = 4x^2 - 12x + 5,$

   **(g)** $y = 5 - 7x - 2x^2,$     **(h)** $y = 5 - 3x^2,$

   **(i)** $y = 3x + 2x^2,$     **(j)** $y = 3 + 2x^2.$

# 7.6 Intersection of a line and curve

When a line intersects a curve, the equations can be solved simultaneously in order to find the point of intersection.

## Worked example 7.11

Calculate the points of intersection of the line with equation $y = 3x + 5$ and the parabola with equation $y = 3x^2 + 2x + 1$.

At a point of intersection, the $x$-coordinates of the line and curve are equal and so are their $y$-coordinates.

### Solution

Substitute $y = 3x + 5$ into $y = 3x^2 + 2x + 1$ so as to eliminate $y$.

$\Rightarrow 3x + 5 = 3x^2 + 2x + 1$

$\Rightarrow 0 = 3x^2 - x - 4$

$\Rightarrow (3x - 4)(x + 1) = 0$

$\Rightarrow x = \dfrac{4}{3}$ or $x = -1$

Because $b^2 - 4ac = 49$ is a perfect square, the quadratic factorises.

Substitute values of $x$ into $y = 3x + 5$.

When $x = \dfrac{4}{3}$, $y = 3 \times \dfrac{4}{3} + 5 = 9$, giving the point $\left(\dfrac{4}{3}, 9\right)$.

When $x = -1$, $y = (3 \times -1) + 5 = 2$ giving the point $(-1, 2)$.

The two points of intersection are $\left(\dfrac{4}{3}, 9\right)$ and $(-1, 2)$.

You could check that these points also satisfy the quadratic: e.g. $3 \times (-1)^2 + 2 \times (-1) + 1 = 3 - 2 + 1 = 2 \checkmark$

**7**

## Worked example 7.12

Determine whether the line $3x - 2y = 9$ and the curve with equation $y = x^2 - 5x + 7$ intersect.

### Solution

Eliminating $y$,

$\Rightarrow 3x - 2(x^2 - 5x + 7) = 9$

$\Rightarrow 3x - 2x^2 + 10x - 14 = 9$

$\Rightarrow 0 = 2x^2 - 13x + 23$

Substitute the expression $y = x^2 - 5x + 7$ into the equation of the line.

Consider the discriminant with $a = 2$, $b = -13$, $c = 23$

$$b^2 - 4ac = (-13)^2 - 4 \times 2 \times 23 = 169 - 184 = -15$$

Because the discriminant is negative, there are no real solutions to the quadratic equation.

The line and curve do not intersect.

Hence there are no real points of intersection of the line and curve.

# 7.7 Intersection of two parabolas

There are situations when two parabolas do not intersect. For example, $y = x^2 + 1$ and $y = x^2 + 3$ have no points in common, because eliminating $y$ gives, $x^2 + 1 = x^2 + 3 \Rightarrow 1 = 3$ which is clearly impossible and so the two parabolas have no points in common.

> The equations for a straight line and a parabola (or two parabolas) can be solved by eliminating $y$ in order to find any points of intersection.

When the parabolas do intersect, the points of intersection can be found in a similar way to the previous section.

## *Worked example 7.13*

Determine the points of intersection of the parabolas with equations $y = x^2 - 5x + 7$ and $y = 5 + 2x - 2x^2$.

## *Solution*

$\Rightarrow x^2 - 5x + 7 = 5 + 2x - 2x^2$

$\Rightarrow 3x^2 - 7x + 2 = 0$

$\Rightarrow (3x - 1)(x - 2) = 0$

$\Rightarrow x = \dfrac{1}{3}$ or $x = 2$

Eliminating y from the two equations.

$b^2 - 4ac = 49 - 24 = 25$ is a perfect square so the quadratic factorises.

Substitute $x = \dfrac{1}{3}$ into first equation $\Rightarrow y = \left(\dfrac{1}{3}\right)^2 - 5\left(\dfrac{1}{3}\right) + 7 = \dfrac{49}{9}$

Substitute $x = 2$ into first equation $\Rightarrow y = 2^2 - 5 \times 2 + 7 = 1$

There are two points of intersection and these are the points $\left(\dfrac{1}{3}, \dfrac{49}{9}\right)$ and $(2, 1)$.

## EXERCISE 7F

**1** Determine the single point of intersection of the following pairs of parabolas

   **(a)** $y = x^2 - 7x + 4$ and $y = x^2 + 3x - 16$,

   **(b)** $y = x^2 + 5x - 3$ and $y = x^2 + 3x - 4$,

   **(c)** $y = x^2 + x - 5$ and $y = x^2 + 4x - 7$.

**2** Find the points of intersection of

   **(a)** the line $y = x + 2$ and the curve $y = x^2 - 4$,

   **(b)** the line $x + y = 4$ and the curve $y = 2x^2 - 7x + 8$,

**(c)** the line $3x - 2y = 7$ and the curve $y = x^2 - 5x - 7$,

**(d)** the line $5x + y + 6 = 0$ and the curve $y = 3x^2 + 5x - 6$,

**(e)** the line $2x + 3y = 4$ and the curve $y = 5x^2 - 3x - 14$.

**3** By considering the discriminant of the resulting quadratic, determine the number of points of intersection of the following lines and curves

**(a)** the line $y = x - 1$ and the curve $y = x^2 - x$,

**(b)** the line $y = x + 4$ and the curve $y = x^2 - 7x + 3$,

**(c)** the line $2x + y = 2$ and the curve $y = 3x^2 - 5x + 3$,

**(d)** the line $2x + y + 6 = 0$ and the curve $y = 4x^2 - 7x - 3$,

**(e)** the line $3x - 2y = 5$ and the curve $y = 3x^2 - 4x - 2$,

**4** Find the coordinates of any points of intersection of the following pairs of parabolas

> If there are no points of intersection you must show why that is the case.

**(a)** $y = x^2 - 7x + 3$ and $y = x^2 - 5x + 1$,

**(b)** $y = x^2 + 3$ and $y = 2x^2 + 4$,

**(c)** $y = x^2 - 3x + 4$ and $y = 2x^2 - 5x + 5$,

**(d)** $y = 2x^2 - 3x + 7$ and $y = 3x^2 - 4x + 1$,

**(e)** $y = x^2 - 13x - 2$ and $y = 2x^2 - 5x + 15$,

**(f)** $y = x^2 - 3x + 5$ and $y = 3x^2 - 4x + 4$,

**(g)** $y = 5x^2 - 2x + 3$ and $y = 3 + 2x - 3x^2$.

**5** Find the exact value of the x-coordinate at each of the points of intersection of the following

> The answers will involve surds.

**(a)** the line $y = 3x + 1$ and the curve $y = 2x^2 - 5x - 7$,

**(b)** the line $2x + y = 7$ and the curve $y = 4x^2 - 8x - 5$,

**(c)** the parabolas $y = 2x^2 - 3x - 4$ and $y = 3x^2 - 8x + 1$,

**(d)** the curves $y = 3x^2 - 7x - 11$ and $y = 5x^2 - 4x - 12$,

**(e)** the curves $y = 4x - 3x^2 + 5$ and $y = x^2 - 2x - 1$.

**6** Show that the quadratic equation resulting from the solution of the simultaneous equations $y = 3x - 5$ and $y = 2x^2 - 5x + 3$ has a single repeated root.

State the geometrical relationship between the curve with equation $y = 2x^2 - 5x + 3$ and the line $y = 3x - 5$.

7 A straight line has equation $y = 4x + k$, where $k$ is a constant, and a parabola has equation $y = 3x^2 + 12x + 7$. Show that the $x$-coordinate of any points of intersection of the line and the parabola satisfy $3x^2 + 8x + 7 - k = 0$. Hence find the range of values of $k$ for which the line and parabola do not intersect.

## Key point summary

**1** An expression of the form $ax^2 + bx + c$ is a *pp100,101*
quadratic and the graph of $y = ax^2 + bx + c$ is
called a parabola .

**2** A quadratic equation that can be written in the form *p101*
$(x - p)(x - q) = 0$ has roots $p$ and $q$.

The graph of $y = (x - p)(x - q)$ crosses the $x$-axis at the
points $(p, 0)$ and $(q, 0)$.

**3** A quadratic can be written in the form $A(x + B)^2 + C$ *p103*
and this is called the completed square form.

This form enables you to find the greatest or least
values of the quadratic.

**4** The formula $x = \dfrac{-b \pm \sqrt{b^2 - 4ac}}{2a}$ can be used to find *p109*

the solutions to any quadratic equation and this
formula must be learned off by heart.

**5** The expression $b^2 - 4ac$ is called the discriminant. *p111*
When $b^2 - 4ac$ is a perfect square, the roots of the
quadratic equation are rational and the quadratic will
factorise.

When $b^2 - 4ac > 0$, the quadratic equation has two
distinct real roots.

When $b^2 - 4ac = 0$, the quadratic equation has one
(repeated) root. This condition is sometimes called
having equal roots.

When $b^2 - 4ac < 0$, the quadratic equation has no
real roots.

**6** The equations for a straight line and a parabola (or *p114*
two parabolas) can be solved simultaneously by
eliminating $y$ in order to find any points of intersection.

| Test yourself | What to review |
|---|---|
| **1** Find the points where the curve with equation $y = 2x^2 - 3x + 1$ crosses the $x$-axis. | *Section 7.2* |
| **2** A parabola has equation $y = x^2 - 8x + 11$. By completing the square, find the coordinates of its vertex. | *Section 7.3* |
| **3** Express $f(x) = 3x^2 + 18x + 20$ in the form $a(x + b)^2 + c$ and hence find the least value of $f(x)$. | *Section 7.3* |
| **4** Find the exact solutions of the equation $x^2 - 8x + 3 = 0$. | *Section 7.4* |
| **5** Use the discriminant to state the number of real roots of each of the following equations.<br>**(a)** $9x^2 - 6x + 1 = 0$,<br>**(b)** $8x^2 - 6x + 1 = 0$,<br>**(c)** $9x^2 - 5x + 1 = 0$. | *Section 7.5* |
| **6** Find the condition on $k$ for the equation $x^2 - 2x + (k - 3) = 0$ to have two real distinct roots. | *Section 7.5* |
| **7** Find the point of intersection of the parabolas with equations $y = x^2 + 3x - 7$ and $y = x^2 - x + 1$. | *Section 7.7* |

7

**Test yourself** ANSWERS

**7** $(2, 3)$.

**6** $k < 4$.

**5 (a)** 1,  **(b)** 2,  **(c)** 0.

**4** $4 \mp \sqrt{13}$.

**3** $a = 3, b = 3, c = -7$; least value is $-7$.

**2** $(4, -5)$.

**1** $(1, 0), (\frac{1}{2}, 0)$.

# CHAPTER 8

# Further differentiation

## Learning objectives

After studying this chapter, you should be able to:
- differentiate expressions which contain brackets and simple fractions
- understand what is meant by turning points and stationary points
- find and distinguish between the stationary points of a curve.

The basic definitions and techniques of differentiation appeared in Chapter 6.

In this chapter you will be dealing with methods for differentiating slightly more complicated expressions as well as looking at special types of points on curves called stationary points.

## 8.1 Simplifying expressions before differentiating

 Sometimes it is necessary to simplify expressions before you can differentiate them. You may have to expand brackets, simplify fractions, use the laws of indices, etc.

Your aim, regardless of how you have to simplify, is to obtain a line of expressions of the form $kx^n$.

### Worked example 8.1

Differentiate the following with respect to $x$:

**(a)** $y = (x - 6)(x + 2)$,        **(b)** $y = (3x + 2)^2$,

**(c)** $y = x(x - 2)(2x + 3)$.

| Multiply out the brackets. |

### Solution

**(a)** $y = (x - 6)(x + 2)$
$y = x^2 - 4x - 12$
$\Rightarrow \dfrac{dy}{dx} = 2x - 4$

| Remember, the expression must be written with terms that are powers of $x$. |

| Now you differentiate |

**(b)** $y = (3x + 2)(3x + 2) = 9x^2 + 12x + 4$

$\Rightarrow \dfrac{dy}{dx} = 18x + 12$

> Expand the brackets first.

**(c)** $y = (x^2 - 2x)(2x + 3) = 2x^3 - x^2 - 6x$

$\Rightarrow \dfrac{dy}{dx} = 6x^2 - 2x - 6$

> $x(x - 2) = x^2 - 2x$

The next example shows how you can deal with certain types of expressions containing fractions.

## Worked example 8.2

Find $\dfrac{dy}{dx}$ for each of the following:

**(a)** $y = \dfrac{x^6 - 8x^3 + 7}{x}$,

**(b)** $y = \dfrac{4x^4 + 9x - 6}{2x^2}$.

## Solution

**(a)** $\quad y = \dfrac{x^6}{x} - \dfrac{8x^3}{x} + \dfrac{7}{x}$

> With this type of expression, it is a simple matter to split the fraction into separate terms.

$\quad y = x^5 - 8x^2 + 7x^{-1}$

> Simplified using the laws of indices.

$\Rightarrow \dfrac{dy}{dx} = 5x^4 - 16x - 7x^{-2}$

$\quad = 5x^4 - 16x - \dfrac{7}{x^2}$

**(b)** $\quad y = \dfrac{4x^4}{2x^2} + \dfrac{9x}{2x^2} - \dfrac{6}{2x^2}$

> Again, split-up the fraction.

$\quad = \dfrac{4}{2}x^2 + \dfrac{9}{2x} - \dfrac{6}{2x^2}$

$\quad = 2x^2 + \dfrac{9}{2}x^{-1} - 3x^{-2}$

> Rewrite terms in the form $kx^n$.

$\Rightarrow \dfrac{dy}{dx} = 4x - \dfrac{9}{2}x^{-2} + 6x^{-3}$

> Now differentiate.

$\quad = 4x - \dfrac{9}{2x^2} + \dfrac{6}{x^3}$

**8**

The following worked example shows how the laws of indices can help you to differentiate some 'nasty-looking' expressions.

## Worked example 8.3

Differentiate each of the following functions with respect to $x$.

**(a)** $y = \sqrt{x}(7\sqrt{x} - 4x^3)$,    **(b)** $y = \dfrac{4x - 3\sqrt{x}}{x^3}$.

## Solution

**(a)** $y = x^{\frac{1}{2}}(7x^{\frac{1}{2}} - 4x^3)$

> Before you attempt to differentiate, you must convert the square roots to powers and then simplify the expression.

Expand the brackets

$$y = 7x^1 - 4x^{\frac{7}{2}}$$    $\boxed{3 + \tfrac{1}{2} = \tfrac{7}{2}}$

> Remember to add the powers of $x$ when multiplying.

$$\Rightarrow \frac{dy}{dx} = 7 - 4\left(\frac{7}{2}x^{\frac{5}{2}}\right)$$

$$= 7 - 14x^{\frac{5}{2}}$$

$$= 7 - 14\sqrt{x^5}$$

> Either of these answers is acceptable.

**(b)**    $$y = \frac{4x}{x^3} - \frac{3x^{\frac{1}{2}}}{x^3}$$

> You have to convert the root to a power.

$$= 4x^{-2} - 3x^{-\frac{5}{2}}$$

> Again, using the laws of indices.

$$\Rightarrow \frac{dy}{dx} = -8x^{-3} - 3\left(-\frac{5}{2}x^{-\frac{7}{2}}\right)$$

$$= -\frac{8}{x^3} + \frac{15}{2\sqrt{x^7}}$$

## EXERCISE 8A

**1** Find $\dfrac{dy}{dx}$ for each of the following:

**(a)** $y = 3x(x - 2)$,

**(b)** $y = (5x + 3)(2x - 3)$,

**(c)** $y = (3x - 2)(4x + 9)$,

**(d)** $y = (6x - 3)^2$,

**(e)** $y = x(2x + 10) - 5x + 2$,

**(f)** $y = 5x(2x^3 + 7x + 5)$,

**(g)** $y = \sqrt{x}(x + 4)$,

**(h)** $y = \sqrt{x}(\sqrt{x} - 2x)$.

**2** Differentiate each of the following with respect to $x$.

**(a)** $y = x^3\left(3x + \dfrac{8}{x}\right)$,

**(b)** $y = \dfrac{4x^3 - 3x^2}{9}$,

**(c)** $y = \dfrac{3x^5 + 4x^3 + 3}{x^2}$,

**(d)** $y = \dfrac{6x(x^2 - 4x)}{2x^3}$,

**(e)** $y = \dfrac{(x + 4)(x - 3)}{x}$,

**(f)** $y = \dfrac{4x^4 - 3x^3 + 1}{10x^4}$,

**(g)** $y = \dfrac{5\sqrt{x} - 3x^7}{x^3}$,

**(h)** $y = \dfrac{(x - 2)(x + 3)}{x^3}$.

**3** Find the gradient of the following curves at the given point:

**(a)** $y = 3x(x - 2)^2$      at the point where $x = 3$,

**(b)** $y = \dfrac{x^2 + 6x^3 - 2}{x^4}$      at the point where $x = -1$,

**(c)** $y = \dfrac{\sqrt{x}(x^3 - \sqrt{x})}{x^2}$      at the point where $x = 1$.

**4** Find $f'(x)$ for each of the following.

**(a)** $f(x) = 2x^4(8x^3 - 2x^4)$,

**(b)** $f(x) = \left(\dfrac{4}{x}\right)\left(\dfrac{3}{\sqrt{x}} + \dfrac{\sqrt{x}}{4}\right)$,

**(c)** $f(x) = x(2\sqrt{x} + 9) - 7\sqrt[3]{x}$,

**(d)** $f(x) = \dfrac{4x^2 - 7\sqrt{x}}{\sqrt[3]{x}} - \dfrac{3}{x}$.

## 8.2 Investigating the graphs of gradient functions

### Worked example 8.4

Consider the graph of the function $y = x^2 - 2x - 8$ given below.

What does the graph of the gradient function look like?

Start at the left-hand side of the graph and imagine the gradient of the curve at that point. Is it negative or positive?

Then move along the curve towards the right and imagine the gradient at each point – is the curve getting steeper or less steep; is the gradient positive or negative?

By asking such questions it is possible to draw the graph of the derivative.

## Solution

So the graph of the gradient function or derivative is a straight line. This is not surprising since the original curve is quadratic and when you differentiate a quadratic expression you end up with a linear expression.

Since the original curve has equation $y = x^2 - 2x - 8$, the derivative is actually $2x - 2$, which is linear.

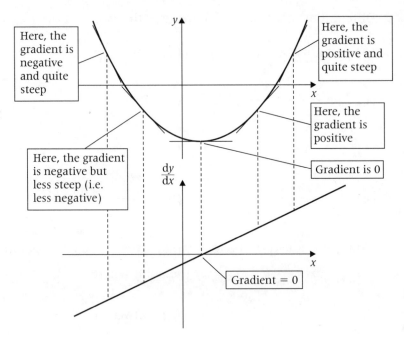

Here, the gradient is negative and quite steep

Here, the gradient is negative but less steep (i.e. less negative)

Here, the gradient is positive and quite steep

Here, the gradient is positive

Gradient is 0

Gradient = 0

## *Worked example 8.5*

The diagram below shows the graph of a cubic function.
Sketch the graph of the gradient function underneath.

## Solution

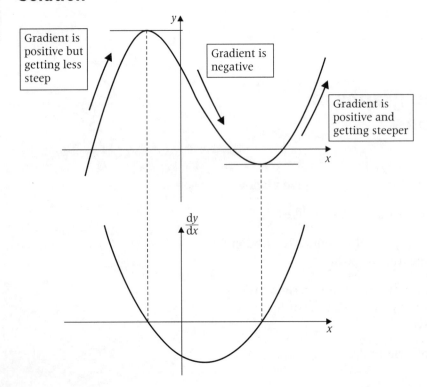

Gradient is positive but getting less steep

Gradient is negative

Gradient is positive and getting steeper

This time the derivative is a quadratic which is what you should expect since when you differentiate a cubic expression you get a quadratic expression.

## EXERCISE 8B

Make a copy of each of the following curves and then sketch the graph of its derivative underneath.

**1**
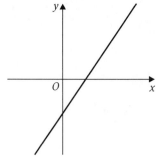

**2**
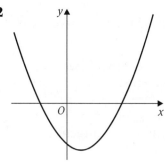

**3**
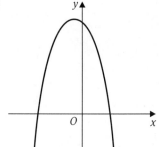

**4**
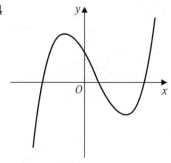

**5**
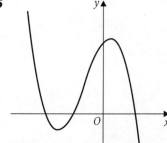

**6**
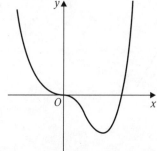

## 'Hills' and 'valleys'

As you have seen in Exercise 8B, some points on the curves are quite distinctive in that they help to define the overall shape of the curve.

These points can be described as the 'hills' and 'valleys' of the curve and you should have recognized that at each of these points the gradient is zero.

The next section considers this in detail.

## 8.3 Turning points

When sketching the graphs of functions, or solving practical problems, there are various points on the curve which are of particular interest.

For example, you may need to consider where the curve crosses the $x$-axis or $y$-axis.

There is another group of points which are very important, particularly when solving 'real-life' problems.

These points are called turning points.

Turning points are points on a curve where the tangent is horizontal .

At turning points, the gradient $\dfrac{dy}{dx} = 0$.

There are two types of turning point, the maximum point and the minimum point.

### Maximum points

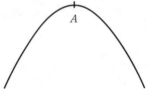

Maximum point, gradient = 0

$A$

Notice that the following applies.

At a maximum point, $A$

| | | |
|---|---|---|
| Just to the left of $A$ | $\dfrac{dy}{dx} > 0$ | (positive gradient) |
| at $A$ | $\dfrac{dy}{dx} = 0$ | (zero gradient) |
| Just to the right of $A$ | $\dfrac{dy}{dx} < 0$ | (negative gradient) |

At a maximum point, the gradient goes from positive to zero to negative.

# Minimum points

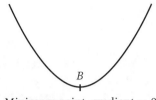

Minimum point, gradient = 0

Notice that the following applies.

At a minimum point, $B$

| Just to the left of $B$ | $\dfrac{dy}{dx} < 0$ | (negative gradient) |

| at $B$ | $\dfrac{dy}{dx} = 0$ | (zero gradient) |

| Just to the right of $B$ | $\dfrac{dy}{dx} > 0$ | (positive gradient) |

> At a minimum point, the gradient goes from negative to zero to positive.

## Worked example 8.6

Find the turning point of the curve with equation

$$y = x^2 - 8x + 14$$

and determine whether it is a maximum or a minimum point.

## Solution

$$\frac{dy}{dx} = 2x - 8$$

**at turning points, gradient = 0**

$\Rightarrow 2x - 8 = 0$

$\Rightarrow x = 4$

when $x = 4$, $y = 4^2 - 8(4) + 14 = -2$

$\Rightarrow$ there is a turning point at $(4, -2)$

> To find the y-coordinate, you substitute into the original equation.

**To decide the nature of the turning point, you have to look at the value of the gradient just to the left and just to the right of the turning point.**

8

Near $x = 4$,

| $x$ | 3.9 | 4 | 4.1 |
|---|---|---|---|
| gradient | $-0.2$ | 0 | 0.2 |

Just to the left of $x = 4$

Just to the right of $x = 4$

negative     0     positive

These values are found by substituting the chosen values of $x$ into the derivative $2x - 8$.

> A diagram like this showing the gradient at three points will help you to visualise whether you have a maximum or minimum point.

$\Rightarrow$ $(4, -2)$ is a minimum point.

$\Rightarrow$ The curve $y = x^2 - 8x + 14$ has one turning point, a minimum point at $(4, -2)$.

## Worked example 8.7

Find the two turning points of the function

$$y = 3x^2(x - 3)$$

and determine which is a maximum and which is a minimum.

## Solution

Now $y = 3x^3 - 9x^2$

> Multiplying out the brackets.

$$\Rightarrow \frac{dy}{dx} = 9x^2 - 18x$$

**At turning points, gradient = 0**

$9x^2 - 18x = 0$

$9x(x - 2) = 0$

> Factorise by taking 9x as a common factor

$\Rightarrow 9x = 0$ or $x - 2 = 0$

$\Rightarrow x = 0$ or $x = 2$

when $x = 0$, $y = 3(0)^3 - 9(0)^2 = 0$

when $x = 2$, $y = 3(2)^3 - 9(2)^2 = -12$

There are two turning points with coordinates $(0, 0)$ and $(2, -12)$.

**To decide the nature of the turning points, you have to look at the value of the gradient just to the left and just to the right of each turning point.**

Near $x = 0$

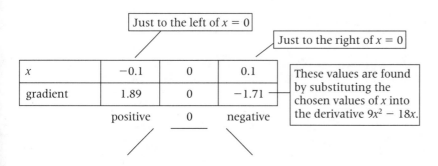

| | Just to the left of $x = 0$ | | Just to the right of $x = 0$ | |
|---|---|---|---|---|
| $x$ | $-0.1$ | $0$ | $0.1$ | These values are found by substituting the chosen values of $x$ into the derivative $9x^2 - 18x$. |
| gradient | $1.89$ | $0$ | $-1.71$ | |
| | positive | $0$ | negative | |

$\Rightarrow$ $(0, 0)$ is a maximum point.

Near $x = 2$

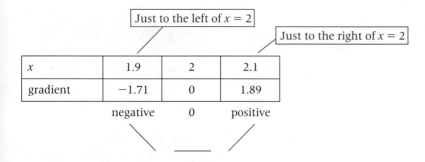

| | Just to the left of $x = 2$ | | Just to the right of $x = 2$ |
|---|---|---|---|
| $x$ | $1.9$ | $2$ | $2.1$ |
| gradient | $-1.71$ | $0$ | $1.89$ |
| | negative | $0$ | positive |

> The values of $x$ chosen should be fairly close to the turning point so that you do not go beyond another turning point.

$\Rightarrow$ $(2, -12)$ is a minimum point.

So the curve $y = 3x^2(x - 3)$ has a maximum point at $(0, 0)$ and a minimum point at $(2, -12)$.

**Note.** Consider the following curve.

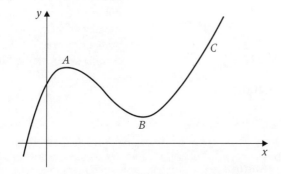

> For this reason $A$ is sometimes called a **local maximum point**. Similarly, $B$ is called a **local minimum point**.

This curve has two turning points: a maximum point at $A$ and a minimum point at $B$. Notice that while there is a maximum point at $A$, this is not the maximum value that the curve reaches.

For example, as $x$ increases beyond point $C$, the curve will continue to grow without limit.

## Worked example 8.8

A function f is defined for $-4 \leqslant x \leqslant 4$, by

$$f(x) = x^3 + x^2 - 16x - 16$$

and is sketched below.

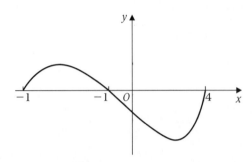

Find the range of the function.

## Solution

$$\frac{dy}{dx} = 3x^2 + 2x - 16$$

at turning points, gradient $= 0$

$\Rightarrow 3x^2 + 2x - 16 = 0$

$\Rightarrow (3x + 8)(x - 2) = 0$

$\Rightarrow x = -\dfrac{8}{3}$ or $x = 2$

when $x = -\dfrac{8}{3}$, $y = \left(-\dfrac{8}{3}\right)^3 + \left(-\dfrac{8}{3}\right)^2 - 16\left(-\dfrac{8}{3}\right) - 16 = \dfrac{400}{27}$

when $x = 2$, $y = (2)^3 + (2)^2 - 16(2) - 16 = -36$

$\Rightarrow$ There are two turning points, one at $\left(-\dfrac{8}{3}, \dfrac{400}{27}\right)$ and the
other at $(2, -36)$.

$\Rightarrow$ The range of the function is $-36 \leqslant f(x) \leqslant \dfrac{400}{27}$.

> Clearly, you need to find the coordinates of the local maximum and local minimum points.

> This is a quadratic equation where the expression will factorise.

> You can easily identify which is the maximum and which is the minimum by looking at the graph, but you could verify this by looking at the sign of the gradient on either side of each turning point.

## EXERCISE 8C

1 Find the turning point of the curve with equation
$y = x^2 - 6x + 7$ and show that it is a minimum point.

2 Find the greatest value of the function f, where

$$f(x) = 6 + 10x - 2x^2$$

and state the value of $x$ at which it occurs.
State the range of f, if the domain is $\mathbb{R}$.

**3** Find the maximum and minimum points of these curves.

(a) $y = 3x^2 - 15x + 15$,

(b) $y = 7 + 12x - 4x^2$,

(c) $y = \dfrac{64}{x} + 4x$.

**4** Find the turning points of the following curves. Determine whether they are maximum or minimum points.

(a) $y = 2x^2(x - 3)$,

(b) $y = 50 - 72x + 15x^2 - x^3$,

(c) $y = \dfrac{108}{x} + 2x^2$.

**5** A curve has equation $y = 8\sqrt{x} - 2x$, where $x > 0$.
Find the turning point on the curve and determine whether it is a maximum or a minimum point.

**6** The curve with equation $y = x^3 - 3x^2 - 9x + 4$ is shown below.

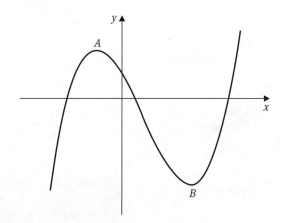

(a) Find the coordinates of the points $A$ and $B$.

(b) The function f is defined for $-2 \leqslant x \leqslant 6$ by

$$f(x) = x^3 - 3x^2 - 9x + 4.$$

Find $f(-2)$ and $f(6)$ and hence obtain the range of f.

**7** A stone is thrown and its height $y$ metres while in the air is given by the equation $y = \dfrac{15x}{2} - x^2$.

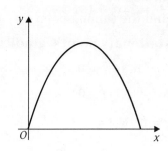

This is shown in the diagram opposite.
Find the maximum height that the stone reaches.
Verify that this point is a maximum point on the curve.

8

## 8.4 Stationary points of inflection

There is a third type of point where the gradient is equal to zero. These are called **stationary points of inflection**.

Stationary points of inflection can appear as two types:

**(i)**

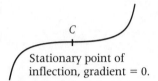

*C*

Stationary point of
inflection, gradient = 0.

**(ii)**

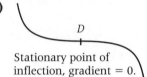

*D*

Stationary point of
inflection, gradient = 0.

Notice that the following applies:

Notice that the following applies:

| At the stationary point of inflection, $C$ |
|---|
| Just to the left of $C$ $\quad \dfrac{dy}{dx} > 0$ |
| at $C$ $\quad \dfrac{dy}{dx} = 0$ |
| Just to the right of $C$ $\quad \dfrac{dy}{dx} > 0$ |

| At a stationary point of inflection, $D$ |
|---|
| Just to the left of $D$ $\quad \dfrac{dy}{dx} < 0$ |
| at $D$ $\quad \dfrac{dy}{dx} = 0$ |
| Just to the right of $D$ $\quad \dfrac{dy}{dx} < 0$ |

So a stationary point of inflection can be recognised since the sign of the gradient is the same on each side of the point.

### Worked example 8.9

Find the coordinates of the stationary points of the curve $y = 4x^3(2 - x)$.

Determine the nature of these stationary points and hence sketch the graph.

> The term 'stationary point' refers to points on a curve where the gradient is zero.
>
> When asked to find stationary points, you will be looking for stationary points of inflection, maximum points or minimum points.

### Solution

$y = 8x^3 - 4x^4$ ——— Expand brackets

$\Rightarrow \dfrac{dy}{dx} = 24x^2 - 16x^3$

**At stationary points, gradient = 0**

$24x^2 - 16x^3 = 0$

$8x^2(3 - 2x) = 0$ ——— $8x^2$ is a common factor

$\Rightarrow x = 0$ or $x = \dfrac{3}{2}$

when $x = 0$, $\quad y = 4(0)^3(2 - 0) = 0$

when $x = \dfrac{3}{2}$, $\quad y = 4\left(\dfrac{3}{2}\right)^3\left(2 - \dfrac{3}{2}\right) = \dfrac{27}{4}$

There are two stationary points with coordinates $(0, 0)$ and $\left(\dfrac{3}{2}, \dfrac{27}{4}\right)$.

> To decide the nature of the stationary points, look at the value of the gradient just to the left and just to the right of each stationary point.

Near $x = 0$,

| $x$ | $-0.5$ | 0 | 0.5 |
|---|---|---|---|
| gradient | 8 | 0 | 4 |
|  | positive | 0 | positive |

Found by substituting the chosen values of $x$ into the derivative $24x^2 - 16x^3$.

$\Rightarrow$ $(0, 0)$ is a point of inflection.

Near $x = \dfrac{3}{2}$,

| $x$ | 1 | 1.5 | 2 |
|---|---|---|---|
| gradient | 8 | 0 | $-32$ |
|  | positive | 0 | negative |

$\Rightarrow \left(\dfrac{3}{2}, \dfrac{27}{4}\right)$ is a maximum point.

In order to sketch the graph, it is helpful to find where the curve crosses the axes.

It crosses the $x$-axis when $y = 0$,

$$4x^3(2 - x) = 0$$
$$\Rightarrow x = 0 \ \text{ or } \ x = 2$$

It crosses the $y$-axis when $x = 0$,

$$y = 8(0)^3 - 4(0)^4 = 0$$

8

You are now in a position to sketch the graph.

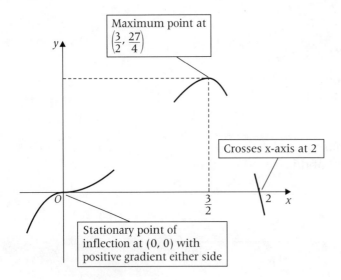

Maximum point at $\left(\dfrac{3}{2}, \dfrac{27}{4}\right)$

Crosses x-axis at 2

Stationary point of inflection at (0, 0) with positive gradient either side

You can now 'fill-in the gaps':

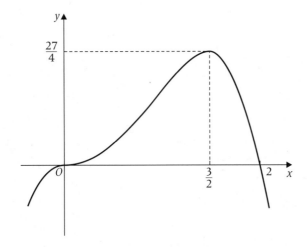

---

### EXERCISE 8D

1  Find the coordinates of the stationary point of the curve
   $y = 16 - 2x^3$.

   Determine the nature of the stationary point and sketch the
   curve.

2  A curve has equation $y = x^3 - 3x^2 + 3x + 1$.
   Find the coordinates of the stationary point on the curve and
   determine whether it is a maximum, minimum or stationary
   point of inflection.

> Try to sketch the curve initially
> without using your graphic
> calculator, and then confirm that
> you have a correct graph.

**3** Find all of the stationary points of the following curves and identify clearly the type of stationary point.

    **(a)** $y = 2x^3 + 9x^2 + 12x - 7$,

    **(b)** $y = 5 + 12x - x^3$.

**4** Find the stationary points on the following curves. Determine the nature of each stationary point.

    **(a)** $y = 3x^2(2x + 1)$,

    **(b)** $y = 16x + \dfrac{1}{x}$,

    **(c)** $y = 3x^4 - 4x^3$.

**5** A curve has equation $y = 4x^3 - 108x$.

    Find all the stationary points on the curve and determine their nature.

    Find where the curve crosses each axis and, hence, sketch the graph. Make sure that you label all important points clearly.

> Work in surd form where necessary.

## MIXED EXERCISE

**1** A curve has equation $y = 4 - x^2$. Find the gradient of the chord joining the points $P$ and $Q$ on the curve where $P$ has $x$-coordinate equal to $-1$ and the $x$-coordinate of $Q$ is 2.

**2** A curve has equation $y = 5x^2 - 12x$. The point $P$ has coordinates $(3, 9)$ and the point $Q$ has $x$-coordinate $3 + h$, where $h$ is small.

    **(a)** Find the y-coordinate of point $Q$ in terms of $h$.

    **(b)** Find the gradient of the chord joining points $P$ and $Q$.

    **(c)** Using your answer to **(b)**, write down the gradient of the curve at the point $P$.

**3** You can differentiate a function from first principles using the following definition.

$$f'(x) = \lim_{h \to 0} \left\{ \frac{f(x + h) - f(x)}{h} \right\}$$

Differentiate: **(a)** $4x^2 - 3x + 12$,   **(b)** $\dfrac{3}{x} - 5$ from first principles.

**8**

**4** Differentiate with respect to $x$:

(a) $y = 6x^3 - 5x^2 + x - 2$,

(b) $y = \dfrac{5x^3}{3} + 4x^2 - \dfrac{x}{2}$,

(c) $y = 7x^4 - 8x^2 + 3$.

**5** Find the derived function of:

(a) $f(x) = \dfrac{4}{x^2} - \dfrac{2}{x} + 4x + 12$,

(b) $g(x) = 6\sqrt{x} - \dfrac{7}{2x^2}$,

(c) $h(x) = \dfrac{x^2 - 3x + 2}{\sqrt{x}}$.

**6** Find the gradient of the following curves at the given point.

(a) $y = 6 + 2x - 5x^2$     at $(0, 6)$,

(b) $y = 2x^3 - 5x + 8$     at $(-1, 11)$,

(c) $y = \dfrac{5}{x^2} - 8x + 2$     at $(1, -1)$,

(d) $y = 4\sqrt{x} + \dfrac{9}{x}$     at $(9, 13)$

**7** Find the coordinates of the points on the curve
$y = x^3 - \dfrac{9x^2}{2} - 20x + 7$ where the gradient equals 10.

**8** Calculate the gradient of the tangent to the curve
$y = 16x + \dfrac{1}{x}$ at the point $(\frac{1}{2}, 10)$.

Calculate also the coordinates of the other point on the curve with the same gradient.

**9** Differentiate the following with respect to $x$

(a) $y = (x + 7)(x - 4)$,

(b) $y = \dfrac{7x^2 - 8x^4 + 2}{x^2}$,

(c) $y = 3\sqrt{x}(9x + 4\sqrt{x})$,

(d) $y = x\left(2x + \dfrac{1}{x}\right)^2$.

**10** Find the points on the curve $y = 4x^3 - 3x^2 - 19$ at which the tangents are parallel to the $x$-axis.

**11** The graph of $y = Ax + Bx^2$ passes through the point $(3, -15)$ and its gradient at that point is $-14$.

   **(a)** Find the values of the constants $A$ and $B$.

   **(b)** Calculate the maximum value of $y$ and state the value of $x$ at which it occurs.

**12** Find the stationary points of the curve with equation

$$y = x^3 - 48x.$$

Determine the nature of each turning point and, hence sketch the curve labelling all important points clearly.

**13** The curve with equation $y = 2x^2 - 1 - \sqrt{x}$ is defined for $x \geqslant 0$ and is shown below.

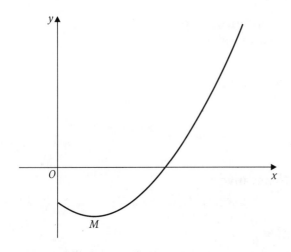

   **(a)** Use differentiation to determine the coordinates of $M$, the minimum point of the curve.

   **(b)** Determine the gradient of the curve at the point where $x = 2.5$, giving your answer correct to three decimal places.　　　　　　　　　　　　[A]

**14** A curve has equation $y = x^2 - \dfrac{54}{x}$.

Find $\dfrac{\mathrm{d}y}{\mathrm{d}x}$ in terms of $x$.

Calculate the coordinates of the stationary point of the curve and determine whether it is a maximum or minimum point.　　　　　　　　　　　　[A]

## Key point summary

1. Sometimes it is necessary to simplify expressions before we can differentiate, e.g. expand brackets or simplify fractions.                                                  *p118*

2. A stationary point is a point on a curve where the gradient is zero, i.e. $\dfrac{dy}{dx} = 0$.                                                  *p124*

3. There are three types of stationary point:                                                  *pp124,130*
   - maximum point
   - minimum point
   - stationary point of inflection

4. Maximum and minimum points are also referred to as turning points.                                                  *p124*

5. To find stationary points, we put the derivative equal to zero and solve the resulting equation.                                                  *p130*

6. The nature of a stationary point can be determined by considering the value of the gradient just to the left and right of the point.                                                  *p131*

   Gradient changes from negative to zero to positive: minimum point.

   Gradient changes from positive to zero to negative: maximum point.

   Gradient changes from positive to zero to positive: stationary point of inflection.

   Gradient changes from negative to zero to negative: stationary point of inflection.

| Test yourself | What to review |
|---|---|
| **1** Differentiate with respect to $x$:<br>    **(a)** $y = (2x - 4)(x + 7)$,<br>    **(b)** $y = \dfrac{2x^3 - 5x^2 + 7}{x^5}$,<br>    **(c)** $y = 3x(6x^3 + 2\sqrt{x})$. | *Section 8.1* |
| **2** Find the gradient of the following curves at the given points:<br>    **(a)** $y = \dfrac{(x - 2)(x - 5)}{x}$      at $x = -2$,<br>    **(b)** $y = 2\sqrt{x}(5x - 3)$      at $x = 9$. | *Section 8.1* |
| **3** Find the minimum value taken by the curve with equation<br>    $y = (x - 7)(x - 6)$<br>and the value of $x$ at which it occurs. | *Section 8.3* |
| **4** A curve has equation $y = x^3 + 6x^2 - 36x + 25$.<br>Find the stationary points of the curve and determine their nature. | *Section 8.4* |

**8**

**Test yourself** **ANSWERS**

**4** $(2, -15)$ minimum, $(-6, 241)$ maximum.

**3** Minimum value of $-0.25$ which occurs at $x = 6.5$.

**2 (a)** $-1.5$,      **(b)** $44$.

**1 (a)** $4x + 10$,      **(b)** $\dfrac{15}{x^4} - \dfrac{4}{x^3} - \dfrac{35}{x^6}$,      **(c)** $72x^3 + 9\sqrt{x}$.

# CHAPTER 9

# Integration

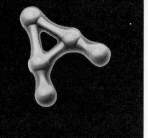

---

## Learning objectives

After studying this chapter, you should be able to:
- understand that integration is the reverse process of differentiation
- be able to integrate expressions of the form $kx^n$, $n \neq -1$
- understand the term 'indefinite integral' and realise the need to add an arbitrary constant
- be able to find the equation of a curve given its derivative and the coordinates of a point on the curve
- understand how to evaluate a 'definite integral'
- use definite integrals to find areas of regions bounded by curves.

## 9.1 Finding a function from its gradient function

You saw earlier how to find a gradient function by differentiation, so that

$$f(x) = 2x^3 - 5x^2 + 3x - 7$$
$$\Rightarrow f'(x) = 6x^2 - 10x + 3$$

Can the process be reversed?

In general, $y = x^n \Rightarrow \dfrac{dy}{dx} = nx^{n-1}$

> You learned to reduce the index by one and to multiply at the front by the index. See Section 6.6 of Chapter 6.

Reversing the process, it would seem that

$$\frac{dy}{dx} = x^m \Rightarrow y = \frac{1}{m+1}x^{m+1}$$

> **Increase** the index by 1 and **divide** at the front by the new index.

> The general process of finding a function from its gradient function is known as **integration**.

As a general guide so that you do not confuse the two techniques,

when you **In**tegrate, you **In**crease the index by 1, whereas

when you **D**ifferentiate, you **D**ecrease the index by 1.

## Worked example 9.1

Given that $\dfrac{dy}{dx} = 12x^2 + 4x - 5$, find an expression for $y$.

> Consider $x^2$ – this integrates to $\dfrac{x^3}{3}$

## Solution

$$\dfrac{dy}{dx} = 12x^2 + 4x - 5 \Rightarrow y = 12 \times \dfrac{x^3}{3} + 4 \times \dfrac{x^2}{2} - 5\dfrac{x^1}{1}$$

It would seem that

> Increase the index by 1 and divide by the new index.

$$y = 4x^3 + 2x^2 - 5x$$

but that is not quite the complete answer.

**Whenever you differentiate a constant you get zero,**

e.g. $y = 7 \Rightarrow \dfrac{dy}{dx} = 0$, *or* $y = -19 \Rightarrow \dfrac{dy}{dx} = 0$

and so the expression for $y$ above could have any constant on the end and still satisfy $\dfrac{dy}{dx} = 12x^2 + 4x - 5$.

The answer to this example is therefore

$$y = 4x^3 + 2x^2 - 5x + c, \text{ where } c \text{ is a constant.}$$

> The constant $c$ is called an **arbitrary constant**.

$$\dfrac{dy}{dx} = x^n \ (n \neq -1) \Rightarrow y = \dfrac{1}{n+1}x^{n+1} + c, \text{ where } c \text{ is an}$$
arbitrary constant.

**9**

## Worked example 9.2

Given that $f'(x) = x^4 - \sqrt{x}$, find an expression for $f(x)$.

## Solution

$$f'(x) = x^4 - \sqrt{x} = x^4 - x^{\frac{1}{2}}$$

> Writing $\sqrt{x}$ as a power of $x$.

$$\Rightarrow f(x) = \dfrac{1}{5}x^5 - \dfrac{1}{\left(\dfrac{3}{2}\right)}x^{\frac{3}{2}} + k = \dfrac{x^5}{5} - \dfrac{2}{3}x^{\frac{3}{2}} + k$$

> *Integrating*: Increase the index by 1 and divide by the new index.

You learned in Section 8.2 of Chapter 8 how to sketch the graph of a gradient function when you were given the graph of the original function. Again this process can be reversed, as indicated below, where you are given the graph of $\dfrac{dy}{dx}$.

> Don't forget the arbitrary constant.

The gradient is zero when $x = -1$, and is positive on the left of this point but negative on the right. There is a maximum point when $x = -1$.

Similarly there is a minimum point at $x = 2$.

These are the only turning points.

For $x > 2$, the gradient is positive and gets steeper as $x$ increases.

You can attempt to sketch the graph of the original curve, but the graph is not unique.

The graph could be translated in the $y$-direction by any amount, and it would still have the same gradient function. There is an infinite number of possible graphs with the same gradient function.

If you are given one point on the curve, you can usually find the actual equation of the curve.

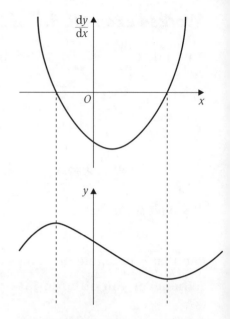

## Worked example 9.3

A curve passes through the point $(2, 5)$ and $\dfrac{dy}{dx} = 10x^7 - \dfrac{6}{x^2}$.

Find its equation.

> You should now see the need for an arbitrary constant and, although you can use any letter, it is common to use $c$ or $k$.

## Solution

Rewriting as powers of $x$, $\dfrac{dy}{dx} = 10x^7 - 6x^{-2}$

> Index is $-2 + 1 = -1$

Integration gives $y = 10 \times \dfrac{x^8}{8} - 6 \times \dfrac{x^{-1}}{-1} + c,$

where $c$ is a constant.

$$\Rightarrow y = \frac{5x^8}{4} + \frac{6}{x} + c$$

Since the curve passes through $(2, 5)$ you can find the value of $c$.

$x = 2$ when $y = 5$, $\Rightarrow 5 = \dfrac{5 \times 2^8}{4} + \dfrac{6}{2} + c \Rightarrow 5 = 320 + 3 + c$

$$\Rightarrow c = -318$$

The equation of the curve is $y = \dfrac{5x^8}{4} + \dfrac{6}{x} - 318.$

## EXERCISE 9A

**1** Find $y$ in terms of $x$ for each of the following:

   **(a)** $\dfrac{dy}{dx} = 12x^5,$         **(b)** $\dfrac{dy}{dx} = 2x^3,$

> Don't forget the arbitrary constant.

**(c)** $\dfrac{dy}{dx} = 4x^7$,

**(d)** $\dfrac{dy}{dx} = 12$,

**(e)** $\dfrac{dy}{dx} = 3x^2 - 2x + 5$,

**(f)** $\dfrac{dy}{dx} = 6x^5 - 18x^2 - x$,

**(g)** $\dfrac{dy}{dx} = 4x^7 - 12x^5 - 4$,

**(h)** $\dfrac{dy}{dx} = 6x^{-4}$,

**(i)** $\dfrac{dy}{dx} = 3x^{\frac{-1}{4}}$

**(j)** $\dfrac{dy}{dx} = \dfrac{3}{x^4} - \dfrac{1}{x^2}$,

**(k)** $\dfrac{dy}{dx} = 6\sqrt{x}$,

**(l)** $\dfrac{dy}{dx} = \dfrac{2}{\sqrt{x}}$.

> You can always check your final answer by differentiating and making sure you get the original expression for $\dfrac{dy}{dx}$ or $f'(x)$.

**2** Find an expression for f($x$) in each of the following cases:

**(a)** $f'(x) = 6x^2 - 4x + 5$,

**(b)** $f'(x) = 3x^2 + 10x + 4$,

**(c)** $f'(x) = 10x^4 - 3x^5 + 7$,

**(d)** $f'(x) = 10x^9 - 8x^3 + 1$,

**(e)** $f'(x) = 2x^{-2} - 3x^{-4}$,

**(f)** $f'(x) = 10x^{-6} - 12x^{-5} + 7x^{-2}$,

**(g)** $f'(x) = \dfrac{3}{x^4} + \dfrac{10}{x^6}$,

**(h)** $f'(x) = \dfrac{2}{x^3} - \dfrac{12}{x^5}$,

**(i)** $f'(x) = \dfrac{18}{x^{10}} - \dfrac{14}{x^8}$,

**(j)** $f'(x) = 6\sqrt{x} + \dfrac{9}{x^2\sqrt{x}}$.

**3** The graph of $y = f(x)$ passes through the point $(1, -3)$ and $f'(x) = 12x^2 + 8x - 3$. Find f($x$).

**4** A curve passes through the point $(-1, 2)$ and is such that $\dfrac{dy}{dx} = 8x^3 - 12x^2 + 3$. Find the equation of the curve.

**5** A curve passes through the point $(-2, 7)$ and is such that $\dfrac{dy}{dx} = \dfrac{4}{x^2} - 8x + 5$. Find the equation of the curve.

**6** The diagrams show the graph of the gradient function. Sketch a possible graph of the original curve in each case.

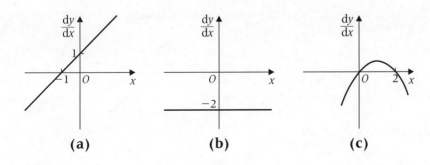

**(a)**          **(b)**          **(c)**

**7** A curve passes through the point (4, 11) and is such that

$\dfrac{dy}{dx} = 3\sqrt{x} + 10x\sqrt{x}$. Find the equation of the curve.

**8** A curve passes through the point (27, 4) and is such that

$\dfrac{dy}{dx} = 8\sqrt[3]{x} - \dfrac{2}{\sqrt[3]{x}}$. Find the equation of the curve.

**9** Given that $\dfrac{dy}{dx} = x^n$, in general $y = \dfrac{1}{n+1}x^{n+1} + c$.

There is, however, one value of $n$ for which this cannot be true. What is this value of $n$?

# 9.2 Simplifying expressions before integrating

Sometimes it is necessary to obtain a series of terms of the form $kx^n$ before integrating.

## *Worked example 9.4* _____

The graph of $y = f(x)$ passes through the point (2, 6) and $f'(x) = (3x - 4)(3 - 2x)$. Find $f(x)$.

## *Solution*

$f'(x) = (3x - 4)(3 - 2x) = 9x - 6x^2 - 12 + 8x = 17x - 6x^2 - 12$

| Multiplying out the brackets. |

$\Rightarrow f(x) = 17 \times \dfrac{x^2}{2} - 6 \times \dfrac{x^3}{3} - 12 \times \dfrac{x^1}{1} + c$

| $c$ is an arbitrary constant. |

$\qquad = \dfrac{17}{2}x^2 - 2x^3 - 12x + c$

When $x = 2$, $y = f(x) = 6$, $\Rightarrow 6 = \left(\dfrac{17}{2} \times 4\right) - (2 \times 8) - (12 \times 2) + c$

$$\Rightarrow 6 = 34 - 16 - 24 + c$$
$$\Rightarrow 6 = -6 + c \Rightarrow c = 12$$
$$\Rightarrow f(x) = \dfrac{17}{2}x^2 - 2x^3 - 12x + 12$$

## *Worked example 9.5* _____

Given that $\dfrac{dy}{dx} = \dfrac{x^3 - 3x + 4}{x^5}$, find an expression for $y$.

## Solution

$$\frac{dy}{dx} = \frac{x^3 - 3x + 4}{x^5} = \frac{x^3}{x^5} - \frac{3x}{x^5} + \frac{4}{x^5}$$

> Writing as separate fractions.

$$\Rightarrow \frac{dy}{dx} = x^{-2} - 3x^{-4} + 4x^{-5}$$

> Each term is now of the form $kx^n$.

$$\Rightarrow y = \left(\frac{x^{-1}}{-1}\right) - \left(3 \times \frac{x^{-3}}{-3}\right) + \left(4 \times \frac{x^{-4}}{-4}\right) + k$$

> $k$ is the arbitrary constant.

$$\Rightarrow y = -x^{-1} + x^{-3} - x^{-4} + k$$

or if you prefer this can be written as

$$y = \frac{1}{x^3} - \frac{1}{x} - \frac{1}{x^4} + k, \text{ where } k \text{ is a constant.}$$

## EXERCISE 9B

1 Find an expression for $y$ in terms of $x$ and a constant in each of the following cases:

(a) $\dfrac{dy}{dx} = x(3x - 2)$,

(b) $\dfrac{dy}{dx} = x^3(10x + 6)$,

(c) $\dfrac{dy}{dx} = 4x^5(2x^2 + 3)$,

(d) $\dfrac{dy}{dx} = x^{-5}(3x + 8)$,

(e) $\dfrac{dy}{dx} = (1 - x)(3x - 2)$,

(f) $\dfrac{dy}{dx} = x(x - 2)(x + 3)$,

(g) $\dfrac{dy}{dx} = x^2(x + 2)(x + 1)$,

(h) $\dfrac{dy}{dx} = x^{-6}(x + 3)(x + 5)$,

(i) $\dfrac{dy}{dx} = \dfrac{(2x + 3)(x + 4)}{x^4}$,

(j) $\dfrac{dy}{dx} = \dfrac{(3x - 4)(x + 2)}{\sqrt{x}}$.

2 Find $f(x)$ in terms of $x$ and an arbitrary constant for each of the following where:

(a) $f'(x) = (2x - 5)(3 - 2x)$,

(b) $f'(x) = \sqrt{x}(5x - 3)$,

(c) $f'(x) = 12x^3(x + 1)(x - 1)$,

(d) $f'(x) = \sqrt{x}(6 - 2\sqrt{x})$,

(e) $f'(x) = \dfrac{x^4 - 3x^2 + 7}{x^2}$,

(f) $f'(x) = \dfrac{x^2 - 3x + 5}{\sqrt{x}}$,

(g) $f'(x) = \dfrac{4x - 5}{\sqrt[3]{x}}$,

(h) $f'(x) = \dfrac{\sqrt{x} - 4x + 6}{\sqrt{x}}$.

3 A curve passes through the point $(-1, 3)$ and is such that $\dfrac{dy}{dx} = x^3(25x - 16)$. Find the equation of the curve.

9

**4** A curve passes through the point $(2, -2)$ and is such that $\dfrac{dy}{dx} = \dfrac{x^5 - 3x^2 + 2}{x^2}$. Find the equation of the curve.

**5** A curve passes through the point $(1, 2)$ and is such that $\dfrac{dy}{dx} = \dfrac{(x - 3)(5 - 2x)}{x^4}$. Find the equation of the curve.

**6** A curve passes through the point $(4, 25)$ and is such that $\dfrac{dy}{dx} = \dfrac{x^2 - 3x + 7}{\sqrt{x}}$. Find the equation of the curve.

**7** A curve passes through the point $(1, -5)$ and is such that $\dfrac{dy}{dx} = \dfrac{(x - 3)(2x + 1)}{\sqrt[3]{x}}$. Find the equation of the curve.

# 9.3 Indefinite integrals

The special symbol $\int$ is used to denote integration.

When you need to integrate $x^3$, for example, you write

$$\int x^3 \, dx = \frac{1}{4}x^4 + c$$

and read as

| the integral | of $x^3$ | with respect to $x$ |

> It is rather like an elongated letter S and, as you will see in the next section, it stands for summation (actually the first letter of the Latin word *summa*). The symbol dates back to the 1600s when a letter S actually looked like this.

> It is a common mistake to forget the dx symbol. Try to remind yourself to include it.

Because the answer contains an arbitrary constant and so does not have a unique value, it is called an **indefinite integral**.

There is nothing new in this section apart from this new notation.

## Worked example 9.6

Find **(a)** $\displaystyle\int x(x - 3) \, dx$, **(b)** $\displaystyle\int \frac{(x + 2)}{\sqrt{x}} \, dx$.

> Notice that you keep the integral sign in your working while you simplify the expression.

## Solution

**(a)** $\displaystyle\int x(x - 3) \, dx = \int x^2 - 3x \, dx$

$$= \frac{x^3}{3} - \frac{3}{2}x^2 + c$$

**(b)** $\int \dfrac{(x+2)}{\sqrt{x}}\,dx = \int \dfrac{x}{\sqrt{x}} + \dfrac{2}{\sqrt{x}}\,dx$

$$= \int x^{\frac{1}{2}} + 2x^{-\frac{1}{2}}\,dx$$

$$= \dfrac{1}{\left(\dfrac{3}{2}\right)} x^{\frac{3}{2}} + \dfrac{2}{\left(\dfrac{1}{2}\right)} x^{\frac{1}{2}} + k$$

$$= \dfrac{2}{3} x^{\frac{3}{2}} + 4x^{\frac{1}{2}} + k, \text{ where } k \text{ is a constant.}$$

## EXERCISE 9C

Find each of the following:

**1** $\int 12x^5\,dx.$      **2** $\int 20x^4\,dx.$

**3** $\int 2x^{-3}\,dx.$      **4** $\int x^2(4x+6)\,dx.$

**5** $\int 88x^{10}\,dx.$      **6** $\int 20x^{-4}\,dx.$

**7** $\int 3x^{-2}\,dx.$      **8** $\int x^{-2}(4+6x^7)\,dx.$

**9** $\int 5x^{-4}\,dx.$      **10** $\int 3x^{\frac{1}{2}}\,dx.$

**11** $\int \dfrac{1}{x^3}\,dx.$      **12** $\int \dfrac{4}{x^2} + \dfrac{6}{x^3}\,dx.$

**13** $\int (x+1)(3x+5)\,dx.$      **14** $\int (x-1)(6x-5)\,dx.$

**15** $\int (3-2x)(x+3)\,dx.$      **16** $\int x(3-2x)(x+3)\,dx.$

**17** $\int (3+2x)^2\,dx.$      **18** $\int (2-3x)^2\,dx.$

**19** $\int x^2\sqrt{x}\,dx.$      **20** $\int (\sqrt{x}-1)^2\,dx.$

**21** $\int \dfrac{x^2-1}{\sqrt{x}}\,dx.$      **22** $\int (x^3-1)\sqrt[3]{x}\,dx.$

**23** $\int (5-6x)^2\,dx.$      **24** $\int \dfrac{2(x^4+1)}{x^3}\,dx.$

**25** $\int 18x^3\sqrt{x}\,dx.$      **26** $\int (\sqrt{x}+3)^2\,dx.$

**27** $\int \dfrac{x^4-3}{x\sqrt{x}}\,dx.$      **28** $\int x(x^3-1)^2\,dx.$

**29** $\int \dfrac{x^5+5}{x^3\sqrt{x}}\,dx.$      **30** $\int x(\sqrt{x}-3)^2\,dx.$

**9**

# 9.4 Interpretation as an area

Consider the curve with equation $y = f(x)$. How can you find the area of the region bounded by the curve, the $x$-axis and the lines with equations $x = a$ and $x = b$?

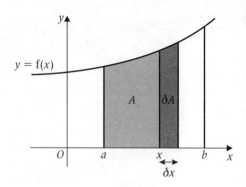

Let the region under the curve from $x = a$ to a general position shown be $A$.

> Now as $x$ increases by $\delta x$, $y$ becomes $y + \delta y$ and $A$ becomes $A + \delta A$.

By considering the two rectangles, it is clear that

$$y \delta x < \delta A < (y + \delta y) \delta x$$

or, dividing throughout by $\delta x$.

$$y < \frac{\delta A}{\delta x} < y + \delta y$$

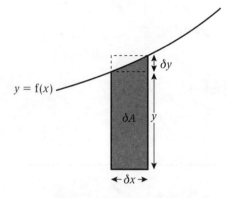

As $\delta x \to 0$, $\delta y \to 0$ and $\dfrac{\delta A}{\delta x} \to \dfrac{dA}{dx}$.

Hence $\dfrac{dA}{dx} = y$

Suppose $\displaystyle\int y\, dx = \int f(x)\, dx = F(x) + c$

then $\qquad\qquad\qquad A = F(x) + c$

Since $A$ is obviously zero when $x = a$,

$$0 = F(a) + c \Rightarrow c = -F(a)$$
$$\Rightarrow A = F(x) - F(a)$$

> So for example when $f(x) = x^2$,
>
> $$F(x) = \frac{x^3}{3}.$$

> The function $F(x)$ is called a primitive of $f(x)$.

Hence the area of the region up to the point where $x = b$ is given by substituting $x = b$ into the formula for $A$.

> Area, $A = F(b) - F(a)$.

## *Worked example 9.7*

Find the area bounded by the curve with equation $y = 8x^3 + 6x + 2$, the $x$-axis and the lines $x = 1$ and $x = 2$, shaded in the diagram.

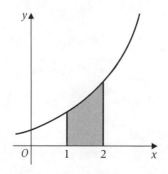

## Solution

Using the notation from above,

$$f(x) = 8x^3 + 6x + 2$$

$$\Rightarrow F(x) = 8 \times \frac{x^4}{4} + 6 \times \frac{x^2}{2} + 2x = 2x^4 + 3x^2 + 2x$$

Area is given by $F(2) - F(1)$

$$F(2) = 32 + 12 + 4 = 48; \qquad F(1) = 2 + 3 + 2 = 7.$$

Area of region is $48 - 7 = 41$.

> Note, there is no need to add $+c$ when finding $F(x)$.
> If you do, it will cancel out when you find $F(b) - F(a)$.

# 9.5 Definite integrals

Finding the area under a curve is made easier by using the notation of a definite integral.

The values of the endpoints $x = a$ and $x = b$ are placed at the bottom and top of the integral sign and these are called **limits**.

A definite integral is of the form $\int_a^b f(x)\, dx$.

> The function $f(x)$ is called the integrand.

The area calculated in Worked example 9.7 is given by the definite integral $\int_1^2 8x^3 + 6x + 2\, dx$.

This example can be reworked using a square bracket notation.

$$\int_1^2 8x^3 + 6x + 2\, dx = [2x^4 + 3x^2 + 2x]_1^2$$

$$= (32 + 12 + 4) - (2 + 3 + 2) = 48 - 7 = 41$$

| Equivalent to F(2) | Equivalent to F(1) |

> The procedure can be streamlined without introducing the function $F(x)$. Instead square brackets are used after integration with the limits placed at the top and bottom of the final bracket.

**9**

> Most graphic calculators find approximate values of definite integrals and this might be a helpful check on your answer

After integrating a definite integral, you obtain $[f(x)]_a^b$ and this is evaluated as $F(b) - F(a)$.

## Worked example 9.8

Find the value of each of the following definite integrals.

**(a)** $\displaystyle\int_2^3 8x^3 + 2x \, dx$   **(b)** $\displaystyle\int_1^4 \sqrt{x}(x + 1) \, dx$

## Solution

**(a)** $\displaystyle\int_2^3 8x^3 + 2x \, dx = [2x^4 + x^2]_2^3$

$$= (2 \times 3^4 + 3^2) - (2 \times 2^4 + 2^2)$$

$$= 171 - 36 = 135$$

> Integrate the expression and put the limits at the end of the square brackets.

> Evaluate at top limit then subtract the value at the bottom limit.

**(b)** $\displaystyle\int_1^4 \sqrt{x}(x + 1) \, dx = \int_1^4 x\sqrt{x} + \sqrt{x} \, dx = \int_1^4 x^{\frac{3}{2}} + x^{\frac{1}{2}} \, dx$

$$= \left[ \frac{2}{5}x^{\frac{5}{2}} + \frac{2}{3}x^{\frac{3}{2}} \right]_1^4$$

$$= \left[ \frac{2}{5} \times 4^{\frac{5}{2}} + \frac{2}{3} \times 4^{\frac{3}{2}} \right] - \left[ \frac{2}{5} \times 1^{\frac{5}{2}} + \frac{2}{3} \times 1^{\frac{3}{2}} \right]$$

$$= \left( \frac{64}{5} + \frac{16}{3} \right) - \left( \frac{2}{5} + \frac{2}{3} \right) = \frac{256}{15}$$

> Write each term as a power of $x$.

> Integrating each term.

> 'top limit value' minus 'bottom limit value'.

## Worked example 9.9

Find the area of the region bounded by the curve with equation $y = x + \dfrac{1}{x^2}$, the lines $x = 1$, $x = 2$ and the $x$-axis from $x = 1$ to $x = 2$.

> Your graphic calculator could be used to get a sketch of the region and give you a check on your answer.

## Solution

Area $= \displaystyle\int_1^2 x + \frac{1}{x^2} \, dx = \int_1^2 x + x^{-2} \, dx$

$$= \left[ \frac{x^2}{2} - \frac{1}{x} \right]_1^2 = \left( \frac{4}{2} - \frac{1}{2} \right) - \left( \frac{1}{2} - \frac{1}{1} \right) = 2$$

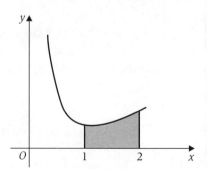

## EXERCISE 9D

Evaluate each of the definite integrals from (1) to (11).

**1** $\displaystyle\int_0^1 6x \, dx.$   **2** $\displaystyle\int_1^3 10x^4 \, dx.$

> Don't worry if some of the final answers are negative.

**3** $\displaystyle\int_0^2 12x^3 \, dx.$  **4** $\displaystyle\int_1^4 2x^3 \, dx.$

**5** $\displaystyle\int_1^3 10x - 6x^2 \, dx.$  **6** $\displaystyle\int_1^2 (x-1)(x+1) \, dx.$

**7** $\displaystyle\int_0^1 (3x-4)(x+1) \, dx.$  **8** $\displaystyle\int_2^4 3x - x^3 \, dx.$

**9** $\displaystyle\int_0^1 \sqrt{x} \, dx.$

**10** $\displaystyle\int_1^4 (2\sqrt{x} - 3)(\sqrt{x} - 1) \, dx.$

> You may wish to sketch the curves and regions using a graphic calculator.

**11** $\displaystyle\int_1^2 \frac{(2x-3)(x+1)}{x^4} \, dx.$

**12** Calculate the area of the region bounded by the curve $y = x^3$, the $x$-axis from the origin to $x = 4$ and the line $x = 4$.

**13** Calculate the area of the region bounded by the curve with equation $y = 2x + 12x^2$, the $x$-axis from $x = 2$ to $x = 3$ and the lines $x = 2$ and $x = 3$.

**14** Calculate the area of the region bounded by the curve with equation $y = x^2 + \dfrac{4}{x^3}$, the $x$-axis from $x = 1$ to $x = 2$ and the lines x $= 1$ and $x = 2$.

**15** Calculate the area of the region bounded by the curve with equation $y = 3\sqrt{x} + \dfrac{2}{\sqrt{x}}$, the $x$-axis from $x = 1$ to $x = 4$ and the lines $x = 1$ and $x = 4$.

**16** Find the areas of the shaded regions shown in the following diagrams.

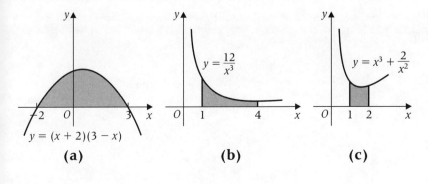

(a)   (b)   (c)

# 9.6 Regions bounded by lines and curves

Sometimes a region is bounded by more than one curve or a curve and a line as the following example illustrates.

## *Worked example 9.10*

Find the points of intersection of the curve $y = x^2 - 3x + 4$ and the line $y = x + 1$.

Calculate the area of the finite region bounded by this curve and this line, shaded in the diagram.

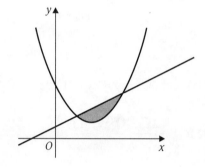

## *Solution*

Eliminating $y$ to find points of intersection,

$$\Rightarrow x + 1 = x^2 - 3x + 4$$
$$\Rightarrow 0 = x^2 - 4x + 3$$
$$\Rightarrow 0 = (x - 1)(x - 3)$$
$$\Rightarrow x = 1 \text{ or } x = 3.$$

when $x = 1$, $y = 2$ and when $x = 3$, $y = 4$.

Points of intersection are $(1, 2)$ and $(3, 4)$.

The area of the shaded region shown in the diagram can be thought of as the difference of two areas.

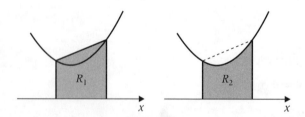

Since $R_1$ is a trapezium, its area could have been found more easily by using

$$\frac{1}{2}(2 + 4) \times (3 - 1) = 6$$

$$\text{Area of } R_1 = \int_1^3 x + 1 \, dx = \left[ \frac{x^2}{2} + x \right]_1^3 = \left( \frac{9}{2} + 3 \right) - \left( \frac{1}{2} + 1 \right) = 6$$

$$\text{Area of } R_2 = \int_1^3 x^2 - 3x + 4 \, dx = \left[ \frac{x^3}{3} - 3\frac{x^2}{2} + 4x \right]_1^3$$

$$= \left( 9 - \frac{27}{2} + 12 \right) - \left( \frac{1}{3} - \frac{3}{2} + 4 \right) = \frac{14}{3}$$

$$\text{Area of shaded region} = 6 - \frac{14}{3} = \frac{4}{3}$$

The area under a curve $y = f(x)$ from $x = a$ to $x = b$ is given by $\int_a^b f(x)\, dx$.

## 9.7 Regions below the x-axis

At times the region being considered lies partly below the $x$-axis. For example, suppose you are finding the area of the shaded region bounded by the curve $y = x(x - 3)$ and the $x$-axis.

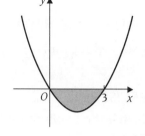

$$\int_0^3 x(x - 3)\, dx = \int_0^3 x^2 - 3x\, dx = \left[\frac{x^3}{3} - 3\frac{x^2}{2}\right]_0^3 = \left(9 - \frac{27}{2}\right) - 0 = -\frac{9}{2}$$

The area is therefore $4\frac{1}{2}$.

Because the summation involves $y$-coordinates that are negative, the integral has a negative value. Care must be taken to consider separately any regions where the $y$-value is negative.

### *Worked example 9.11*

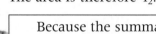

The curve with equation $y = 4x - x^2$ cuts the $x$-axis at the points $O$ and $P$, and also intersects the line $y + 2x = 0$ at the point $Q$. Calculate the area of the finite region bounded by the curve and the line, shaded in the diagram.

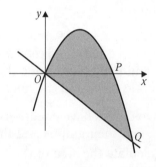

### *Solution*

On the $x$-axis, $y = 0$. So $4x - x^2 = 0 \Rightarrow x(4 - x) = 0$

$\Rightarrow x = 0, x = 4$.

Therefore $P$ is the point $(4, 0)$.

Eliminating $y$ to find the intersection of the line and curve,

$-2x = 4x - x^2 \Rightarrow x^2 - 6x = 0 \Rightarrow x(x - 6) = 0$
$\Rightarrow x = 0, x = 6$. When $x = 6$, $y = -12$.

Coordinates of $Q$ are $(6, -12)$.

Considering regions separately.

Substitute in line equation – check in the curve equation.

Area of $R_1 = \int_0^4 4x - x^2\, dx = \left[2x^2 - \frac{x^3}{3}\right]_0^4 = \left(2 \times 16 - \frac{64}{3}\right) - 0 = \frac{32}{3}$

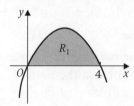

To find area of $R_2$, consider

$$\int_4^6 4x - x^2\, dx = \left[2x^2 - \frac{x^3}{3}\right]_4^6 = \left(2 \times 36 - \frac{216}{3}\right)$$
$$- \left(2 \times 16 - \frac{64}{3}\right) = -\frac{32}{3}$$

**9**

Therefore area of $R_2 = \dfrac{32}{3}$

But $R_2 + R_3$ is a triangle and has area $= \dfrac{1}{2} \times 6 \times 12 = 36$

Hence $R_3$ has area $36 - \dfrac{32}{3} = \dfrac{76}{3}$

The original shaded region consists of $R_1 + R_3$ and so the area of this shaded region is $\dfrac{32}{3} + \dfrac{76}{3} = 36$.

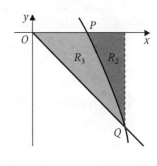

## EXERCISE 9E

**1** Sketch the graph of the parabola with equation $y = x^2 + 1$ and the line with equation $y = 3x - 1$. Find the two points of intersection of the line and the curve. Calculate the area of the finite region bounded by the parabola and the line.

**2** Show that the curve with equation $y = 18 + 3x - x^2$ and the line with equation $y = 18 - 3x$ intersect on the $x$-axis and on the $y$-axis, and state the points of intersection.

Calculate the area of the finite region bounded by the line and the curve.

**3** The line $x + y = 9$ and the curve with equation $y = x^2 - 2x + 3$ intersect at the points $P$ and $Q$. Find the coordinates of $P$ and $Q$ and hence determine the area of the finite region bounded by the curve and the line.

**4** Two curves have equations $y = x^2 + 8$ and $y = x(10 - x)$. Sketch their graphs and find their points of intersection.

Calculate the area of the finite region bounded by the two curves.

**5** The two curves $y = x^2 - 2x + 3$ and $y = 3 - 4x - x^2$ intersect at $A$ and $B$. Sketch their graphs and find the points $A$ and $B$.

Calculate the area of the finite region bounded by the two curves.

**6** Find the points where the curve $y = x^2 + x - 6$ crosses the $x$-axis. Sketch the curve and determine the area of the finite region bounded by the curve and the $x$-axis.

**7** The two curves $y = x(x - 5)$ and $y = 10x - 2x^2$ intersect at the origin and the point $F$. Sketch the curves and state the coordinates of $F$.

Calculate the area of the finite region bounded by the two curves.

**8** Find the area of the finite region bounded by the parabola with equation $y = x(x - 4)$ and the line $x + y = 0$.

**9** The graph of $y = \sqrt{x}$ (defined for $x > 0$) is sketched together with the line $y = \dfrac{1}{2}x$. Find the coordinates of the point of intersection $A$, other than the origin $O$.

Calculate the area of the finite region bounded by the line and the curve.

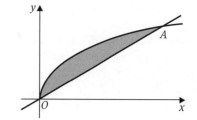

**10** Sketch the graphs of the curves with equations $y = 16 - x^2$ and $y = x^2 - 5x + 13$ on the same axes. Find the coordinates of the two points of intersection.

Calculate the area of the finite region bounded by the two curves

**11** The sketch shows the graph of the curve with equation $y = (x + 2)(x + 1)(x - 1)$.

Find the total area of the two regions, shaded on the diagram, bounded by the curve and the $x$-axis.

Why would you not obtain the correct answer by simply finding

$$\int_{-2}^{1} (x + 2)(x + 1)(x - 1)\, \mathrm{d}x?$$

**12** The diagram shows a sketch of the curve $y = x^2 - 4$ and the line $y = x - 2$. The curve intersects the $x$-axis at the points $A$ and $B$ and the curve and line intersect at a further point $C$.

**(a)** Find the coordinates of the points $A$, $B$ and $C$.

**(b)** Calculate the area of the shaded region bounded by the line and curve.

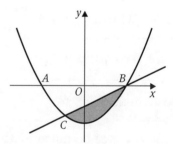

**9**

---

## Key point summary

**1** Integration is the reverse process of differentiation.    *p138*

**2** $\dfrac{\mathrm{d}y}{\mathrm{d}x} = x^n\ (n \neq -1) \Rightarrow y = \dfrac{1}{n+1}x^{n+1} + c$, where $c$ is an    *p139*
arbitrary constant.

**3** An indefinite integral has no limits and is of the form    *p144*
$\displaystyle\int \mathrm{f}(x)\, \mathrm{d}x$. You must remember to include an arbitrary constant in your answer.

**4** A definite integral is of the form $\displaystyle\int_{a}^{b} \mathrm{f}(x)\, \mathrm{d}x$, where    *p147*
$a$ and $b$ are the limits.

**5** After integrating a definite integral, you obtain      *p147*
$[F(x)]_a^b$ and this is evaluated as $F(b) - F(a)$.

**6** The area under a curve $y = f(x)$ from $x = a$ to $x = b$     *p151*
is given by

$$\int_a^b f(x) \, dx$$

**7** When a region lies below the *x*-axis, the value of the     *p151*
definite integral is negative. Separate integrals may be
needed to find the area of a region when part of it lies
below the *x*-axis.

| Test yourself | What to review |
|---|---|
| **1** Obtain the equation of the curve passing through $(-1, 5)$ which has gradient $\dfrac{dy}{dx} = 6x^2 - \dfrac{2}{x^3}$. | *Section 9.1* |
| **2** Find $f(x)$ when $f'(x) = \dfrac{(6x + 5)}{\sqrt{x}}$. | *Section 9.2* |
| **3** Find $\int (x - 3)(3x + 5) \, dx$ | *Section 9.3* |
| **4** Evaluate $\int_0^1 5x^4 - 6x \, dx$. | *Section 9.4* |
| **5** Find the area bounded by the curve with equation $y = \sqrt[3]{x}$, the *x*-axis and the lines $x = 1$ and $x = 8$. | *Section 9.5* |
| **6** Find the area of the finite region bounded by the *x*-axis and the curve with equation $y = (x + 1)(x - 2)$. | *Section 9.6* |

Test yourself   **ANSWERS**

**1** $y = 2x^3 + 1/x^2 + 6$.

**2** $f(x) = 4x^{\frac{3}{2}} + 10x^{\frac{1}{2}} + c$.

**3** $x^3 - 2x^2 - 15x + c$.

**4** $-2$.     **5** $\dfrac{45}{4}$.     **6** $4.5$

# CHAPTER 10

# Further equations and quadratic inequalities

## Learning objectives

After studying this chapter, you should be able to:
- locate roots of equations by a change of sign
- find exact points of intersection of lines and curves when the resulting equation is quadratic
- determine approximate values of points of intersection in more difficult cases
- solve quadratic inequalities.

## 10.1 Exact solutions to equations

You have learned how to solve linear equations of the form $ax + b = 0$, and quadratic equations of the form $ax^2 + bx + c = 0$, where $a$, $b$ and $c$ are constants.

In the sixteenth century in Italy various formulae were developed to solve cubic equations.
Cardano derived a formula to solve equations of the form

$$x^3 + cx = d.$$

His solution was

$$x = \sqrt[3]{u} - \sqrt[3]{v}$$

where $u = \sqrt{\left(\dfrac{d}{2}\right)^2 + \left(\dfrac{c}{3}\right)^3} + \dfrac{d}{2}$ and $v = \sqrt{\left(\dfrac{d}{2}\right)^2 + \left(\dfrac{c}{3}\right)^3} - \dfrac{d}{2}$.

> Look at a History of Maths website and consider the interesting contest between Fiore and Tartaglia.

### Worked example 10.1

Use Cardano's formula to find the exact root of $x^3 - 6x = 6$.

### Solution

$c = -6$, $d = 6$ and so $\left(\dfrac{d}{2}\right)^2 + \left(\dfrac{c}{3}\right)^3 = (3)^2 + (-2)^3 = 9 - 8 = 1$

$x = \sqrt[3]{1 + 3} - \sqrt[3]{1 - 3} = \sqrt[3]{4} - \sqrt[3]{(-2)}$

$\quad = \sqrt[3]{4} + \sqrt[3]{2}$

> You can check this answer because $\sqrt[3]{4} + \sqrt[3]{2} \approx 2.847$ and $2.847^3 - 6 \times 2.847 \approx 6.$

10

Sometimes, the answer produced by this method is rather complicated. For example the solution to $x^3 + 6x = 20$ is

$$\sqrt[3]{\sqrt{108} + 10} - \sqrt[3]{\sqrt{108} - 10}.$$

> Check this on a calculator and you may get a surprise!

Cardano's method and other similar formulae do not always provide all the solutions to a cubic equation and as equations become as complicated as $x^5 - 3x^2 + 2x - 3 = 0$, there is no known analytical solution and so numerical methods have to be used.

## 10.2 Numerical methods

Suppose you draw the graph of $y = f(x)$ and it crosses the $x$-axis between $x = a$ and $x = b$.

The situation may be as in diagram (1) or as in diagram (2).

Diagram (1)

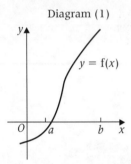

Diagram (2)

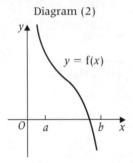

In diagram (1) f($a$) < 0 and f($b$) > 0.

In diagram (2) f($a$) > 0 and f($b$) < 0.

In each case there is a change in sign, either going from positive to negative or from negative to positive.

> Provided the graph is continuous over the interval $a < x < b$, there must be a point in this interval for which $f(x) = 0$.

### *Worked example 10.2*

Show that the root of the equation $x^5 - 3x^2 + 2x - 3 = 0$ lies between 1.44 and 1.45.

> You could check this on your graphics calculator by drawing the graph and using the trace facility to see where the curve crosses the $x$-axis.

### Solution

Let $f(x) = x^5 - 3x^2 + 2x - 3$.

$f(1.44) = 1.44^5 - 3(1.44)^2 + 2 \times 1.44 - 3 = -0.149\ldots$

$f(1.45) = 1.45^5 - 3(1.45)^2 + 2 \times 1.45 - 3 = 0.002234\ldots$

> The change in sign indicates that the root lies between 1.44 and 1.45.

## Worked example 10.3

Find two consecutive negative integers between which the root of the equation $x^3 - 17x + 32 = 0$ lies.

### Solution

Let $f(x) = x^3 - 17x + 32$.

The graph of $y = f(x)$ is continuous for all values of $x$.

$f(-1) = -1 + 17 + 32 = 48$

$f(-5) = -125 + 85 + 32 = -8$

$f(-4) = -64 + 68 + 32 = 36$

There is now a change of sign between these last two values of $x$.

Two consecutive negative integers between which the root lies are

$\qquad$ $-5$ and $-4$.

> Always set up a function first.

> The root must lie between $-1$ and $-5$ and is likely to be nearer $-5$.

## Worked example 10.4

Given that $f(x) = \dfrac{1}{x}$. Find $f(2)$ and $f(-1)$.

Can you deduce that a root of $\dfrac{1}{x} = 0$ lies between $-1$ and $2$?

### Solution

$f(2) = \dfrac{1}{2}$;  $f(-1) = -1$.

Although there is a change in sign, you need to consider the graph of $y = f(x)$.

The graph is **not** continuous between $-1$ and $2$. It has a discontinuity when $x = 0$. You can **not** deduce that the equation has a root between $-1$ and $2$.

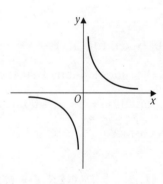

**10**

## EXERCISE 10A

1 Verify that the equation $x^5 + 7x - 10 = 0$ has a root between 1.1 and 1.2.

2 Show that the equation $x^3 - 3x + 5 = 0$ has a root between $-2.3$ and $-2.1$.

3 Prove that the equation $x^5 + 2x - 7 = 0$ has a root between 1.3 and 1.4.

4 Verify that the equation $x^3 + 12x - 39 = 0$ has a root between 2.2 and 2.3.

**5** Find two consecutive integers between which the root of the equation $x^7 + 2x^2 + 3 = 0$ lies.

**6** Prove that one root of the equation $x^4 - 23x + 19 = 0$ lies between 0 and 1 and find two consecutive integers between which the other root lies.

**7** The equation $x^3 + 7x - 19 = 0$ has a root close to 1.8. Determine whether the root lies between 1.75 and 1.80 or between 1.80 and 1.85.

**8** Consider the equation $x^5 - 9x - 7 = 0$.

   **(a)** Show that the equation has a root between $-1.5$ and $-1.4$.

   **(b)** Given that $g(x) = x^5 - 9x - 7$ show that $g(-1)$ and $g(2)$ have the same sign.
   
   **(i)** Does that mean there are no roots of the equation between $-1$ and 2?

   **(ii)** Find $g(-\frac{1}{2})$ and $g(1\frac{1}{2})$. What can you deduce about roots of the equation?

**9** Use Cardano's formula given in section 10.1 to find the exact solutions to the equations

   **(a)** $x^3 + 12x = 12$,

   **(b)** $x^3 + 6x = 2$,

   **(c)** $x^3 - 6x = 40$.

**10** Given that $f(x) = \dfrac{1}{2x - 1}$, find $f(0)$ and $f(1)$.

A student claims that the change in sign proves that the equation $\dfrac{1}{2x - 1} = 0$ has a root between 0 and 1. Is she correct?

# 10.3 Points of intersection of graphs

You have already considered the intersection of two straight lines, a line and a parabola or two parabolas. The idea can be extended to find the intersection points of a line and other curves.

If, after eliminating one of the variables, the resulting equation is a quadratic, this can be factorised or it can be solved using the quadratic equation formula.

> The point of intersection of two curves or a curve and a line is found by eliminating one variable, such as $y$, and solving for the other variable.

## Worked example 10.5

Determine the points of intersection of the line $3x - 2y = 4$ and the curve with equation $x^2 + 2y^2 = 6$.

## Solution

Rearranging the equation of the line gives $y = \dfrac{3x - 4}{2}$.

> You may have preferred to eliminate $x$ instead.

Substituting into $x^2 + 2y^2 = 6$ gives

$$x^2 + 2\left(\frac{3x - 4}{2}\right)^2 = 6$$

$$\Rightarrow x^2 + 2\left(\frac{9x^2 - 24x + 16}{4}\right) = 6$$

Multiplying throughout by 2 to clear fractions

$$\Rightarrow 2x^2 + 9x^2 - 24x + 16 = 12$$

$$\Rightarrow 11x^2 - 24x + 4 = 0$$

$$\Rightarrow (11x - 2)(x - 2) = 0$$

$$\Rightarrow x = 2 \text{ or } x = \tfrac{2}{11}$$

> If you could not easily see the factors here, you could have solved the equation using the quadratic equation formula.

Since $y = \dfrac{3x - 4}{2}$, when $x = 2$, $y = 1$

and when $x = \tfrac{2}{11}$, $y = -1\tfrac{8}{11}$.

Coordinates of points of intersection are $(2, 1)$ and $(\tfrac{2}{11}, -1\tfrac{8}{11})$.

## Worked example 10.6

Find the $x$-coordinates of the points of intersection of the line $y = 3x + 5$ and the curve with equation

$$20x^2 - 2y^2 + 53x + y + 27 = 0.$$

**10**

## Solution

Substitute $y = 3x + 5$ into $20x^2 - 2y^2 + 53x + y + 27 = 0$

$$\Rightarrow 20x^2 - 2(3x + 5)^2 + 53x + (3x + 5) + 27 = 0$$

$$\Rightarrow 20x^2 - 2(9x^2 + 30x + 25) + 56x + 5 + 27 = 0$$

$$\Rightarrow 20x^2 - 18x^2 - 60x - 50 + 56x + 32 = 0$$

$$\Rightarrow 2x^2 - 4x - 18 = 0$$

$$\Rightarrow x^2 - 2x - 9 = 0$$

Using the quadratic equation formula

$$x = \frac{-b \pm \sqrt{b^2 - 4ac}}{2a} \quad \text{where } a = 1, b = -2, c = -9$$

$$x = \frac{2 \pm \sqrt{(-2)^2 - 4(-9)}}{2} = \frac{2 \pm \sqrt{40}}{2}$$

$$\Rightarrow x = \frac{2 \pm 2\sqrt{10}}{2} = 1 \pm \sqrt{10}$$

The $x$-coordinates of the points of intersection are

$$1 + \sqrt{10} \text{ and } 1 - \sqrt{10}.$$

### EXERCISE 10B

1 Find the points of intersection of the line $y = 3x + 4$ and the curve with equation $xy = 20$.

2 Determine the points of intersection of the line $x + y = 3$ and the curve with equation $x^2 + y^2 = 5$.

3 Calculate the points of intersection of the line $y = 2x - 7$ and the curve with equation $xy + x^2 = 6$.

4 Find the points of intersection of the line $y = x - 5$ and the curve with equation $6y^2 = x$.

5 Show that the straight line $x + y = 8$ does not intersect the curve with equation $x^2 + y^2 = 4$.

> Recall that when the discriminant is negative, the quadratic equation has no real roots.

6 Determine whether the curve with equation $x^2 - y^2 = 9$ intersects the following lines. If they do intersect, find the points of intersection.

(a) $y = 2x$,     (b) $y = 2x - 6$,     (c) $y = 2x + 1$.

7 Determine the values of $x$ where the curve with equation $x^2 - y^2 - 7xy + 8x - 5 = 0$ crosses the $x$-axis, leaving your answers in surd form.

8 Find the $y$-coordinates of the points of intersection of the line $x + 3y = 7$ and the curve $x^2 + 6y - 3y^2 = 7$, leaving your answers in surd form.

# 10.4 Approximate values for points of intersection

In the last section, you found that the points of intersection were often determined by solving a quadratic equation. This is not always possible and you may have to use the numerical methods introduced in Section 10.2.

> If the point of intersection cannot be found exactly then form an equation of the form f($x$) = 0 and look for a change of sign to locate the root.

## Worked example 10.7

The $x$-coordinate of the point of intersection of the line $y = 3x - 5$ and the curve $y = x^3 - 5x + 7$ is $\alpha$. Show that $-3.4 < \alpha < -3.3$.

## Solution

Point of intersection is given by equating the two expressions for $y$.

$\Rightarrow 3x - 5 = x^3 - 5x + 7$

$\Rightarrow x^3 - 8x + 12 = 0$ where $x = \alpha$ is the root of the equation.

Let f($x$) = $x^3 - 8x + 12$

$\quad \Rightarrow$ f($-3.4$) = $(-3.4)^3 - 8 \times 3.4 + 12 = -0.104$

$\quad \Rightarrow$ f($-3.3$) = $(-3.3)^3 - 8 \times 3.3 + 12 = 2.463$

Change in sign.

The graph of $y = x^3 - 8x + 12$ is continuous for all values of $x$, so the change in sign means that $-3.4 < \alpha < -3.3$.

## Worked example 10.8

The two curves with equations $y = 2^x$ and $y = x^3 - 5$ intersect at the point ($\alpha$, $\beta$). Determine two consecutive integers between which $\alpha$ lies.

## Solution

You could plot the graphs on your graphics calculator and verify that curves have a single point of intersection where the $x$-coordinate is less than 5.

It is important to follow this procedure, though.

For the point of intersection $2^x = x^3 - 5$

$$\Rightarrow 2^x - x^3 + 5 = 0$$

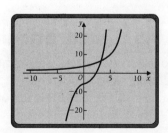

You must rearrange the equation so it is of the form f($x$) = 0.

**10**

Create a new function $f(x) = 2^x - x^3 + 5$

$\quad f(1) = 2^1 - 1^3 + 5 = 6;$

$\quad f(2) = 2^2 - 2^3 + 5 = 1;$

$\quad f(3) = 2^3 - 3^3 + 5 = -14.$

Since $y = f(x)$ is continuous for all values of $x$ and there is a change of sign between $x = 2$ and $x = 3$, $\alpha$ must lie between the consecutive integers 2 and 3.

### EXERCISE 10C

**1** Prove that the curve with equation $y = x^3$ and the curve with equation $y = x^2 + 1$ intersect at a point whose $x$-coordinate lies between 1.4 and 1.5.

**2** Show that the line with equation $y = 2x - 7$ and the curve with equation $y = x^5 + 3$ intersect at a point whose $x$-coordinate lies between $-1.8$ and $-1.6$.

**3** Verify that the line with equation $x + 3y = 1$ and the curve with equation $y = x^3 - x + 2$ intersect at a point whose $x$-coordinate lies between $-1.4$ and $-1.3$.

**4** Prove that the curve with equation $y = x^5$ and the curve with equation $y = x^2 - 5$ intersect at a point whose $x$-coordinate lies between $-1.3$ and $-1.2$.

**5** The two curves with equations $y = x^5 - x^3 + 1$ and $y = x^2 + 3$ intersect at the point $(p, q)$. Show that $1.50 < p < 1.51$.

**6** The two curves with equations $y = 3^x$ and $y = x^7$ intersect at the point $(r, s)$. Prove that $1.20 < r < 1.21$.

**7** The two curves with equations $y = 19 - 2^x$ and $y = 5^x$ intersect at the point $(t, u)$. Show that $1.71 < t < 1.72$.

**8** The curves $y = x^4 - 3$ and $y = 5x - x^6$ intersect at the points $(a, b)$ and $(c, d)$, where $a \approx -0.57$ and $c \approx 1.36$.

   **(a)** Determine whether $-0.58 < a < -0.57$
       or $-0.57 < a < -0.56$.

   **(b)** Determine whether $1.35 < c < 1.36$ or $1.36 < c < 1.37$.

## 10.5 Quadratic inequalities

You learned how to solve linear inequalities in Chapter 3. In this section, you will extend the idea to quadratic inequalities. These can be solved algebraically or by consideration of a graph.

> Quadratic inequalities can be solved by drawing a graph and considering when the graph is above or below the $x$-axis.

## Worked example 10.9

Solve the inequality $(2x - 3)(1 - 5x) > 0$

## Solution

Let $f(x) = (2x - 3)(1 - 5x)$ and consider the graph of $y = f(x)$.

The graph is a parabola and you need to know when the graph is above the $x$-axis, or when $y > 0$.

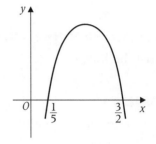

The graph of $y = (2x - 3)(1 - 5x)$ cuts the $x$-axis when $2x - 3 = 0$ and when $1 - 5x = 0$, namely at $(\frac{3}{2}, 0)$ and at $(\frac{1}{5}, 0)$.

Also when $x = 0$, $y = -3$ so the parabola passes through $(0, -3)$. You can sketch its graph.

From the graph, you can see when $y > 0$. This is when $x$ lies between $\frac{1}{5}$ and $\frac{3}{2}$. The original inequality is strict. It does not include an equals sign.

Solution is $\frac{1}{5} < x < \frac{3}{2}$.

> You can check your answer by choosing values in this interval. For instance, $x = 1 \Rightarrow (2x - 3)(1 - 5x) = (-1) \times (-4) = 4 > 0.$ ✓

## Worked example 10.10

Solve the inequality $3x^2 + 5x - 2 \geqslant 0$.

> You can simplify matters so that you do not actually need to draw a graph.
>
> Instead, you consider the sign of the expression over the different intervals.

## Solution

Factorising the quadratic gives $(3x - 1)(x + 2) \geqslant 0$.

Let $f(x) = (3x - 1)(x + 2)$.

$f(x) = 0$ when $x = \frac{1}{3}$ or when $x = -2$

> These are called **critical values**.

Consider a number line with these critical values marked on.

There are now three separate zones to consider.

Choose a value in each of these zones and work out $f(x)$.

For $x < -2$, choose $x = -3$, say. $f(-3) = (-10)(-1) = 10 > 0$.

For $x$ between $-2$ and $\frac{1}{3}$, choose $x = 0$ so $f(0) = -2 < 0$.

For $x > \frac{1}{3}$, choose $x = 1$, say. $f(1) = 2 \times 3 = 6 > 0$.

> These are the only values of $x$ when the expression is zero.
>
> Therefore the expression must always be positive or always negative throughout the separate intervals shown.

You can now draw a diagram indicating when $f(x)$ is positive or negative.

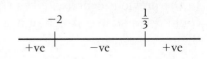

**10**

The question asks when the expression is greater than or equal to zero.

There are two separate intervals forming the solution.

$$x \leqslant -2 \ \text{ or } \ x \geqslant \tfrac{1}{3}$$

> When you get your final answer you can always check you have put the signs the right way round.
>
> Solution predicts $x = 2$ lies in the solution interval.
> $$3 \times 2^2 + 5 \times 2 - 2 = 20$$
> $$(>0 \text{ so } \checkmark)$$
> Also $x = -4$ should satisfy the inequality
> $$3 \times (-4)^2 + 5 \times (-4) - 2 = 26$$
> $$(>0 \text{ so } \checkmark)$$

## Worked example 10.11

Solve the inequality $2x^2 < 15 - x$.

## Solution

Rearrange the inequality $2x^2 + x - 15 < 0$

Factorising $(x + 3)(2x - 5) < 0$

Critical values are $x = -3$ and $x = 2\tfrac{1}{2}$

Indicating on a diagram the sign of $(x + 3)(2x - 5)$

Solution to $2x^2 + x - 15 < 0$ is $-3 < x < 2\tfrac{1}{2}$

> Critical values are given by $x + 3 = 0$ and $2x - 5 = 0$.

In the following exercise, the quadratics will all factorise.

### EXERCISE 10D

Solve each of the following inequalities.

**1** $(x - 3)(2x + 7) < 0$,   **2** $(1 - x)(2x - 3) \leqslant 0$.

**3** $x^2 - x - 6 > 0$,   **4** $x^2 - 5x - 6 < 0$,

**5** $x^2 + 3x - 10 \geqslant 0$,   **6** $x^2 + 7x + 12 < 0$,

**7** $2x^2 - x - 1 > 0$,   **8** $x^2 - 16 > 0$,

**9** $3x^2 - 4x - 4 \leqslant 0$,   **10** $4x^2 - 5x + 1 > 0$,

**11** $2x^2 > 3x + 9$,   **12** $x^2 \leqslant 25$.

**13** $2x + 3 \leqslant x^2$,   **14** $5x^2 + 3 > 8x$,

**15** $3x + 7 < 4x^2$,   **16** $11x - 3 > 8x^2$,

**17** $5x + 2x^2 > 3$,   **18** $12x^2 - 13x < 22$,

**19** $20x^2 + 3 > 16x$,   **20** $5 + 9x^2 \geqslant 18x$.

> You may find a sketch helpful in the first instance, but examiners will regard a diagram showing the sign of the expression as sufficient working, provided you state the critical values.

## 10.6 Quadratics with irrational roots

In the previous exercise, all the quadratics factorised, and you could use a simple sketch or a sign diagram to help you solve them.

> The values of $x$ for which the quadratic is equal to zero are the critical values. You can easily solve a quadratic inequality by means of a sign diagram, indicating when the expression is positive or negative.

If the quadratic has two irrational roots then you can proceed in a similar way.

Suppose the two critical values are $p$ and $q$ where $p < q$.

Mark the critical values on a diagram.

Consider the value of the expression for each of the three zones and solve the inequality.

## Worked example 10.12

Solve the inequality $2x^2 < 3x + 7$

## Solution

Rearrange to get $2x^2 - 3x - 7 < 0$

Solving the quadratic equation $2x^2 - 3x - 7 = 0$,

$$\Rightarrow x = \frac{-b \pm \sqrt{b^2 - 4ac}}{2a} \text{ where } a = 2, b = -3, c = -7$$

$$\Rightarrow x = \frac{3 \pm \sqrt{9 + 56}}{4}$$

$$\Rightarrow x = \frac{3 + \sqrt{65}}{4} \approx 2.77 \text{ or } x = \frac{3 - \sqrt{65}}{4} \approx -1.27$$

The critical values are $\frac{1}{4}(3 + \sqrt{65})$ and $\frac{1}{4}(3 - \sqrt{65})$ but the decimal approximations are easier to deal with on a sign diagram.

Let    $f(x) = 2x^2 - 3x - 7$

$f(-3) = 18 + 9 - 7 = 20 > 0$

$f(0) = 0 + 0 - 7 = -7 < 0$

$f(10) = 200 - 30 - 7 = 163 > 0$

The inequality $2x^2 - 3x - 7 < 0$ has solution[1]

$\frac{1}{4}(3 - \sqrt{65}) < x < \frac{1}{4}(3 + \sqrt{65})$.

**10**

-1.27          2.77
──────┼──────────┼──────
+ve        -ve        +ve

> You have probably realised that after finding a **single** value of the function, you can complete the sign diagram. A second value is useful as a check.

# 10.7 Completing the square

All quadratic inequalities can be solved by completing the square. You need to make use of one of the following standard results.

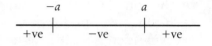

Consider the inequality $y^2 > a^2$.

$$y^2 - a^2 > 0 \;\Rightarrow\; (y - a)(y + a) > 0$$

$$\boxed{y^2 > a^2 \;\Rightarrow\; y > a \text{ or } y < -a}$$

Similarly you can use the sign diagram to solve the inequality $y^2 < a^2$.

$$\boxed{y^2 < a^2 \;\Rightarrow\; -a < y < a}$$

## Worked example 10.13 ____

By completing the square, solve the inequalities

**(a)** $x^2 + 4x - 1 \geqslant 0$,  **(b)** $2x^2 - 12x - 5 < 0$.

## Solution

**(a)** $x^2 + 4x - 1 = (x + 2)^2 - 4 - 1$
$\Rightarrow x^2 + 4x - 1 \geqslant 0 \;\Rightarrow\; (x + 2)^2 \geqslant 5$

Using the result in the first box above

$$x + 2 \geqslant \sqrt{5} \text{ or } x + 2 \leqslant -\sqrt{5}$$
$$x \geqslant \sqrt{5} - 2 \text{ or } x \leqslant -\sqrt{5} - 2$$

> Subtracting 2 from both sides of each linear inequality.

**(b)** $2x^2 - 12x - 5 = 2(x^2 - 6x) - 5 = 2[(x - 3)^2 - 9] - 5$
$$= 2(x - 3)^2 - 23$$
$$2x^2 - 12x - 5 < 0 \;\Rightarrow\; 2(x - 3)^2 - 23 < 0$$

$$\Rightarrow (x - 3)^2 < \frac{23}{2} \;\Rightarrow\; (x - 3)^2 < \left(\sqrt{\frac{23}{2}}\right)^2$$

Using the result in the second box above,

$$\Rightarrow -\sqrt{\frac{23}{2}} < x - 3 < \sqrt{\frac{23}{2}}$$

$$\Rightarrow 3 - \sqrt{\frac{23}{2}} < x < 3 + \sqrt{\frac{23}{2}}$$

> Adding 3 to both sides of each linear inequality.

## EXERCISE 10E

Solve each of the following inequalities.

**1** $x^2 - 6x - 4 < 0$.  **2** $x^2 + 8x + 3 \leqslant 0$.

**3** $x^2 - 4x - 1 > 0$.  **4** $x^2 - 2x - 5 < 0$.

**5** $x^2 - 10x + 3 \geqslant 0$.  **6** $x^2 + 3x + 1 < 0$.

**7** $2x^2 - 4x - 1 > 0$.  **8** $3x^2 - 6x - 7 > 0$.

**9** $3x^2 - 12x - 5 \leqslant 0$.  **10** $4x^2 - 12x + 3 > 0$.

# 10.8 Discriminant revisited

At times, it is necessary to solve quadratic inequalities when you are considering the conditions for a quadratic equation to have real roots, for example.

Recall from Chapter 7 that the quadratic $ax^2 + bx + c = 0$ has

* two distinct real roots when $b^2 - 4ac > 0$;
* two equal roots when $b^2 - 4ac = 0$.

Therefore the condition for real roots is $b^2 - 4ac \geqslant 0$.

## Worked example 10.14

Find the possible values of $k$ for the quadratic equation

$$(2k - 1)x^2 + 8kx + 2(5k + 3) = 0$$

to have real roots.

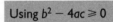

Using $b^2 - 4ac \geqslant 0$

Divide both sides by $-8$ and reverse the inequality sign.

**10**

## Solution

$(8k)^2 - 4(2k - 1) \times 2(5k + 3) \geqslant 0$

$\Rightarrow 64k^2 - 8(10k^2 + k - 3) \geqslant 0$

$\Rightarrow -8k^2 + (10k^2 + k - 3) \leqslant 0$

$\Rightarrow 2k^2 + k - 3 \leqslant 0$

$\Rightarrow (2k + 3)(k - 1) \leqslant 0$

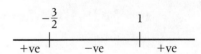

Critical points are $k = -\frac{3}{2}$ and $k = 1$. Sign diagram is shown in the margin.

Solution is $-1\frac{1}{2} \leqslant k \leqslant 1$.

## Worked example 10.15

Find the condition on $k$ for the quadratic equation

$$3kx^2 - (k + 3)x + (k - 2) = 0$$

to have **no** real roots.

## Solution

$\Rightarrow (k + 3)^2 - 4 \times 3k \times (k - 2) < 0$

$\Rightarrow (k + 3)^2 < 12k(k - 2)$

$\Rightarrow k^2 + 6k + 9 < 12k^2 - 24k$

$\Rightarrow 0 < 11k^2 - 30k - 9$

$\Rightarrow 0 < (11k + 3)(k - 3)$

Critical points are $k = 3$ and $k = -\frac{3}{11}$ with sign diagram for the expression $(11k + 3)(k - 3)$ drawn at the side.

Solution is $k > 3$, $k < -\frac{3}{11}$.

> Using $b^2 - 4ac < 0$

> A different approach from multiplying by a negative number is to take terms to the opposite side of the inequality.

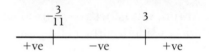

## EXERCISE 10F

**1** Find the values of $k$ for which the quadratic equation

$$(k - 3)x^2 + (k + 2)x + (2k + 1) = 0$$

has real roots.

**2** Determine the condition on $k$ for the quadratic equation

$$(k + 1)x^2 + (3k + 2)x - (k + 6) = 0$$

to have real roots.

**3** Find the possible values of $k$ for the quadratic equation

$$2kx^2 - (k + 2)x + (3 - k) = 0$$

to have two distinct real roots.

**4** Find the values of $k$ for which the quadratic equation

$$(k + 3)x^2 - 4kx + (5 - 4k) = 0$$

has no real roots.

**5** Determine the condition on $k$ for the quadratic equation

$$(2k - 5)x^2 - (k - 1)x + (k - 2) = 0$$

to have two distinct real roots.

**6** Determine the condition on $k$ for the quadratic equation

$$(3k + 4)x^2 - (3 + k)x + (2k + 3) = 0$$

to have real roots.

## Key point summary

**1** The equation $f(x) = 0$ has a root in the interval     *p156*
$a < x < b$ when $f(a)$ and $f(b)$ have opposite signs,
provided that the graph of $y = f(x)$ is continuous over
the interval $a < x < b$.

**2** The point of intersection of two curves or a curve     *p158*
and a line is found by eliminating one variable, such
as $y$, and solving for the other variable.

**3** If the point of intersection cannot be found exactly     *p161*
then form an equation of the form $f(x) = 0$ and look
for a change of sign to locate the root.

**4** Quadratic inequalities can be solved by drawing a     *p162*
graph and considering when the graph is above or
below the $x$-axis.

**5** The values of $x$ for which the quadratic is equal to     *p165*
zero are the critical values. You can easily solve a
quadratic inequality by means of a sign diagram,
indicating when the expression is positive or negative.

| Test yourself | What to review |
|---|---|
| **1** Determine whether the equation $x^3 - 7x + 9 = 0$ has a root between (a) $-3.15$ and $-3.14$, or (b) $-3.14$ and $-3.13$. | *Section 10.2* |
| **2** Find the points of intersection of the line $y = 3x - 2$ and the curve with equation $xy = 8$. | *Section 10.3* |
| **3** Prove that the line with equation $y = 3 - x$ and the curve with equation $y = 3x^5 - 2x^2 + 2$ intersect at a point whose $x$-coordinate lies between 0.8 and 0.9. | *Section 10.4* |
| **4** Solve the inequality $3x^2 < 4x + 4$ | *Section 10.5* |
| **5** Solve the inequality $x^2 - 12x > 4$ by completing the square. | *Section 10.7* |
| **6** Find the values of $k$ for which the quadratic equation $2x^2 - (k + 1)x + (3k - 7) = 0$ has real roots. | *Section 10.8* |

**10**

## Test yourself ANSWERS

**6**   $k \geqslant 19,\ k \leqslant 3$.
**5**   $x > 6 + 2\sqrt{10},\ x < 6 - 2\sqrt{10}$.
**4**   $-\frac{2}{3} < x < 2$.
**2**   $(2, 4),\ (-\frac{4}{3}, -6)$.
**1**   (a).

# CHAPTER 11

# Trigonometry

---

## Learning objectives

After studying this chapter you should:
- be familiar with the sine, cosine and tangent functions
- recognise the graphs of the sine cosine and tangent functions, their symmetries and their periodicity
- know and be able to use $\tan \theta = \dfrac{\sin \theta}{\cos \theta}$ and $\sin^2 \theta + \cos^2 \theta = 1$ to simplify trigonometrical equations
- be able to solve simple trigonometrical equations.

---

## 11.1 Introduction

Trigonometry originally meant the study of triangles, or three points. You have no doubt used trigonometry before, considering mainly right-angled triangles. It does, however, have a wide variety of applications including surveying, navigation and engineering. The sine, cosine and related functions can model the behaviour of natural phenomena such as sound, music and many aspects of our physical environment including planetary motion.

> It is usual to use variables such as the Greek letter $\theta$ pronounced 'theta' or $x$ for an angle, although any variable can be used.

## 11.2 The sine function – an informal approach

You will recall that $\sin \theta = \dfrac{\text{side opposite } \theta}{\text{hypotenuse}} = \dfrac{o}{h}$ in a right-angled triangle where the angle $\theta$ is less than 90°.

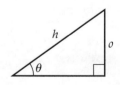

From a calculator in degree mode, $\sin 140° = 0.642\ldots$, $\sin(-55)° = -0.819\ldots$, $\sin 370° = 0.173\ldots$, etc.
It is possible to calculate the sine of any angle and so a definition of $\sin \theta$ is required that is valid for any angle.

> The angle can be greater than 360° or less than zero. Try it and see – any angle!

If you have a graphics calculator and you plot $y = \sin x$ in degree mode between $-360$ and $360$ degrees you will get:

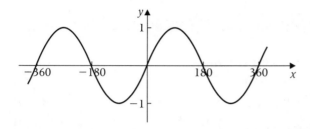

This is not surprising because the word **sine** comes from the Latin word 'sinus' meaning a curve or bay.

Next a diversion to the funfair, where you are going to take a ride on a special type of Ferris Wheel. You have to enter from a platform that is level with the horizontal diameter of the wheel. You travel in an anticlockwise direction and consider your distance from the platform as the angle you turn through varies.

Imagine that you are very small so that you are always on the circumference of the wheel.

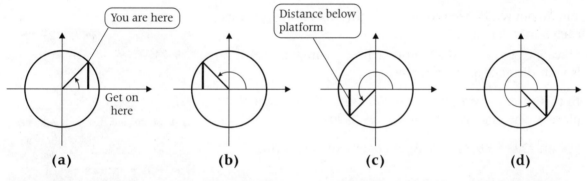

**(a)**

Travel in an anticlockwise direction. Here you have turned through about 50°

**(b)**

Here you have travelled through about 140° and you are still above the platform.

**(c)**

Here the angle is about 240° and you are below the platform.

**(d)**

About 330° travelled. No need to get off after one revolution (360°). You can go round as often as you like.

Various methods can be used to find your position, such as estimation or scale drawings. You could say that when you are at the maximum distance above the platform, then this is one unit.

This distance is equal to the radius of the wheel.

**11**

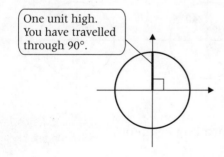

One unit high. You have travelled through 90°.

## Worked example 11.1

How far above or below the platform are you in each of the diagrams above?

### Solution

**The sine of the angle that you have travelled through gives your height above or below the platform.**

Let $y$ be the vertical distance in each particular case.

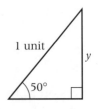

1 unit

$y$

50°

**(a)** You can probably see that $y$ can be found using

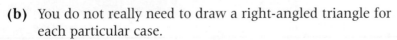

$$\sin \theta = \frac{\text{side opposite } \theta}{\text{hypotenuse}}$$

Since the hypotenuse is one unit long, then
$y = \sin 50° = 0.766$ (three decimal places). This is your distance above the platform.

> 0.766 of a unit

**(b)** You do not really need to draw a right-angled triangle for each particular case.

Since $y = \sin 140° = 0.623$ units (three decimal places), this is your distance above the platform.

**(c)** In this case, $y = \sin 240° = -0.866$ units (three decimal places). The negative sign indicates 'below'.

**(d)** $y = \sin 330° = -0.5$ units. Again below the platform.

> If you write sin 50°, sin 140°, sin 240° then these are exact values, just as $\sqrt{2}$ is exact.
>
> Generally, these values are rounded when you work them out on a calculator. A few angles do have a sine that has an exact decimal form. For example, sin 330° = −0.5 exactly.

## 11.3 The cosine function – an informal approach

You are still at the funfair, riding on the Ferris Wheel. The wheel has a radius of 1 unit.
You travel in an anticlockwise direction and consider your distance from the **vertical diameter**.
Call this distance $x$.
To the right of the vertical diameter is positive, to the left is negative.

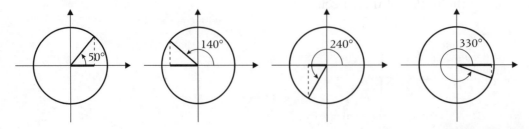

The **cosine function** will give this distance, depending again on the angle that you have turned through.

> The sine function and the cosine function are closely related.

## *Worked example 11.2*

Work out your distance from the vertical diameter for each of the above (as a fraction of 1 unit):

### *Solution*

**(a)** $\cos 50° = 0.643$ units (three decimal places)

> Positive, so to the right.

**(b)** $\cos 140° = -0.766$ units (three decimal places)

**(c)** $\cos 240° = -0.5$

> Negative, so to the left.

**(d)** $\cos 330° = 0.866$ (three decimal places)

# 11.4 Definition of the sine and cosine function

The sine and cosine functions are called **circular functions** for the following reason.

Take a circle with radius one unit, centred at the origin with the $x$ and $y$ axis positioned in the usual way. This is called a **unit circle**.

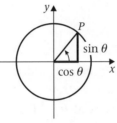

**Positive** angles are measured in an **anticlockwise** direction.

**Negative** angles are measured in a **clockwise** direction.

## Sine

The **sine** of an angle is the **vertical** distance from the $x$-axis of a point $P$ as it travels around a unit circle.

> **It can be defined as the $y$ coordinate of $P$.**

For example, $\sin 240° = -0.866$ (three decimal places)

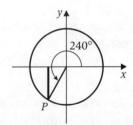

> Locate a journey of 240°. Does this look right?

## Cosine

The **cosine** of an angle is the **horizontal** distance from the $y$-axis of a point $P$ as it travels around a unit circle.

> **It can be defined as the $x$ coordinate of $P$.**

For example, $\cos 240° = -0.5$

> **Point $P$ has coordinates $(\cos \theta , \sin \theta)$**

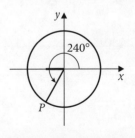

> The point $P$ is uniquely defined by the coordinates $(\cos \theta, \sin \theta)$

# 11.5 The graph of the sine function

For this section, you should make good use of your graphics calculator or graph plotting software to plot the graphs.

### The graph of $y = \sin \theta$

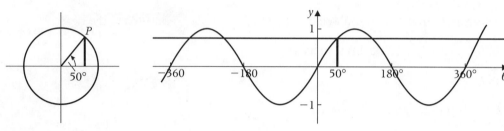

From the graph

$$\sin 50° = \sin 130° = \sin 410° = \sin -230°, \text{ etc.}$$

## Key features of the graph of $y = \sin \theta$

**(a)** The graph is **periodic**, The graph of $y = \sin \theta$ has a **period** of 360°. It repeats itself in every 360° interval.

**(b)** The maximum value of $\sin \theta$ is 1.
The minimum value of $\sin \theta$ is $-1$.

**(c)** The sine function is **many–one**.

**(d)** The graph has rotational symmetry, of order 2 about the origin. Hence, $\sin \theta$ is an **odd** function.

**(e)** Vertical lines of symmetry occur at $\theta = 90°$, $\theta = 270°$, $\theta = -90°...$, etc.

> Just as you repeat your position on the Ferris Wheel every 360° no matter what your starting position.

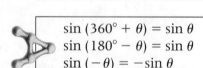
> To solve $\sin x = a$, where $-1 \leqslant a \leqslant 1$, for a given interval, use $\sin^{-1} a$ to find one other value of $x$. Use the graph of $y = \sin x$ to find other solutions within the interval.

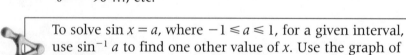
> $\sin (360° + \theta) = \sin \theta$
> $\sin (180° - \theta) = \sin \theta$
> $\sin (-\theta) = -\sin \theta$

# 11.6 The graph of the cosine function

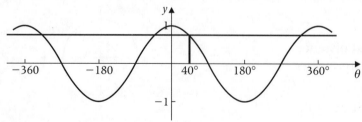

From the graph of $y = \cos \theta$

$$\cos 40° = \cos (-40°) = \cos 320° ..., \text{ etc.}$$

## Key features of the graph of y = cos θ

**(a)** The graph is periodic, with period 360°.

**(b)** The maximum value of cos θ is 1.
The minimum value of cos θ is −1.

**(c)** The cosine function is **many–one**.

**(d)** The graph of $y = \cos \theta$ has reflective symmetry in the $y$-axis. Hence, cos θ is an **even** function.

**(e)** Vertical lines of symmetry occur at $\theta = 0°$, $\theta = 180°$, $\theta = -360°$, …, etc.

> To solve cos $x = b$, where $-1 \leqslant b \leqslant 1$, for a given interval, use $\cos^{-1} b$ to find one value of $x$. Use the graph of $y = \cos x$ to find other solutions within the interval.

> $\cos (360° + \theta) = \cos \theta$
> $\cos (360° − \theta) = \cos \theta$
> $\cos (−\theta) = \cos \theta$

## EXERCISE 11A

**1** Make a copy of the unit circle and for each angle state:

> Only use your calculator to **check** your answers.

    **(i)** whether the sine is positive or negative,
    **(ii)** whether the cosine is positive or negative:

    **(a)** 70°,     **(b)** 130°,     **(c)** 300°,
    **(d)** 200°,     **(e)** −60°,     **(f)** −100°.

**2** Make a copy of the sketch of the unit circle and the graph of $y = \sin \theta$.

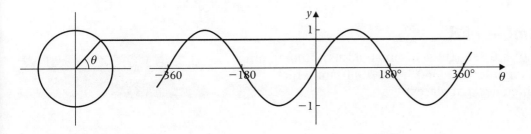

**(a)** On your sketch, mark the point $(\theta, \sin \theta)$ for each of the values of $\theta$ given:

    **(i)** $\theta = 20°$,     **(ii)** $\theta = 160°$,     **(iii)** $\theta = 50°$,
    **(iv)** $\theta = -200°$,     **(v)** $\theta = 230°$,     **(vi)** $\theta = 140°$,
    **(vii)** $\theta = -340°$,     **(viii)** $\theta = 130°$,     **(ix)** $\theta = -20°$,
    **(x)** $\theta = -230°$,     **(xi)** $\theta = 200°$,     **(xii)** $\theta = -130°$.

**(b)** Identify values of $\theta$ above for which:

    **(i)** $\sin \theta = \sin 20°$     **(ii)** $\sin \theta = \sin 50°$

**11**

**3** Make a copy of the sketch of the graph of $y = \cos \theta$.

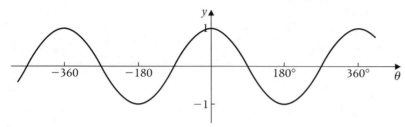

**(a)** On your sketch, mark the point $(\theta, \cos \theta)$ for each of the values of $\theta$ given

    **(i)**  $\theta = 50°$,         **(ii)**  $\theta = 40°$,        **(iii)**  $\theta = -50°$,

    **(iv)**  $\theta = 310°$,      **(v)**  $\theta = 220°$,      **(vi)**  $\theta = 140°$,

    **(vii)** $\theta = 320°$,     **(viii)** $\theta = -40°$,     **(ix)**  $\theta = 230°$,

    **(x)**  $\theta = -410°$,    **(xi)**  $\theta = 400°$,     **(xii)** $\theta = -220°$.

**(b)** Identify values of $\theta$ above for which

    **(i)**   $\cos \theta = \cos 50°$   **(ii)**   $\cos \theta = \cos 140°$

# 11.7 Finding angles with the same sine or cosine

You can work out on your calculator that $\sin 30° = 0.5$. There are, however, other angles that have the same sine as $30°$, as you have already seen. For example, $\sin 150° = 0.5$, $\sin 390° = 0.5$, etc.

Sometimes it is necessary to find all of the angles within a given interval that have the same sine or cosine.

> If no interval were specified, there would be an infinite number of solutions.

> To solve equations with multiple angles, be aware that if you are looking for values of $\theta$ within a particular interval, then you will need to consider values of $5\theta$ in an interval five times as large.

## Worked example 11.3

Given that $\sin 60° = 0.866$ (three decimal places), find all other angles $\theta$ within the interval $-360° \leqslant \theta \leqslant 360°$ for which $\sin \theta = 0.866$ (three decimal places)

> $\theta$ can take any value between $-360°$ to $360°$ inclusive

## Solution

The best method is probably to sketch a graph of $y = \sin \theta$ for the interval given.

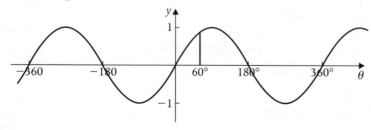

> It can become confusing if you use the idea of a circle over a large interval.

It is now quite an easy task to use the symmetry and periodicity properties of the function to locate the other angles.

The angle 60° is located on the $\theta$-axis 60° to the right of the origin.

You could also say that 60° is 30° to the left of 90° etc.

Another angle with the same sine as 60° within the given interval is $(180 - 60)°$, 60° to the left of 180°.

From the graph, you can see that there are two more solutions between $-360° \leqslant \theta \leqslant -180°$, namely $(-360 + 60)°$ and $(-180 - 60)°$.

The other angles within the interval $-360° \leqslant \theta \leqslant 360°$ that have the same sine as 60° are:

$\theta = (180 - 60)° = 120°$ — | 60° to the left of 180° |

$\theta = (-180 - 60)° = -240°$ — | 60° to the left of $-180°$ |

$\theta = (-360 + 60)° = -300°$ — | 60° to the right of $-360°$ |

Check using a calculator that the sine of each angle does equal sin 60°

## Worked example 11.4

Find all values of $\theta$ within the interval $-360° \leqslant \theta \leqslant 360°$ for which $\cos 130° = \cos \theta$.

## Solution

Sketch the graph of $y = \cos \theta$.

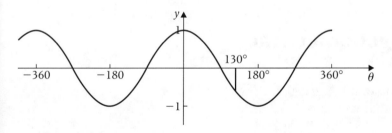

One solution is $\theta = 130°$.

Locate 130° on the $\theta$ axis. This is $(180 - 50)°$

Other solutions within the given interval are

$\theta = (180 + 50)° = 230°$ — | 50° to the left of 180° |

$\theta = (-180° + 50)° = -130°$ — | 50° to the left of $-180°$ |

$\theta = (-180 - 50)° = -230°$ — | 50° to the right of $-180°$ |

Now check the solutions!
$\cos 130° = -0.6427...$

## EXERCISE 11B

**1** Find all possible angles $\theta$ for which

**(a)** $\sin \theta = \sin 50°$, in the interval $-360° \leqslant \theta \leqslant 180°$,

**(b)** $\sin \theta = \sin -20°$, in the interval $-180° \leqslant \theta \leqslant 180°$,

**(c)** $\sin \theta = \sin 90°$, in the interval $-360° \leqslant \theta \leqslant 360°$,

**(d)** $\sin \theta = \sin 0°$, in the interval $-360° < \theta < 360°$,

**(e)** $\sin \theta = \sin 170°$, in the interval $-360° \leqslant \theta \leqslant 180°$,

**(f)** $\sin \theta = \sin -130°$, in the interval $-180° \leqslant \theta \leqslant 360°$.

**2** Find all possible angles $\theta$ for which

**(a)** $\cos \theta = \cos -40°$, in the interval $-180° \leqslant \theta \leqslant 180°$,

**(b)** $\cos \theta = \cos 70°$, in the interval $0° \leqslant \theta \leqslant 360°$,

**(c)** $\cos \theta = \cos 110°$, in the interval $0° \leqslant \theta \leqslant 360°$,

**(d)** $\cos \theta = \cos 0°$, in the interval $-360° \leqslant \theta < 360°$,

**(e)** $\cos \theta = \cos 90°$, in the interval $-90° < \theta \leqslant 360°$,

**(f)** $\cos \theta = \cos 20°$, in the interval $-180° \leqslant \theta \leqslant 180°$.

**3** Use the graphs of $y = \cos \theta$ and $y = \sin \theta$ to state the smallest **positive** angle $\theta$ for which

**(a)** $\cos -35° = \cos \theta$, **(b)** $\cos 380° = \cos \theta$,

**(c)** $\sin -180° = \sin \theta$, **(d)** $\sin -45° = \sin \theta$,

**(e)** $\sin 310° = \sin \theta$, **(f)** $\cos -225° = \cos \theta$.

# 11.8 Solving simple trigonometrical equations

Suppose you are told that the cosine of an angle $\theta$ is 0.7. How could a value of the angle $\theta$ be found that would give 0.7 as its cosine?

The equation is $\cos \theta = 0.7$ and

$\theta$ is 'the angle whose cosine is 0.7'.

Using the idea of a flow diagram

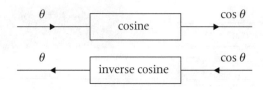

**Important**: 'Inverse cosine' is written as $\cos^{-1}$. $\cos^{-1}$ means *'undo taking the cosine of an angle'* or *'do the inverse operation to taking the cosine'* or *'inverse cos'*.

It **does not** mean $\dfrac{1}{\cos \theta}$

While a calculator will give the cosine of any angle, reversing the process does not give all of the angles with a given cosine.

A calculator considers a specific interval and returns one angle. This is called the **principal value**.

Because there is an infinite number of angles having the same cosine!

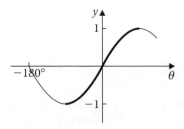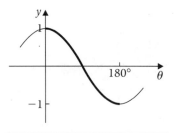

For $\sin^{-1}\theta$ a calculator gives angles $-90° \leqslant \theta \leqslant 90°$

For $\cos^{-1}\theta$ a calculator gives angles $0° \leqslant \theta \leqslant 180°$

## Worked example 11.5

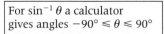

Solve the equation $\cos\theta = 0.5$, in the interval $0° \leqslant \theta \leqslant 360°$

Which angles within the given interval have a cosine of 0.5?

## Solution

Using the 'inverse cos' key on a calculator gives $\theta = 60°$.

So $\cos 60° = 0.5$

Other solutions within the interval can be found by considering the graph of $y = \cos\theta$ and this should now be a familiar process.

One angle that has a cosine of 0.5

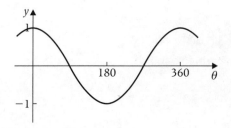

Using the symmetry properties of the graph, $(360 - 60)°$ is also a solution. There are two solutions within the given interval and these are $\theta = 60°$ and $\theta = 300°$.

Check with your calculator that $\cos 300° = 0.5$

**11**

## Worked example 11.6

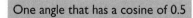

Solve the equation $5\sin x = 1$, in the interval $-360° \leqslant x \leqslant 0°$ giving your answers to the nearest $0.1°$.

## Solution

By now you should be quite familiar with the graph of $\sin x$ so rearrange to give

$$\sin x = \frac{1}{5} \quad \text{or} \quad \sin x = 0.2$$

Solving $\sin x = 0.2$ on a calculator gives $x = 11.536\ldots°$ which is outside the given interval since $-360° \leqslant x \leqslant 0°$.

> If you input $\sin^{-1}\left(\frac{1}{5}\right)$ remember the brackets.

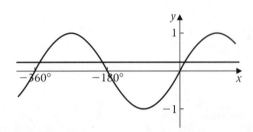

> If you have a graphics calculator you can use the zoom and trace facilities to find approximate values for the solutions.

The graph shows that $x$ can be found using the symmetry properties of $\sin x$ and so in this case

either $\quad x = -180° - 11.536\ldots° \quad \Rightarrow x = -191.536\ldots°$

or $\quad\quad x = -360° + 11.536\ldots° \quad \Rightarrow x = -348.463\ldots°$

There are two solutions, $x = -191.5°$

$\quad\quad\quad\quad\quad\quad\quad\quad\quad x = -348.5°$ both to the nearest $0.1°$

> Always use your full calculator display to evaluate inverse cosine and inverse sine or you may lose accuracy.

## Problems involving quadratic equations

## Worked example 11.7

Solve the equation $3\cos^2\theta - 5\cos\theta + 2 = 0$, in the interval $-360° \leqslant \theta \leqslant 360°$ giving your answers to the nearest $0.1°$

> $(\cos\theta)^2$ is usually written as $\cos^2\theta$
> $(\sin\theta)^2$ is usually written as $\sin^2\theta$
> Otherwise you may be tempted to write $\cos\theta^2$ or $\sin\theta^2$ **which are not the same as** $(\cos\theta)^2$ and $(\sin\theta)^2$
> **Think: '$\cos^2\theta$ is $\cos\theta$ squared' or $\cos\theta \times \cos\theta$.**

## Solution

Factorising gives $(3\cos\theta - 2)(\cos\theta - 1) = 0$

**either**

$3\cos\theta - 2 = 0 \Rightarrow \cos\theta = \frac{2}{3} \Rightarrow \cos^{-1}\frac{2}{3} = \theta = 48.189\ldots°$

from which the other solutions are:

$\theta = (360 - 48.189\ldots)° = 311.810\ldots°$

$\theta = (-360 + 48.189\ldots)° = -311.810\ldots°$

> You may not at first glance notice that this is a quadratic equation. If you write the equation as
> $\quad 3(\cos\theta)^2 - 5\cos\theta + 2 = 0$
> and compare with
> $\quad 3x^2 - 5x + 2 = 0$
> then this is seen more easily, with '$x$' replaced by '$\cos\theta$'

**or**

$\cos \theta - 1 = 0 \Rightarrow \cos \theta = 1 \Rightarrow \theta = 0°$

other solutions are

$\theta = 360°$ or $\theta = -360°$

If $-360° < \theta < 360°$ then these two solutions would be outside the range.

The solutions are (to the nearest 0.1°),

$\theta = -360°, -311.8°, -48.2°, 0°, 48.2°, 311.8°, 360°.$

> **N.B.** If you are solving $7 \cos^2 \theta - 16 \cos \theta + 4 = 0$, for example, this factorises to give $(7 \cos \theta - 2)(\cos \theta - 2) = 0$. $(\cos \theta - 2) = 0$ does not give solutions. **Why?** The solutions are given by $(7 \cos \theta - 2) = 0$.

Sometimes the equation will not factorise and so in this case the quadratic formula is used, where $\cos \theta = \dfrac{-b \pm \sqrt{b^2 - 4ac}}{2a}$.

Write $x = \cos \theta$ to see this more clearly.

## Worked example 11.8

Solve the equation $2\cos^2 \theta - 7\cos \theta + 1 = 0$, in the interval $0 \leqslant \theta \leqslant 360°$ giving your answer to the nearest 0.1°.

## Solution

$a = 2, b = -7, c = 1.$ $\cos \theta = \dfrac{7 \pm \sqrt{(-7)^2 - 4 \times 2 \times 1}}{2 \times 2} = \dfrac{7 \pm \sqrt{41}}{4}$

either $\cos \theta = \dfrac{7 + \sqrt{41}}{4} = 3.3507...$ for which there are no solutions

or $\cos \theta = \dfrac{7 - \sqrt{41}}{4} = 0.1492...$ which gives

$\theta = 81.4°$ or $278.6°$

## EXERCISE 11C

**1** Solve the following equations for the given interval, giving answers to the nearest 0.1°

  **(a)** $\sin \theta = 0.25$, in the interval $0° \leqslant \theta \leqslant 360°$,

  **(b)** $\cos x = \dfrac{4}{5}$, in the interval $-360° \leqslant x \leqslant 90°$,

  **(c)** $\sin x = 0.4$, in the interval $-360° \leqslant x \leqslant 360°$,

  **(d)** $\cos \theta = -0.7$, in the interval $-360° \leqslant \theta \leqslant 360°$,

  **(e)** $\cos x = 0.3$, in the interval $-360° \leqslant x \leqslant 0°$,

  **(f)** $\sin \theta = -0.5$, in the interval $0° \leqslant \theta \leqslant 360°$,

  **(g)** $\sin x = 0$, in the interval $0° < x < 360°$

  **(h)** $\cos \theta = 1$, in the interval $-360° \leqslant \theta \leqslant 360°$

When the answer is an exact whole number of degrees, such as 30°, there is no need to write 30.0°.

The idea of asking for answers to the nearest 0.1°, which will appear in exam questions, is to prevent you from leaving your answer as a full calculator display.

**2** Find the first four positive solutions of the following equations, giving your answers to the nearest 0.1°.

    **(a)** $10 \sin \theta = 5$,

    **(b)** $7 \sin x + 4 = 0$,

    **(c)** $5 \cos x + 2 = 0$

    **(d)** $\dfrac{\sin \theta}{2} + \dfrac{3}{10} = \dfrac{1}{5}$,

    **(e)** $4 \cos \theta - \cos \theta = 2$,

    **(f)** $2 \sin x - \dfrac{1}{2} \sin x = 1$.

**3** Solve the following equations in the interval $0° \leqslant \theta < 360°$, to the nearest 0.1°.

    **(a)** $2 \cos^2 \theta - \cos \theta - 1 = 0$,

    **(b)** $3 \sin^2 \theta - \sin \theta = 0$,

    **(c)** $\cos^2 \theta - 1 = 0$,

    **(d)** $5 \cos^2 \theta + \cos \theta = 0$,

    **(e)** $6 \sin^2 \theta - \sin \theta = 1$,

    **(f)** $4 \cos^2 \theta + 7 \cos \theta = 2$,

    **(g)** $6 \cos^2 \theta + \cos \theta - 1 = 0$,

    **(h)** $4 \sin^2 \theta + 3 \sin \theta = 1$.

**4** Use the quadratic equation formula to solve the following equations in the interval $0° \leqslant x \leqslant 360°$ to the nearest 0.1°.

    **(a)** $\cos^2 x + \cos x - 1 = 0$,

    **(b)** $\sin^2 x + 6 \sin x + 1 = 0$,

    **(c)** $\sin^2 x + 2 \sin x = 2$,

    **(d)** $3 \cos^2 x + 6 \cos x - 2 = 0$,

    **(e)** $2 \sin^2 x + 4 \sin x = 3$,

    **(f)** $4 \cos^2 x + 24 \cos x + 17 = 0$.

# 11.9 Multiple angles

Sometimes, trigonometrical equations involve terms such as

$$\sin (2\theta)$$

or

$$\cos (3x + 40°).$$

Comparing $\sin \theta$ and $\sin 2\theta$, $0° \leqslant \theta \leqslant 180°$:

> Take $\theta$ then multiply by 2 **then** take the sine.
> Take $x$ then multiply by 3 then add 40° **then** take the cosine.

| $\theta$ | $\sin \theta$ | $2\theta$ | $\sin 2\theta$ |
|---|---|---|---|
| 0° | 0 | 0° | 0 |
| 45° | 0.71 | 90° | 1.00 |
| 90° | 1.00 | 180° | 0 |
| 135° | 0.71 | 270° | −1.00 |
| 180° | 0 | 360° | 0 |

If $\theta$ varies between 0° and 180°, $\sin \theta$ completes half a period. However, $2\theta$ will vary between 0° and 360° and $\sin 2\theta$ completes one full period. A few values of $\theta$, $\sin \theta$, $2\theta$ and $\sin 2\theta$ are given.

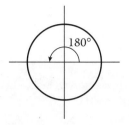

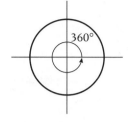

| | |
|---|---|
| $\theta$ turns through 180° so sin $\theta$ completes half a period. | $2\theta$ turns through 360° so sin $2\theta$ completes one full period. |

You go twice as fast with $2\theta$

Comparing $\cos x$ and $\cos (3x + 40°)$, $0° \leqslant x \leqslant 180°$

If $x$ varies between 0° and 180°, $\cos x$ completes half a period and starts at 0°. However, $(3x + 40°)$ will vary between 40° and 580° and $\cos (3x + 40°)$ completes three full periods.

Three times as fast as $\cos x$. $\cos (3x + 40°)$ finishes its journey as 580° $(3 \times 180 + 40)°$

| $x$ | $\cos x$ | $(3x + 40°)$ | $\cos(3x + 40°)$ |
|---|---|---|---|
| 0° | 1 | 40° | 0.77 |
| 45° | 0.71 | 175° | −1.00 |
| 90° | 0 | 310° | 0.64 |
| 135° | −0.71 | 445° | 0.09 |
| 180° | −1 | 580° | −0.77 |

A few values of $x$, $\cos x$, $(3x + 40°)$ and $\cos (3x + 40°)$ are given in the table opposite, all to two decimal places.

When considering equations such as $\sin 2\theta = 0.4$ or $\cos (3x + 40°) = 0.75$ for a given interval, it is important therefore, to realise that a larger interval should be considered for $2\theta$ or $3x + 40°$, etc .

If $\cos x$ starts at, say, $x = -180°$, then $\cos (3x + 40°)$ would start at $x = [3 \times (-180) + 40]° = -500°$

## *Worked example 11.9*

Solve the equation $\cos 2x = \frac{1}{2}$, in the interval $0° \leqslant x \leqslant 360°$.

## *Solution*

### **Method 1**

If you plot the graphs of $y = \cos 2x$ and $y = \frac{1}{2}$ you can see how many solutions there are within the given interval. The solutions are found at the points where the two graphs intersect.

Using your graphics calculator.

**11**

The function $y = \cos 2x$ goes 'twice as fast' as the function $y = \cos x$ so expect 'twice as many' solutions within the given interval.

$\cos 2x = \frac{1}{2} \Rightarrow 2x = 60°$, from a calculator.

If $2x = 60°$, then $x = 30°$.

You have found one solution to the equation.

Now use the symmetries of the graph of $y = \cos 2x$ to find the other solutions.

$$x = (180 - 30)° = 150°$$

$$x = (180 + 30)° = 210°$$

$$x = (360 - 30)° = 330°$$

Solutions are 30°, 150°, 210°, 330°

All four solutions have now been found.

> Substitute all solutions into the original equation to make sure that they are correct.
> $\cos(2 \times 30)° = \cos 60° = 0.5$ ✓
> $\cos(2 \times 210)° = \cos 420° = 0.5$ ✓
> $\cos(2 \times 150)° = \cos 300° = 0.5$ ✓
> $\cos(2 \times 330)° = \cos 660° = 0.5$ ✓

## Method 2

To solve $\cos \theta = \frac{1}{2}$ you would use the $\cos^{-1}$ key on your calculator to find one solution, then you can use the symmetry properties of the graph to find the other solutions. The same method is used here, only now substitute $\theta = 2x$.

$\cos \theta = \frac{1}{2} \Rightarrow \theta = 60°$, from a calculator.

If $\theta = 2x = 60°$, then $x = 30°$.

You have found one solution to the equation.

Consider the interval for $\theta$ :

when   $x = 0°$,  $\theta = 0°$ and when $x = 360°$, $\theta = 720°$

so      $0° \leqslant \theta \leqslant 720°$

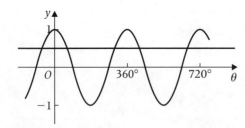

From the graph of $y = \cos \theta$, the other solutions are

$$\theta = 2x = 300° \Rightarrow x = 150°$$

$$\theta = 2x = 420° \Rightarrow x = 210°$$

$$\theta = 2x = 660° \Rightarrow x = 330°$$

Solutions are 30°, 150°, 210°, 330°

With practice, you can use Method 2 without actually making a substitution.

## *Worked example 11.10*

Solve the equation $\sin 3x = 0.4$, in the interval $0° < x < 180°$, giving your answers to the nearest $0.1°$.

### Solution

From your calculator, $\sin 3x = 0.4$

$$\Rightarrow 3x = \sin^{-1} 0.4 = 23.578...°$$

Use the graph of $y = \sin \theta$ to find other values of $3x$ with the same sine.

$$3x = 180° - 23.578...° = 156.422...°$$
$$3x = 360° - 23.578...° = 383.578...°$$
$$3x = 540° - 23.578...° = 516.422...°$$

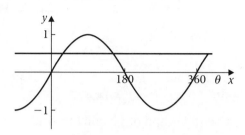

Dividing by three gives the values of $x$:

$$x = \frac{23.578...}{3} = 7.859...°; \quad x = \frac{156.422...}{3} = 52.14...°;$$

$$x = \frac{383.578...}{3} = 127.859...°; \quad x = \frac{516.422...}{3} = 172.14...°;$$

Remember to explore values within three times the original interval, from $0°$ to $540°$.

The solutions are $7.9°$, $52.1°$, $127.9°$, $172.1°$ (to the nearest $0.1°$)

## *Worked example 11.11*

Solve the equation $\sin (3\theta - 20°) = 0.25$, in the interval $-90° \leqslant \theta \leqslant 90°$ giving your answer to the nearest $0.1°$.

### Solution

Here, plotting $y = \sin (3\theta - 20°)$ and $y = 0.25$ for the given interval produces the following graphs:

Expect three solutions. These can be seen from the graphs.

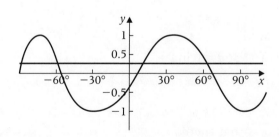

Substitute a single variable for the term in the bracket. Let $(3\theta - 20) = t$ and then solve $\sin t = 0.25$.

Consider the interval required for $t$:

When $\theta = -90°$, $(3\theta - 20°) = -290°$

When $\theta = 90°$, $(3\theta - 20°) = 250°$

so $-290° \leqslant t \leqslant 250°$

The graphs of $y = \sin t$ and $y = 0.25$ are shown below.

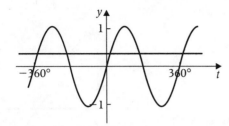

$\sin^{-1} 0.25$ gives $t = 14.477\ldots$

Use the graph of $y = \sin t$ to find the other values of $t$

| either | or | or |
|---|---|---|
| $t = 14.477\ldots°$ | $t = (-180 - 14.477\ldots)°$ | $t = (180 - 14.477\ldots)°$ |
| $3\theta - 20° = 14.477\ldots°$ | $t = -194.477\ldots°$ | $t = 165.522\ldots°$ |
| $3\theta = 34.477\ldots°$ | $3\theta - 20° = -194.477\ldots°$ | $3\theta - 20° = 165.522\ldots°$ |
| $\theta = \dfrac{34.477\ldots°}{3}$ | $\theta = -58.2°$ to the nearest $0.1°$ | $\theta = 61.8°$ to the nearest $0.1°$ |

and $\theta = 11.5°$ to
the nearest $0.1°$

> Check now to see if these solutions are correct
> $\sin (3 \times 11.5 - 20)° = 0.25$ (two decimal places)
> Since $\theta$ was rounded, this is correct.
>
> Check the others for yourself.

Solutions are $-58.2°$, $11.5°$, $61.8°$ to the nearest $0.1°$

With experience, it will not be necessary to substitute a single
variable for the term in brackets.

## Worked example 11.12 _____

Solve the equation $\cos (2x + 10°) = 0.6$, $0° \leqslant x \leqslant 360°$ giving
your answer to the nearest $0.1°$.

## Solution

A sketch of $y = \cos (2x + 10°)$ and $y = 0.6$ shows that there are
four solutions within the given interval.

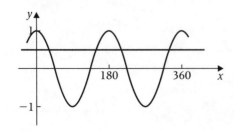

When $x = 0°$,        $(2x + 10°) = 10°$

When $x = 360°$,      $(2x + 10°) = 730°$

so $10° \leqslant (2x + 10°) \leqslant 730°$

$\cos^{-1} 0.6 = 53.130...°$

$2x + 10° = 53.130...°$           $\Rightarrow x = 21.6°$ to the nearest $0.1°$

$2x + 10° = 360° - 53.130...°$   $\Rightarrow x = 148.4°$ to the nearest $0.1°$.

$2x + 10° = 360° + 53.130...°$   $\Rightarrow x = 201.6°$ to the nearest $0.1°$

$2x + 10° = 720° - 53.130...°$   $\Rightarrow x = 328.4°$ to the nearest $0.1°$.

> It is, of course, possible to find more solutions, but these will be outside of the given interval. If in doubt, better to find too many solutions and then discard the ones outside the interval.
>
> **Check** to make sure that these solutions satisfy the original equation, allowing for rounding.

## EXERCISE 11D

1   Find all solutions in the interval $0° < \theta < 180°$ of the
    equation $2 \sin (3\theta - 48°) - 1 = 0$.                    [A]

Solve the equations in questions 2 to 15 for the given interval
giving your answers to the nearest $0.1°$.

2   $\sin 2x = 0.42$,                    $0° \leqslant x \leqslant 360°$.

3   $\cos 3\theta = 0.6$,                  $-180° \; \theta \leqslant 90°$.

4   $4 \sin 2\theta = 1$,                   $-180° \leqslant \theta \leqslant 180°$.

5   $3 \cos 3\theta + 2 = 0$,            $-90° \leqslant \theta \leqslant 90°$.

6   $\sin (2\theta + 40°) = 1$,          $0° \leqslant \theta \leqslant 360°$.

7   $\cos (2x + 30°) = -0.3$,       $0° \leqslant x \leqslant 360°$.

8   $5 \cos (3\theta - 40°) = 1$,       $-90° \leqslant \theta \leqslant 90°$.

9   $4 \sin (2x - 35°) - 3 = 0$,      $-180° \leqslant x \leqslant 90°$.

10  $\sin (3x - 58°) = -0.4$,        $0° \leqslant x \leqslant 180°$.

11  $10 \cos (3\theta + 20°) - 8 = 0$,   $0° \leqslant \theta \leqslant 180°$.

12  $5 \sin (5x + 75°) = 2$,          $0° \leqslant x \leqslant 180°$.

13  $2 \sin \dfrac{\theta}{2} = 0.6$,            $0° \leqslant \theta \leqslant 360°$.

> Interval $0° \leqslant \dfrac{\theta}{2} \leqslant 180°$

14  $\cos \left( \dfrac{x}{3} + 10° \right) = 0.4$,      $-180° \leqslant x \leqslant 180°$.

15  $3 \cos \left( \dfrac{\theta}{2} - 30° \right) = 2$,      $0° \leqslant \theta \leqslant 720°$.

**11**

# 11.10 The tangent function

Draw a unit circle with a vertical tangent on the right of the circle. The radius travels through an angle $\theta$ in an anticlockwise (positive) direction starting at the *x*-axis. Think of the radius as a double-ended torch with a ray of light shining from both ends. Think of the tangent as a screen that the light from the torch hits in different places, depending on the angle that it travels through.

What is the distance of the beam of light, as it hits the screen, from the *x*-axis?

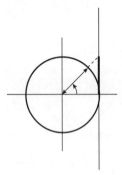 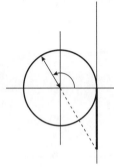 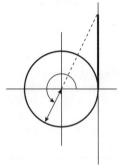 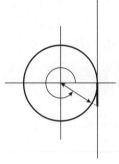

The torch has travelled through about 50°. The beam of light is more than 1 unit above the *x*-axis (positive).

The torch has travelled through about 110°. The beam of light is about 2.5 units below the *x*-axis (negative).

The torch has travelled through about 240°. The beam of light is about 2 units above the *x*-axis (positive).

The torch has travelled through about 330°. The beam of light is about half a unit below the *x*-axis (negative).

The exact distance of the beam of light from the *x*-axis is found using the tangent function, again with positive values for 'above' and negative values for 'below'. Try working out the tangent for these four angles using a calculator.

A more formal definition of the tangent function is given later.

Use your calculator to work out the tangent of any angle between 0° and 360°, considering the idea outlined above. Then try angles outside this interval.

'tangent' is abbreviated to 'tan'

If you tried to work out the tangent of 90° or 270° you would receive an 'error' message. It is obvious that, when the torch is at 90° or 270° (180 + 90) °, for example, the beam of light will not hit the screen and so for these angles, the tangent is not defined.

Also for (360 + 90)° (540 + 90)°, −90° (−90 − 180)° etc.

Below is a table of values of $\theta$ and approximate values for tan $\theta$ in the region of 90°

| $\theta$ | 89.00° | 89.10° | 89.20° | 89.30° | 89.40° | 89.50° | 89.60° | 89.70° | 89.80° | 89.90° | 89.91° | 89.92° | 89.93° | 89.94° | 89.95° | 89.96° | 89.97° | 89.98° | 89.99° |
|---|---|---|---|---|---|---|---|---|---|---|---|---|---|---|---|---|---|---|---|
| tan $\theta$ | 57.3 | 63.7 | 71.6 | 81.8 | 95.5 | 115 | 143 | 191 | 286 | 573 | 637 | 716 | 819 | 955 | 1146 | 1432 | 1910 | 2865 | 5730 |
| $\theta$ | 90.01° | 90.02° | 90.03° | 90.04° | 90.05° | 90.06° | 90.07° | 90.08° | 90.09° | 90.10° | 90.20° | 90.30° | 90.40° | 90.50° | 90.60° | 90.70° | 90.80° | 90.90° | 91.00° |
| tan $\theta$ | −5730 | −2865 | −1910 | −1432 | −1146 | −955 | −819 | −716 | −637 | −573 | −286 | −191 | −143 | −115 | −95.5 | −81.8 | −71.6 | −63.7 | −57.3 |

Notice how quickly tan $\theta$ becomes very large and positive as the angle $\theta$ approaches 90° and how large and negative tan $\theta$ is when $\theta$ is just over 90°.

# 11.11 The graph of the tangent function

## The graph of $y = \tan \theta$

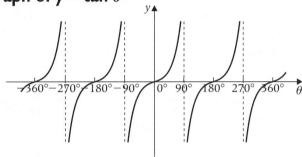

The dotted vertical lines are called asymptotes. You can see from the table that $\tan \theta$ becomes 'large positive' or 'large negative' close to either side of the asymptotes. The value of $\tan \theta$ 'tends towards plus or minus infinity' or is said to be undefined wherever there is an asymptote.

## Key features of the graph of $y = \tan \theta$

(a) The graph is periodic with period $180°$.
(b) $\tan \theta$ can take any value, it is not restricted in the same way that $\sin \theta$ and $\cos \theta$ are.
(c) The tangent function is **many–one**.
(d) The graph has rotational symmetry of order 2 about the origin. Hence $\tan \theta$ is an odd function.

$\tan (180° + \theta) = \tan \theta$
$\tan (-\theta) = -\tan \theta$

 The equation $\tan x = d$ has solutions for all values of $d$.

 $\tan (180° + \theta) = \tan \theta$, $\tan (-\theta) = -\tan \theta$.

## *Worked example 11.13*

Find all angles in the interval $-270° \leqslant \theta \leqslant 360°$ that have the same tangent as $-35°$.

## *Solution*

The graph of $y = \tan \theta$ repeats itself every $180°$, so once you have sketched $\tan \theta$ for the given range, it is quite a simple task to identify all of the angles.

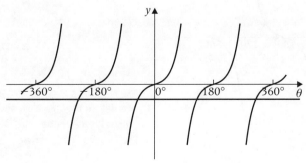

In the same way that you solved equations such as $\sin x = 0.3$ and $\cos (2\theta + 10°) = 0.4$, you can solve similar equations involving the tangent function.

**11**

The other angles are

$$\theta = (-180 - 35)° = -215°$$

35° to the left of −180°

$$\theta = (180 - 35)° = 145°$$

35° to the left of 180°

$$\theta = (360 - 35)° = 325°$$

35° to the left of 360°

Check using a calculator that the tangent of each angle does equal tan (−35)°.

## Worked example 11.14

Solve the equation tan $(2x - 10°) = 100$ in the interval $-180° \leqslant x \leqslant 180°$ to the nearest 0.1°

## Solution

From the graph of $y = \tan (2x - 10°)$, four solutions are expected.

It is difficult, in this case, to plot $y = \tan (2x - 10°)$ and $y = 100$ on the same set of axes. Plot $y = \tan (2x - 10°)$ and estimate, by eye, $y = 100$.

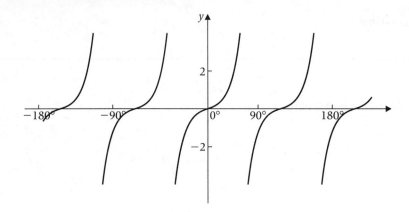

Consider the interval for $2x - 10°$:

when $x = -180°$, $2x - 10° = -370°$

when $x = 180°$, $2x - 10° = 350°$

$-370° \leqslant (2x - 10°) \leqslant 350°$.

$y = \tan \theta$

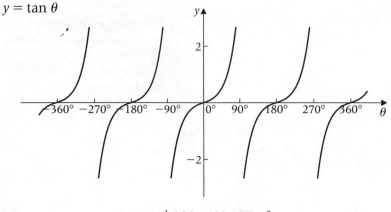

$$\tan^{-1} 100 = 89.427...°$$

The method is exactly the same as the one used for the sine and cosine functions. You should not mistake the value '100' in $\tan^{-1} 100$ for an angle.

$2x - 10° = 89.427...° \Rightarrow x = 49.7°$

$2x - 10° = (180 + 89.427...)° \Rightarrow x = 139.7°$

$2x - 10° = (-180 + 89.427...)° \Rightarrow x = -40.3°$

$2x - 10° = (-360 + 89.427...)° \Rightarrow x = -130.3°$

all to the nearest 0.1°.

> Using the graph of $y = \tan \theta$.

> A small error due to rounding means a large error, in this case, when checking accuracy of answers. Why?

## EXERCISE 11E

**1** Find all angles $\theta$ for which:

   **(a)** $\tan \theta = \tan 50°$, in the interval $-180° \leqslant \theta \leqslant 360°$,

   **(b)** $\tan \theta = \tan (-20)°$, in the interval $0° \leqslant \theta \leqslant 360°$,

   **(c)** $\tan \theta = \tan 120°$, in the interval $-360° \leqslant \theta \leqslant 180°$,

   **(d)** $\tan \theta = \tan 20°$, in the interval $-360° \leqslant \theta \leqslant 0°$,

   **(e)** $\tan \theta = \tan 230°$, in the interval $-180° \leqslant \theta \leqslant 360°$,

   **(f)** $\tan \theta = \tan (-60)°$, in the interval $-360° \leqslant \theta \leqslant 180°$.

**2** Solve the following equations, giving your answers to the nearest 0.1°.

   **(a)** $\tan x = 0.5$ in the interval $0° \leqslant x \leqslant 360°$,

   **(b)** $4 \tan \theta = 4$ in the interval $0° \leqslant \theta \leqslant 360°$,

   **(c)** $\tan x = 0$ in the interval $0° \leqslant x \leqslant 360°$,

   **(d)** $6 \tan x = 1$ in the interval $0° \leqslant x \leqslant 180°$,

   **(e)** $10 \tan \theta + 3 = 0$ in the interval $-180° \leqslant \theta \leqslant 180°$.

**3** Solve the following equations, giving your answers to the nearest 0.1°.

   **(a)** $\tan^2 \theta = \frac{1}{4}$ in the interval $-180° \leqslant \theta \leqslant 270°$,

   **(b)** $\tan^2 x + 14 \tan x + 40 = 0$ in the interval $-180° \leqslant x \leqslant 0°$,

   **(c)** $\tan^2 \theta - \tan \theta - 2 = 0$ in the interval $-180° \leqslant \theta \leqslant 180°$

   **(d)** $2 \tan^2 \theta - 7 \tan \theta + 2 = 0$ in the interval $0° \leqslant \theta \leqslant 360°$

   **(e)** $3 \tan^2 x + 3 \tan x = 1$ in the interval $-180° \leqslant x \leqslant 180°$.

**4** Solve each of the following, giving your answers to the nearest 0.1°.

   **(a)** $\tan 2x - 1 = 0$ in the interval $0° \leqslant x \leqslant 180°$,

   **(b)** $\tan 3\theta = -8$ in the interval $0° \leqslant \theta \leqslant 180°$,

   **(c)** $2 \tan 2\theta - 3 = 0$ in the interval $-180° \leqslant \theta \leqslant 180°$,

   **(d)** $\tan (2\theta + 25°) = 1$ in the interval $-180° \leqslant \theta \leqslant 180°$,

   **(e)** $\tan (3x - 10°) = 2$ in the interval $-90° \leqslant x \leqslant 90°$,

   **(f)** $2 \tan (2x + 10°) = 4$ in the interval $0° \leqslant x \leqslant 180°$,

   **(g)** $\tan (3\theta - 45°) - \frac{1}{2} = 1$ in the interval $-90° \leqslant \theta \leqslant 90°$,

   **(h)** $\tan \left( \dfrac{x}{2} - 30° \right) = 1.4$ in the interval $0° \leqslant x \leqslant 360°$,

   **(i)** $3 \tan \left( \dfrac{\theta}{3} + 10° \right) + 7 = 0$ in the interval $-540° \leqslant \theta \leqslant 540°$.

**11**

# 11.12 The relationship $\cos^2\theta + \sin^2\theta = 1$

*P* has coordinates $(\cos\theta, \sin\theta)$ on a unit circle

Taking the right-angled triangle *OPQ* gives

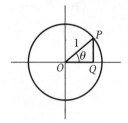
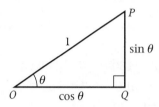

Applying Pythagoras' theorem to the triangle gives

$$(OQ)^2 + (PQ)^2 = 1^2$$
$$(\cos\theta)^2 + (\sin\theta)^2 = 1^2$$
$$\cos^2\theta + \sin^2\theta = 1$$

This is an identity (because it is true for all values of $\theta$) and so

$$\cos^2\theta + \sin^2\theta \equiv 1$$

> You can also write
> $\cos^2\theta \equiv 1 - \sin^2\theta$
> $\sin^2\theta \equiv 1 - \cos^2\theta$

# 11.13 The relationship between sin $\theta$, cos $\theta$ and tan $\theta$

Taking the right-angled triangles *OAB* and *OPQ* and using the idea of similar triangles

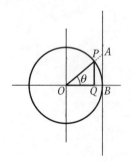
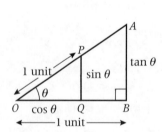

$$\frac{AB}{OB} = \frac{PQ}{OQ} \quad \text{so that} \quad \frac{\tan\theta}{1} = \frac{\sin\theta}{\cos\theta},$$

since *P* has coordinates $(\cos\theta, \sin\theta)$.

more simply $\qquad \tan\theta = \dfrac{\sin\theta}{\cos\theta}$

The relationship $\tan \theta = \dfrac{\sin \theta}{\cos \theta}$, is also an identity.

Hence,

$$\tan \theta \equiv \frac{\sin \theta}{\cos \theta}$$

This is generally given as the definition of $\tan \theta$.

Knowing $\tan \theta \equiv \dfrac{\sin \theta}{\cos \theta}$ means that given any two of these values, the third value can be found.

> An identity is true for all values of the variable, in this case $\theta$, whereas an equation is possibly satisfied by only a few values of the variable.

> Provided $\cos \theta \neq 0$.

## Worked example 11.15

Find the value of $\tan \theta$ when $\sin \theta = \dfrac{3}{5}$ and $\cos \theta = -\dfrac{4}{5}$,

## Solution

$$\tan \theta \equiv \frac{\sin \theta}{\cos \theta} = \frac{3}{5} \div -\frac{4}{5} = \frac{3}{5} \times -\frac{5}{4} = -\frac{3}{4}$$

It is also possible to create further identities using $\tan \theta \equiv \dfrac{\sin \theta}{\cos \theta}$.

> If you use your calculator to work with fractions, always use the fraction button. Do not be tempted to convert fractions to decimals since some fractions do not have an exact decimal representation. For example,
>
> $$\frac{5}{13} = 0.384615384615$$
>
> ↑       ↑
> exact   approximate

## Worked example 11.16

Show that $\dfrac{1 - \sin \theta}{\cos \theta} \equiv \dfrac{1}{\cos \theta} - \tan \theta$.

## Solution

LHS: $\dfrac{1 - \sin \theta}{\cos \theta} \equiv \dfrac{1}{\cos \theta} - \dfrac{\sin \theta}{\cos \theta} \equiv \dfrac{1}{\cos \theta} - \tan \theta$, since

$$\tan \theta \equiv \frac{\sin \theta}{\cos \theta}.$$

> If you are asked to 'show that' or 'prove that' then consider one side of the identity and, step by step, reduce it to the same form as the other side of the identity.

> You could just as easily have started with the RHS, in this case, and reduced it to the LHS.

**11**

The identity $\cos^2\theta + \sin^2\theta \equiv 1$ can be used to simplify other identities.

## Worked example 11.17 ────────────

Show that $\dfrac{2 - \cos^2 x}{1 + \sin^2 x} \equiv 1$

Since the numerator and denominator contain $\cos^2 x$ and $\sin^2 x$ it makes sense to try the identity $\cos^2\theta + \sin^2\theta \equiv 1$.

For this example, start with the LHS and reduce it to 1.

## Solution

$$\boxed{\cos^2 x = 1 - \sin^2 x}$$

LHS: $\dfrac{2 - \cos^2 x}{1 + \sin^2 x} \equiv \dfrac{2 - (1 - \sin^2 x)}{1 + \sin^2 x} \equiv \dfrac{1 + \sin^2 x}{1 + \sin^2 x} \equiv 1$

You could also consider the denominator using
$$\sin^2 x \equiv 1 - \cos^2 x$$

The identity $\cos^2\theta + \sin^2\theta \equiv 1$ can also be used to manipulate equations into a form whereby they can be solved more easily.

## Worked example 11.18 ────────────

Solve the equation $\sin^2 x + \cos x + 1 = 0$, giving all answers in degrees in the interval $0° < x < 360°$.

Contains both sine and cosine terms **but** $\sin^2 x \equiv 1 - \cos^2 x$ so this equation can be written in terms of cosine only by replacing $\sin^2 x$ with $1 - \cos^2 x$.

## Solution

Using $\cos^2 x + \sin^2 x \equiv 1$, so that $\sin^2 x \equiv 1 - \cos^2 x$ enables the equation to be written as a quadratic in $\cos x$, so that

$$\underbrace{1 - \cos^2 x}_{\sin^2 x} + \cos x + 1 = 0$$

Rearrange to give

$$\cos^2 x - \cos x - 2 = 0.$$

Factorising

$$(\cos x - 2)(\cos x + 1) = 0.$$

**Either** $\cos x - 2 = 0$, which does not give any solutions.

**or** $\cos x = -1 \Rightarrow x = \cos^{-1}(-1) = 180°$

which is the only solution for the given interval as the graph of $y = \sin^2 x + \cos x + 1$ would confirm.

## Worked example 11.19

Solve the equation $4 \sin 2x = 3 \cos 2x$, giving all solutions in degrees to the nearest $0.1°$ in the interval $-180° \leqslant x \leqslant 180°$.

## Solution

Dividing both sides by $\cos 2x$

$$\Rightarrow 4 \frac{\sin 2x}{\cos 2x} = 3 \Rightarrow \frac{\sin 2x}{\cos 2x} = \frac{3}{4}$$

$$\Rightarrow \tan 2x = \frac{3}{4}$$

> Use the identity $\tan \theta \equiv \dfrac{\sin \theta}{\cos \theta}$.

Find one value for $2x = \tan^{-1} 0.75 = 36.8699...°$

The interval to be considered is $-360° \leqslant 2x \leqslant 360°$.

Other values are $2x = 180° + 36.87° = 216.87°$

$$\text{and } 2x = -180° + 36.87° = -143.13°$$

$$\text{and } 2x = -360° + 36.87° = -323.13°$$

> Other values of $2x$ are obtained by adding and subtracting $180°$ using the symmetries of the graph of $y = \tan \theta$.

Hence the values of $x$ are given by dividing by 2

$$\Rightarrow x = -161.6°, -71.6°, 18.4°, 108.4°.$$

> It is customary to present the final answers in ascending order, but provided you have found all the solutions the order does not matter.

## EXERCISE 11F

**1** Find the value of

**(a)** $\tan \theta$ when $\sin \theta = -\dfrac{4}{5}$ and $\cos \theta = \dfrac{3}{5}$,

**(b)** $\tan x$ when $\cos x = \dfrac{5}{13}$ and $\sin x = \dfrac{12}{13}$,

**(c)** $\sin \theta$ when $\tan \theta = -\dfrac{5}{12}$ and $\cos \theta = -\dfrac{12}{13}$,

**(d)** $\sin x$ when $\cos x = -\dfrac{3}{5}$ and $\tan x = \dfrac{4}{3}$,

**(e)** $\tan x$ when $\cos x = \dfrac{24}{25}$ and $\sin x = -\dfrac{7}{25}$,

**(f)** $\cos \theta$ when $\tan \theta = \dfrac{24}{7}$ and $\sin \theta = \dfrac{24}{25}$,

**(g)** $\cos x$ when $\sin x = \dfrac{3}{5}$ and $\tan x = -\dfrac{3}{4}$.

**11**

**2** Use the identities $\tan \theta \equiv \dfrac{\sin \theta}{\cos \theta}$ and $\cos^2 x + \sin^2 x \equiv 1$ to show that

**(a)** $(\cos x + \sin x)^2 \equiv 1 + 2 \cos x \sin x$

**(b)** $1 + \cos^2 x \equiv 2 - \sin^2 x$

**(c)** $\sin^2 \theta + 2 \cos^2 \theta \equiv 2 - \sin^2 \theta$

**(d)** $\sin^2 \theta - \cos^2 \theta \equiv 2 \sin^2 \theta - 1$

**(e)** $\dfrac{1 - \sin x}{\tan x} \equiv \dfrac{1}{\tan x} - \cos x$

**(f)** $\dfrac{\cos x \sin x}{\tan x} \equiv 1 - \sin^2 x$

**(g)** $\dfrac{\tan x \cos^2 x}{\sin x \cos x} \equiv 1$

**(h)** $\dfrac{5 - \sin^2 \theta}{4 + \cos^2 \theta} \equiv 1$

**(i)** $\dfrac{3 + \sin^2 \theta}{2 + \cos \theta} \equiv 2 - \cos \theta$

**(j)** $\dfrac{\tan \theta \sin \theta}{1 - \cos \theta} \equiv 1 + \dfrac{1}{\cos \theta}$

> Although these are identities and the symbol $\equiv$ has been used, it is very common to switch to an equals sign ($=$) instead. It is important to realise that these relations are valid for all values of the variable. You are not solving an equation.
>
> However, you rarely write $2x + 3x \equiv 5x$, but usually write $2x + 3x = 5x$ and so in a similar way, you can write
> $$\cos^2 x + \sin^2 x = 1.$$

> LHS: put numerator in terms of cosine, then factorise

**3** Solve the following equations giving your answers in degrees to the nearest $0.1°$:

**(a)** $2 \sin^2 x + 3 \cos x + 1 = 0$ in the interval $0° \leqslant x \leqslant 360°$,

**(b)** $\sin^2 \theta + 3 \cos \theta = 2$ in the interval $0° \leqslant \theta \leqslant 360°$,

**(c)** $2 \cos^2 x + 4 \sin x - 3 = 0$ in the interval $-360° \leqslant x \leqslant 180°$,

**(d)** $\tan x + \cos x = 0$ in the interval $-180° \leqslant x \leqslant 180°$,

**(e)** $\tan \theta \sin \theta - \cos \theta = 0$ in the interval $0° \leqslant \theta \leqslant 360°$.

**4** Solve each of the following equations, giving all solutions between $0°$ and $180°$ to the nearest $0.1°$.

**(a)** $5 \sin 3x = 7 \cos 3x$,

**(b)** $2 \sin 2x + 5 \cos 2x = 0$.

**5 (a)** Express $\dfrac{8 + \cos^2 \theta}{3 - \sin \theta}$

in the form $a + b \sin \theta$, where $a$ and $b$ are integers.

**(b)** Hence find all solutions of the equation

$$\frac{8 + \cos^2 2x}{3 - \sin 2x} = \frac{5}{2}$$

in the interval $0° \leqslant x \leqslant 360°$.

**6 (a)** Prove the identity $\dfrac{\sin \theta}{1 + \cos \theta} + \dfrac{1 + \cos \theta}{\sin \theta} \equiv \dfrac{2}{\sin \theta}$.

**(b)** Hence find all solutions of the equation

$$\frac{\sin 3x}{1 + \cos 3x} + \frac{1 + \cos 3x}{\sin 3x} = 5$$

in the interval $0° \leqslant x \leqslant 360°$, giving your answers to the nearest $0.1°$.

**7 (a)** On one diagram sketch the graphs of $y = \cos x$ and $y = \tan x$ for values of $x$ between $0°$ and $360°$.

**(b)** Show that the $x$-coordinates of the points of intersection of the graphs of $y = \cos x$ and $y = \tan x$ satisfy the equation

$$\sin^2 x + \sin x - 1 = 0.$$

**(c)** Hence find the $x$-coordinates of the points of intersection of the two graphs in the interval $0° \leqslant x \leqslant 360°$, giving your answers to the nearest $0.1°$. [A]

**8** Find all solutions in the interval $0° < x < 360°$ of the equation
$$3 \tan x + 2 \cos x = 0.$$ [A]

---

## Key point summary

**1** To solve $\sin x = a$, where $-1 \leqslant a \leqslant 1$, for a given interval, use $\sin^{-1} a$ to find one value of $x$. Use the graph of $y = \sin x$ to find other solutions within the interval.     *p174*

**2** $\sin (360° + \theta) = \sin \theta$     *p174*
$\sin (180° - \theta) = \sin \theta$
$\sin (-\theta) = -\sin \theta$

**3** To solve $\cos x = b$, where $-1 \leqslant b \leqslant 1$, for a given interval, use $\cos^{-1} b$ to find one value of $x$. Use the graph of $y = \cos x$ to find other solutions within the interval.     *p175*

**4** $\cos (360° + \theta) = \cos \theta$
$\cos (360° - \theta) = \cos \theta$
$\cos (-\theta) = \cos \theta$

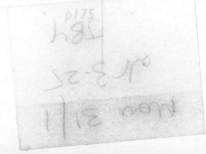

**5** To solve equations with multiple angles, such as $\cos 5\theta = c$, be aware that if you are looking for values of $\theta$ within a particular interval, then you will need to consider values of $5\theta$ in an interval five times as large. *p176*

**6** A graphics calculator can help you determine how many solutions to expect within a given interval. You can also use the zoom and trace facilities to find approximate values of the solutions in order to check your answers. *p179*

**7** The equation $\tan x = d$ has solutions for all values of $d$. Use your calculator to find one solution using $\tan^{-1} d$ and use the symmetries of the graph to find all other solutions. *p189*

**8** $\tan (180° + \theta) = \tan \theta$, $\tan (-\theta) = -\tan \theta$. *p189*

**9** The Pythagoras identity is $\cos^2 \theta + \sin^2 \theta \equiv 1$, and this relationship is true for all possible values of $\theta$. *p192*

**10** $\tan \theta \equiv \dfrac{\sin \theta}{\cos \theta}$, $(\cos \theta \neq 0)$ *p193*

**11** To prove an identity, consider the expression on one side and try to reduce it to the expression on the other side. If this proves too difficult then try to show that the RHS and the LHS are equivalent to a third expression. *p193*

| Test yourself | What to review |
|---|---|

**1** Find all the angles $\theta$ for which:

    **(a)** $\sin\theta = \sin(-45)°$, in the interval $-180° \leqslant \theta \leqslant 360°$,

    **(b)** $\cos\theta = \cos 100°$, in the interval $-270° \leqslant \theta \leqslant 0°$.

*Section 11.7*

**2** Find all the solutions in the given interval, giving answers to the nearest 0.1°:

    **(a)** $\sin\theta = 0.3$, in the interval $-360° \leqslant \theta \leqslant 360°$,

    **(b)** $\cos x = -\dfrac{2}{7}$, in the interval $0° \leqslant x \leqslant 360°$.

*Section 11.8*

**3** Solve the following equations, giving your answers to the nearest 0.1°.

    **(a)** $2\sin 2\theta = 0.5$, in the interval $0° \leqslant \theta \leqslant 90°$.

    **(b)** $2\cos 3\theta + 1 = 0$, in the interval $-90° \leqslant \theta \leqslant 90°$

    **(c)** $\sin(2\theta + 20°) = 0.3$, in the interval $0° \leqslant \theta \leqslant 360°$

*Section 11.9*

**4** Solve $3\tan(4\theta) = 4$, giving your answers to the nearest 0.1° in the interval $-90° \leqslant \theta \leqslant 90°$.

*Section 11.11*

**5** Solve $\tan^2 x - \tan x - 6 = 0$, giving your answers to the nearest 0.1° in the interval $0° \leqslant x \leqslant 360°$.

*Section 11.11*

**6** Given that $\sin\theta = \dfrac{24}{25}$ and that $\cos\theta = -\dfrac{7}{25}$, find $\tan\theta$.

*Section 11.13*

**7** Prove the identity $\dfrac{1}{1+\cos\theta} + \dfrac{1}{1-\cos\theta} \equiv \dfrac{2}{\sin^2\theta}$.

*Section 11.2*

**Test yourself ANSWERS**

**6** $-\dfrac{24}{7}$

**5** $71.6°$, $116.6°$, $251.6°$, $296.6°$

**4** $-76.7°$, $-31.7°$, $13.3°$, $58.3°$.

**3 (a)** $7.2°$, $82.8°$; **(b)** $\mp 40°$, $\mp 80°$; **(c)** $71.3°$, $178.7°$, $251.3°$, $358.7°$.

**2 (a)** $-342.5°$, $-197.5°$, $17.5°$, $162.5°$; **(b)** $106.6°$, $253.4°$.

**1 (a)** $-45°$, $-135°$, $225°$, $315°$; **(b)** $-260°$, $-100°$.

CHAPTER 12

# Transformation of graphs

---

## Learning objectives

After studying this chapter you should be able to:
- transform graphs using translations
- reflect graphs in different axes to produce new graphs
- use compositions of simple transformations such as translations, reflections, stretches to sketch graphs
- relate the ideas of odd, even and periodic functions to graphs.

---

## 12.1 Translations parallel to the *x*-axis

The graph of $y = x^2$ is sketched in diagram **(a)** and the graph of $y = (x - 2)^2$ is shown in diagram **(b)**.

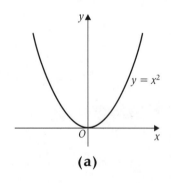

**(a)**

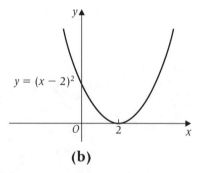

**(b)**

The vertex of $y = (x - 2)^2$ is at $(2, 0)$, whereas the vertex of $y = x^2$ is at the origin $(0, 0)$. A translation by the vector $\begin{bmatrix} 2 \\ 0 \end{bmatrix}$ moves the vertex of parabola **(a)** to the vertex of parabola **(b)**. In fact every point on $y = x^2$ is mapped onto the corresponding point on $y = (x - 2)^2$ by a translation through $\begin{bmatrix} 2 \\ 0 \end{bmatrix}$.

Similarly a translation with vector $\begin{bmatrix} -3 \\ 0 \end{bmatrix}$ maps the parabola
$y = x^2$ onto the new parabola $y = (x + 3)^2$.

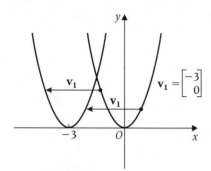

Similarly, if a translation of $\begin{bmatrix} 5 \\ 0 \end{bmatrix}$ is applied to the graph of $y = x^3$,
the new curve has equation $y = (x - 5)^3$.

Sketch the curves on your graphics calculator or on graph plotting software.

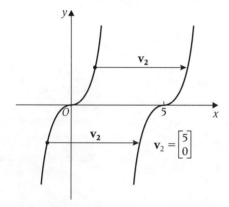

In general, a translation of $\begin{bmatrix} a \\ 0 \end{bmatrix}$ transforms the graph of
$y = f(x)$ into the graph of $y = f(x - a)$.

## Worked example 12.1

The graph of $y = (x - 5)^4$ is translated by $\begin{bmatrix} -4 \\ 0 \end{bmatrix}$. Find the
equation of the new graph.

## Solution

Replace the variable $x$ by $x - (-4) = x + 4$

New graph has equation $y = (\{x + 4\} - 5)^4 = (x - 1)^4$.

Use the result from the box above.

12

## 12.2 General translations of graphs

Where is the vertex of the parabola with equation
$y = (x - 4)^2 + 5$?

From what you discovered in Chapter 7, the vertex
is at $(4, 5)$.

In order to draw its graph you could draw the graph

of $y = x^2$ and translate it through the vector $\begin{bmatrix} 4 \\ 5 \end{bmatrix}$.

The reason for this is seen if you rearrange the equation
in the form $y - 5 = (x - 4)^2$.

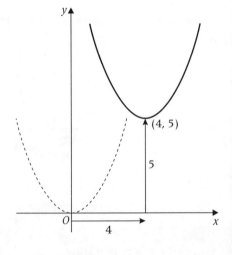

> In general, a translation of $\begin{bmatrix} a \\ b \end{bmatrix}$ transforms the graph of
> $y = f(x)$ into the graph of $y - b = f(x - a)$.

### EXERCISE 12A

**1** The second graph has been transformed from the first by a
translation. State the vector of the translation in each case.

   **(a)** **(i)** $y = x^2$,            **(ii)** $y = (x - 7)^2$,

   **(b)** **(i)** $y = x^2$,            **(ii)** $y = (x + 1)^2$,

   **(c)** **(i)** $y = x^5$,            **(ii)** $y = (x - 6)^5$,

   **(d)** **(i)** $y = x^7$,            **(ii)** $y = (x + 2)^7$,

   **(e)** **(i)** $y = x^2$,            **(ii)** $y - 5 = (x - 1)^2$,

   **(f)** **(i)** $y = x^2$,            **(ii)** $y = 3 + (x + 2)^2$,

   **(g)** **(i)** $y = x^5$,            **(ii)** $y = (x - 1)^5 - 7$,

   **(h)** **(i)** $y = x^4$,            **(ii)** $y = 3 + (x + 8)^4$.

> A useful strategy is to find the
> point on the second graph that
> corresponds to the origin in the
> first graph.
>
> If you need to, sketch the graphs
> on your graphics calculator.

**2** Find the equation of the graph after it has been translated by
the vector given in each case.

   **(a)** $y = x$, $\begin{bmatrix} 4 \\ 0 \end{bmatrix}$,    **(b)** $y = x$, $\begin{bmatrix} 0 \\ 3 \end{bmatrix}$,    **(c)** $y = x$, $\begin{bmatrix} 2 \\ 5 \end{bmatrix}$,

   **(d)** $y = x^2$, $\begin{bmatrix} -1 \\ -1 \end{bmatrix}$,    **(e)** $y = x^3$, $\begin{bmatrix} 3 \\ 2 \end{bmatrix}$,    **(f)** $y = x^5$, $\begin{bmatrix} -1 \\ -3 \end{bmatrix}$,

   **(g)** $y = x^7$, $\begin{bmatrix} -3 \\ -4 \end{bmatrix}$,    **(h)** $y = \sqrt{x}$, $\begin{bmatrix} 1 \\ -5 \end{bmatrix}$    **(i)** $y = \dfrac{2}{x}$, $\begin{bmatrix} 3 \\ 4 \end{bmatrix}$.

**3** The graph of $y = f(x)$ for $0 \leqslant x \leqslant 3$ is sketched below and $f(x) = 0$ for $x < 0$ and for $x > 3$.

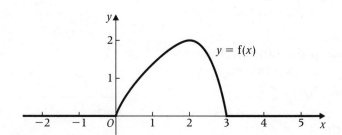

On separate sets of axes, sketch the graph of:

**(a)** $y = f(x - 1)$,      **(b)** $y = f(x + 2)$,

**(c)** $y - 3 = f(x + 2)$,      **(d)** $y = f(x - 3) + 2$,

**(e)** $y = f(x - 1) - 2$.

**4** Sketch the graph of:

**(a)** $y = \sin x$,

**(b)** $y = \sin (x - 10°)$,

**(c)** $y = \sin (x + 70°)$,

**(d)** $y = 2 + \sin (x - 30°)$.

State the transformation that has taken place in mapping graph **(a)** onto each of graphs **(b)**, **(c)** and **(d)**.

**5** Sketch the graph of:

**(a)** $y = \cos x$,

**(b)** $y = \cos (x + 120°)$,

**(c)** $y = \cos (x - 50°)$,

**(d)** $y = \cos (x - 80°) - 3$.

State the transformation that has taken place in mapping graph **(a)** onto each of graphs **(b)**, **(c)** and **(d)**.

**6** Sketch the graph of:

**(a)** $y = \tan x$,

**(b)** $y = \tan (x + 20°)$,

**(c)** $y = \tan (x - 30°)$,

**(d)** $y = \tan (x - 30°) + 5$.

State the transformation that has taken place in mapping graph **(a)** onto each of graphs **(b)**, **(c)** and **(d)**.

**7** State all the possible values of $k$ between 0 and 1000 for which $\sin (x - k°) \equiv \cos x$.

Explain the result geometrically with reference to the graphs of $y = \sin x$ and $y = \cos x$.

12

# 12.3 Reflections

You have already discovered that the graph of an inverse function can be obtained from the graph of the original function by reflection in the line $y = x$.

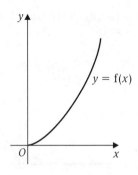

So, for instance, by reducing the domain of the function f given by $f(x) = x^2$ to $x \geqslant 0$, the function is one–one and the graph of $y = f(x)$ is shown on the right. The range is $f(x) \geqslant 0$.

The graph of the inverse function, namely $y = \sqrt{x}$, $x \geqslant 0$ is shown below and is obtained by reflection in the line $y = x$.

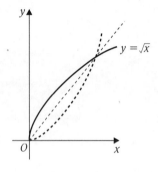

> Recall that you interchange $x$ and $y$ when finding an inverse function and this is equivalent to reflecting in the line $y = x$.

In general, the graph of $x = f(y)$ is obtained from the graph of $y = f(x)$, by reflection in the line $y = x$.

## Worked example 12.2

Sketch the graph of $y = x^3$.
Hence sketch the graph of $y = \sqrt[3]{x}$

### Solution

The graph of $y = x^3$ is sketched below.

$$y = \sqrt[3]{x} \Leftrightarrow y^3 = x$$

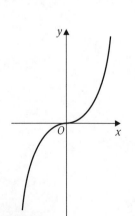

> Draw the line $y = x$ and reflect original curve in this line to obtain graph of $y = \sqrt[3]{x}$

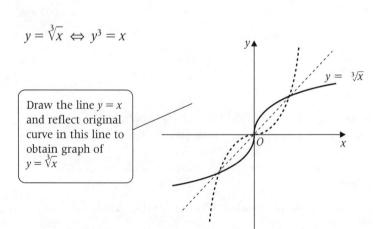

## Worked example 12.3

Draw the graphs of $y = x^4$ and $y = -x^4$ on the same axes and state a transformation that maps one graph onto the other.

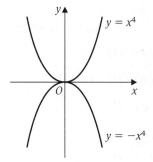

## Solution

Each graph is mapped onto the other graph by a reflection in the line $y = 0$ (or the $x$-axis).

## Worked example 12.4

Draw the graphs of $y = x^2$ and $y = 4 - x^2$ on the same axes and state a transformation that maps one graph onto the other.

## Solution

Each graph is mapped onto the other graph by a reflection in the line $y = 2$.

> In general, the graph of $y = f(x)$ is transformed into the graph of $y = 2b - f(x)$ by a reflection in the line $y = b$.

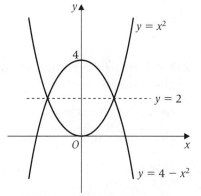

## Worked example 12.5

Draw the graphs of $y = x^3$ and $y = (6 - x)^3$ on the same axes and state a transformation that maps one graph onto the other.

You may need to use your graphics calculator to obtain these graphs.

## Solution

Each graph is mapped onto the other graph by a reflection in the line $x = 3$.

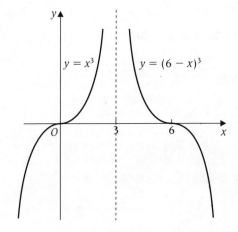

> In general, the graph of $y = f(x)$ is transformed into the graph of $y = f(2a - x)$ by a reflection in the line $x = a$.

12

## EXERCISE 12B

1 Describe the transformation that has taken place in mapping the first graph onto the second in each case:

You may need to sketch some of the graphs, but hopefully you can describe some of the transformations without doing so.

(a) (i) $y = x^2$,      (ii) $y = 2 - x^2$,

(b) (i) $y = x^2$,      (ii) $y = 2 + x^2$,

(c) (i) $y = x^5$,      (ii) $y = (4 - x)^5$,

(d) (i) $y = x^7$,      (ii) $y = (-2 - x)^7$,

(e) (i) $y = x^5$,      (ii) $y = x^{\frac{1}{5}}$,

(f) (i) $y = x^2$,      (ii) $y = 8 - x^2$,

(g) (i) $y = x^5$,      (ii) $y = (2 - x)^5$,

(h) (i) $y = x^4$,      (ii) $y = 10 - x^4$.

2 Find the new equation in each case after it has undergone the given transformation:

(a) $y = x$, reflection in the line $y = 2$,

(b) $y = x^5$, reflection in the line $x = 1$,

(c) $y = x^4$, translation with vector $\begin{bmatrix} 1 \\ 2 \end{bmatrix}$,

(d) $y = x^7$, reflection in the line $y = x$,

(e) $y = x + 3$, reflection in the line $y = 1$,

(f) $y = x^5 + x$, reflection in the line $x = 3$,

(g) $y = (x - 3)^5$, translation with vector $\begin{bmatrix} -3 \\ 4 \end{bmatrix}$,

(h) $y = x^3 - 2x + 2$, reflection in the line $y = 1$.

3 Describe the transformation that maps the graph of $y = \sin x$ onto:

(a) $y = \sin(40° - x)$,

(b) $y = \sin(90° - x)$,

(c) $y = 2 - \sin x$.

4 Describe the transformation that maps the graph of $y = \cos x$ onto:

(a) $y = \cos(120° - x)$,

(b) $y = 2 + \cos x$,

(c) $y = 6 - \cos x$.

# 12.4 One-way and two-way stretches

The graph of $y = 5x^2$ is similar to the graph of $y = x^2$, but each $y$-coordinate corresponding to a given $x$ value is five times as large. The transformation mapping $y = x^2$ onto $y = 5x^2$ is a **one-way stretch** with scale factor 5 in the $y$-direction.

## Worked example 12.6

Draw the graphs $y = x^3$ and $y = \left(\dfrac{x}{2}\right)^3$ on the same axes and state a transformation that maps the first graph onto the second.

## Solution

As you consider the graphs, you can see that in the $x$-direction, the second graph is stretched 2 times as much as the first graph.

A rearrangement of the equation in the form $x = 2\sqrt[3]{y}$ perhaps makes this clearer.

The transformation is a one-way stretch of scale factor 2 in the $x$-direction.

**Note**. Because $y = \left(\dfrac{x}{2}\right)^3 = \dfrac{x^3}{8} = \dfrac{1}{8}x^3$

You could also describe this as a one-way stretch with scale factor $\dfrac{1}{8}$ in the $y$-direction.

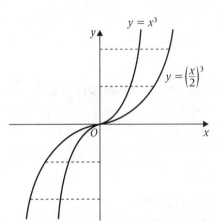

Sometimes, the stretch is two-way as illustrated in the next example.

## Worked example 12.7

Find the equation of the curve that is the result of transforming the graph of $y = x^5$ by a factor 3 in the $x$-direction and a factor 4 in the $y$-direction.

It is common to use the term 'factor 3' instead of 'scale factor 3'.

## Solution

Rearranging the equation in the form $x = \sqrt[5]{y}$ helps you to see that a stretch of factor 3 in the $x$-direction would have equation

$$x = 3y^{\frac{1}{5}} \text{ or } y = \left(\frac{x}{3}\right)^5.$$

Including a stretch in the $y$-direction of scale factor 4 would give

$$y = 4\left(\frac{x}{3}\right)^5.$$

In general, the graph of $y = f(x)$ is transformed into the graph of $y = d\, f\left(\dfrac{x}{c}\right)$ by a stretch of scale factor $c$ in the $x$-direction and a stretch of scale factor $d$ in the $y$-direction.

12

## Enlargements

When a two-way stretch has the same scale factor, $k$, in both the $x$- and $y$-directions, the transformation is an **enlargement** with scale factor $k$, centre the origin. It is called an enlargement, even when $0 < k < 1$, so that there is actually a reduction in size. The value of $k$ may also be negative.

# 12.5  Composite transformations

When the simple transformations described in the previous sections are performed successively on a graph, the transformation is said to be **composite** and, in general, the order in which the transformations are applied is important.

## *Worked example 12.8*

The graph of $y = x^5$ is reflected in the line $y = 3$ and is then reflected in the line $y = 1$. Find the equation of the resulting curve and describe geometrically the single transformation which maps $y = x^5$ onto this new curve.

## Solution

After reflection in $y = 3$, the curve has equation $y = 6 - x^5$.

Now performing the reflection in $y = 1$ gives

$$y = 2 - (6 - x^5)$$

or    $y = x^5 - 4$.

The single transformation mapping $y = x^5$ onto $y = x^5 - 4$ is

a translation of $\begin{bmatrix} 0 \\ -4 \end{bmatrix}$.

> Reflection in $y = 3$ maps $y = f(x)$ onto $y = 6 - f(x)$.

**Note**. If you had not done the transformations in this order you would have obtained the graph with equation $y = x^5 + 4$ where the graph has been translated 4 units in the positive $y$-direction.

## *Worked example 12.9*

The graph of $y = x^3$ is reflected in the line $x = 2$, and then a two-way stretch with scale factor 3 in the $x$-direction and factor 27 in the $y$-direction is applied. Find the equation of the resulting curve.

## Solution

After reflection in $x = 2$, curve has equation

$$y = (4 - x)^3.$$

> Reflection in $x = 2$ takes $y = f(x)$ to $y = f(4 - x)$.

Two way stretch produces the new curve

$$y = 27 \times \left(4 - \frac{x}{3}\right)^3$$

or $\quad y = (12 - x)^3$

## Half-turns

The composite transformation of a reflection in the line $x = a$ and a reflection in the line $y = b$ is a half-turn about the point $(a, b)$, irrespective of the order in which the reflections take place.

Reflecting $y = f(x)$ in the line $x = a$ gives $y = f(2a - x)$. Now reflecting $y = g(x)$ in the line $y = b$ gives $y = 2b - g(x)$. Therefore reflecting $y = f(2a - x)$ in the line $y = b$ gives $y = 2b - f(2a - x)$.

> As a special case, the curve $y = f(x)$ is mapped onto the curve $y = -f(-x)$ by a half-turn about the origin.

## *EXERCISE 12C*

**1** Each of the following transformations of the first curve onto the second can be produced by a one-way stretch. State the value of the scale factor when the stretch is:

      **(i)** parallel to the *x*-axis,   **(ii)** parallel to the y-axis.

**(a)** $y = x^2, y = 4x^2,$          **(b)** $y = x^3, y = 8x^3,$

**(c)** $y = x^2, y = \dfrac{9}{16}x^2,$     **(d)** $y = \sqrt{x}, y = \sqrt{3x}.$

**2** Describe the sequence of transformations that maps the curve $y = \sin x$ onto:

**(a)** $y = 3 \sin (x - 30°),$     **(b)** $y = 2 + \sin 3x,$

**(c)** $y = 4 - \sin 5x,$         **(d)** $y = 5 \sin (40° - x).$

**3** Describe the sequence of transformations that maps the curve $y = \cos 2x$ onto:

**(a)** $y = 5 \cos (2x - 30°),$     **(b)** $y = 7 + \cos 3x,$

**(c)** $y = 1 - \cos 4x,$         **(d)** $y = 3 \cos (40° - 2x).$

**12**

**4** Find the equation of the curve which results from transforming the graph of $y = x^2$ by:

    **(a)** reflection in $x = 2$ followed by a stretch in the $y$-direction of factor 5,

    **(b)** reflection in $y = 1$ followed by a stretch in the $x$-direction of factor 2,

    **(c)** a stretch in the $x$-direction of factor $\dfrac{1}{2}$ followed by a reflection in the line $x = 4$,

    **(d)** a stretch in the $y$-direction of factor 3 followed by a reflection in the line $x = -2$,

    **(e)** a reflection in the line $x = 1$ followed by a translation of $\begin{bmatrix} 2 \\ 3 \end{bmatrix}$.

**5** Find the equation of the curve obtained from transforming the graph of $y = x^3$ by:

    **(a)** reflection in $x = 2$ followed by a reflection in $y = 1$,

    **(b)** a half turn about the point $(3, 5)$,

    **(c)** a stretch in the $x$-direction of factor $\dfrac{1}{2}$ followed by a reflection in the line $x = 4$,

    **(d)** a stretch in the $y$-direction of factor 3 followed by a reflection in the line $x = -2$.

    **(e)** a reflection in the line $y = x$, followed by a reflection in the line $x = 1$.

## 12.6 Periodic functions

In the chapter on trigonometry, you were introduced to the term **periodic function** in relation to the sine and cosine functions.

> In general, the function f is said to have period $p$, when $p$ is the smallest positive number such that
>
> $f(x+p) = f(x)$ for all values of $x$.

Consider the graphs of the periodic functions f and g.

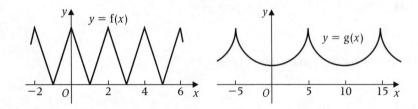

The period of f is 2 and the period of g is 10.

# 12.7 Odd and even functions

## *Worked example 12.10*

A definition of odd and even functions was given in section 5.7 of chapter 5.

You are given the following periodic functions

(a) $f : x \mapsto \sin 3x$,     (b) $g : x \mapsto \cos 5x$     (c) $h : x \mapsto \tan 2x$.

For each function

(i) sketch the graph for $-180° \leqslant x \leqslant 180°$,

(ii) state its period,

(iii) determine whether it is an odd or even function.

Use your graphics calculator to confirm the following sketches.

## *Solution*

(a) (ii) From the sketch, the period is
$$360° \div 3 = 120°.$$

(iii) the graph has half-turn symmetry about the origin. This means that $\sin 3x$ is an odd function.

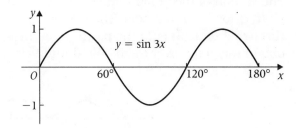

(b) (ii) From the sketch, the period is
$$360° \div 5 = 72°.$$

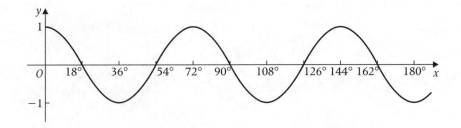

(iii) the graph has reflective symmetry in the *y*-axis. This means that $\cos 5x$ is an even function.

(c) (ii) From the sketch, the period is
$$180° \div 2 = 90°.$$

(iii) the graph has rotational symmetry of order 2 about the origin. This means that $\tan 2x$ is an odd function.

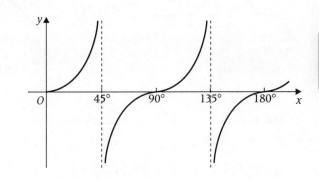

12

## Worked example 12.11

The function f is defined by $f(x) = \dfrac{1}{2}x$ for $0 \leqslant x \leqslant 2$.

The function is even and periodic with period 4.
Sketch the graph of $y = f(x)$ for $-4 \leqslant x \leqslant 8$.

## Solution

For $0 \leqslant x \leqslant 2$, the graph is a straight line with gradient $\dfrac{1}{2}$.

By reflecting in the *y*-axis, the portion of the graph for $-2 \leqslant x \leqslant 0$ can be obtained, because f is an even function.

The section of the graph for $-2 \leqslant x \leqslant 2$ must be the graph of $y = f(x)$ for one full period. The graph can now be translated through 4 units in both the positive and negative *x*-directions to obtain the graph over the required interval.

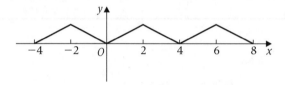

### EXERCISE 12D

**1** State the period of each of the functions sketched below.

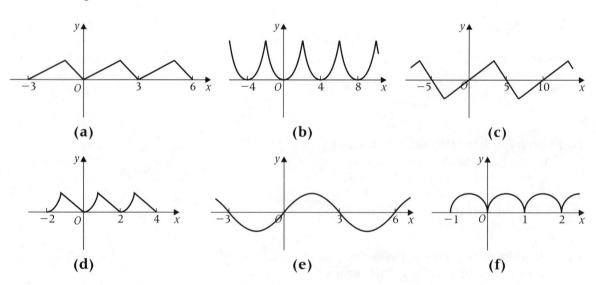

| (a) | (b) | (c) |
|---|---|---|

| (d) | (e) | (f) |
|---|---|---|

**2** The function f is periodic with period 2 and is defined by:

$$f(x) = x^2 \text{ for } -1 \leqslant x \leqslant 1.$$

Sketch the graph of $y = f(x)$ for $-3 \leqslant x \leqslant 7$.

**3** Find the period, in degrees, of each of the following graphs:

    **(a)** $y = \sin 6x,$     **(b)** $y = \sin \frac{1}{4}x,$     **(c)** $y = \cos 15x,$

    **(d)** $y = \cos \frac{3}{4}x,$     **(e)** $y = \sin (3x - 40°),$     **(f)** $y = \cos (5x - 100°),$

    **(g)** $y = \tan 4x.$

**4** The graph of $y = g(x)$ is sketched for $-2 \leqslant x \leqslant 0$. Given that g is an odd function with period 4, sketch the graph of $y = g(x)$ for $-4 \leqslant x \leqslant 6$.

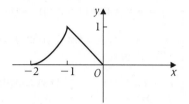

**5** The function h is defined by $h(x) = \sin x$ for $0° \leqslant x \leqslant 90°$. Given that h is an even function with period 180°, sketch the graph of $y = h(x)$ for $-360° \leqslant x \leqslant 360°$.

**6** The voltage $V$ volts in a component of an electric circuit at time $t$ seconds after the current is switched on satisfies the formula

$$V(t) = \begin{cases} t^2 + 1, & 0 \leqslant t \leqslant 1 \\ 3 - t, & 1 < t \leqslant 2. \end{cases}$$

    **(a)** Sketch the graph of $V$ against $t$ for $0 \leqslant t \leqslant 2$.

    **(b)** Given that $V(t)$ is periodic with period 2 seconds, sketch the graph of $V$ for $2 \leqslant t \leqslant 6$ and find the values of

        **(i)** $V(2.5),$     **(ii)** $V(5.8).$         [A]

**7** The function f is defined for $0 \leqslant x \leqslant 2$ by

$$f(x) = \begin{cases} x + 2, & 0 \leqslant x \leqslant 1 \\ 4 - x^2, & 1 < x \leqslant 2. \end{cases}$$

    **(a)** Sketch the graph of $y = f(x)$ for $0 \leqslant x \leqslant 2$.

    **(b)** Given that f is an even function, sketch the graph of $y = f(x)$ for $-2 \leqslant x \leqslant 2$.

    **(c)** Given that f is periodic with period 4, sketch the graph of $y = f(x)$ for $-6 \leqslant x \leqslant 6$ and find the values of

        **(i)** $f(2.5),$     **(ii)** $f(-2.5),$     **(iii)** $f(3.5).$

## Key point summary

**1** A translation of $\begin{bmatrix} a \\ 0 \end{bmatrix}$ transforms the graph of     *p201*
    $y = f(x)$ into the graph of $y = f(x - a)$.

**2** A translation of $\begin{bmatrix} a \\ b \end{bmatrix}$ transforms the graph of     *p204*
    $y = f(x)$ into the graph of $y - b = f(x - a)$.

**3** The graph of $x = f(y)$ is obtained from the graph     *p204*
    of $y = f(x)$, by reflection in the line $y = x$.

**4** The graph of $y = f(x)$ is transformed into the graph     *p205*
    of $y = 2b - f(x)$ by a reflection in the line $y = b$.

**12**

**5** The graph of $y = f(x)$ is transformed into the graph of $y = f(2a - x)$ by a reflection in the line $x = a$.  *p205*

**6** The graph of $y = f(x)$ is transformed into the graph of $y = d\,f\!\left(\dfrac{x}{c}\right)$ by a stretch of scale factor $c$ in the $x$-direction and a stretch of scale factor $d$ in the $y$-direction.  *p207*

**7** The curve $y = f(x)$ is mapped onto the curve $y = -f(-x)$ by a half-turn about the origin.  *p209*

**8** The function f is periodic when  *p210*
$$f(x + p) = f(x)$$
for all values of $x$. When $p$ is the smallest positive number satisfying this relation, the period is $p$.

| Test yourself | What to review |
|---|---|
| **1** Find the equation of the curve resulting from translating the graph of $y = x^7$ through $\begin{bmatrix} 2 \\ -1 \end{bmatrix}$. | *Section 12.2* |
| **2** Determine the transformation that maps $y = x^3$ onto $y = 6 - x^3$. | *Section 12.3* |
| **3** The graph of $y = x^3$ can be mapped onto the graph of $y = 8x^3$ by means of a one-way stretch. State the scale factor of the stretch when it is parallel to the **(a)** $y$-axis, **(b)** $x$-axis. | *Section 12.4* |
| **4** Describe the sequence of transformations that maps the curve $y = \sin x$ onto $y = 5\sin(20° - x)$. | *Section 12.5* |
| **5** The function f is defined by $f(x) = x$ for $0 \leqslant x \leqslant 3$. Given that f is even and periodic with period 6, sketch the graph for $0 \leqslant x \leqslant 12$. | *Section 12.6* |

**Test yourself   ANSWERS**

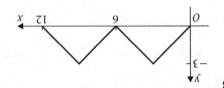

**5**

**4** Reflection in $x = 10°$ followed by a stretch in the $y$-direction scale factor 5.

**3** (a) 8, (b) $\dfrac{1}{2}$.

**2** Reflection in the line $y = 3$.

**1** $y = (x - 2)^7 - 1$

# CHAPTER 13

# Sequences and series

---

## Learning objectives

After studying this chapter, you should be able to:
- generate sequences using formulae or inductive definitions
- understand the difference between sequences and series
- understand what is meant by an arithmetic series
- find the $n$th term and the sum of the first $n$ terms of an arithmetic series
- find the sum of the first $n$ natural numbers
- use formulae for the sum of the squares and cubes of the first $n$ natural numbers.

---

## 13.1 Sequences

Probably from an early age you will have been presented with puzzles such as the following.

Find the next term in each of the following

   **(a)**  1, 8, 27, 64, _____

   **(b)**  0, 3, 8, 15, _____

> These patterns of numbers, separated by commas, are called **sequences**.

Provided you could justify your answer, you could insert almost any number in the missing space.

For instance, although most people might argue that 125 is *the* answer to puzzle sequence **(a)** above, you might have been using the formula

$$n^3 + 7(n-1)(n-2)(n-3)(n-4)$$

to generate the terms 1, 8, 27, 64 in which case substituting $n = 5$ gives 293.

No doubt you can invent many more formulae which would give a different value for the 5th term.

> Try to make up some formulae which would lead to an answer different from **24** for the missing term in sequence **(b)** above.

## 13.2 Suffix notation

> The most common notation for the terms of a sequence is the suffix notation.
>
> The first term is often written as $t_1$, the second term $t_2$, the third $t_3$ and so on, with the $n$th term being $t_n$.

This is very similar to function notation, so that if

$$t_n = n^2 + 1$$

then $t_1 = 1^2 + 1 = 2$,  $t_2 = 2^2 + 1 = 5$, etc.

A sequence can be thought of as a function with domain consisting of a subset of the set of natural numbers

$$\mathbb{N} = \{1, 2, 3, 4, \ldots\}.$$

Any letter with suffices can be used to represent the terms of a sequence, but the most common letter used is $u$ and the terms of the sequence are $u_1, u_2, u_3, \ldots$

> Rather like $f(n) = n^2 + 1$, so that $f(1) = 1^2 + 1 = 2$ and $f(2) = 2^2 + 1 = 5$.

### *Worked example 13.1*

Given that $u_n = n(n + 2)$, find $u_3$ and $u_5$.

Find an expression for $u_n - u_{n-1}$ and simplify your answer.

### *Solution*

$u_3 = 3(3 + 2) = 15$, $u_5 = 5(5 + 2) = 35$

To find $u_{n-1}$ it is necessary to replace $n$ by $n - 1$ in the formula.

$$u_{n-1} = (n - 1)(n - 1 + 2) = (n - 1)(n + 1) = n^2 - 1.$$

$$u_n = n(n + 2) = n^2 + 2n$$

Hence $u_n - u_{n-1} = n^2 + 2n - (n^2 - 1) = 2n + 1$.

> Substituting $n = 3$, $n = 5$ in turn into the formula for $u_n$.

## 13.3 Inductive definition

> The previous worked example showed that
> $u_n - u_{n-1} = 2n + 1$.
>
> This can be rewritten as $u_n = u_{n-1} + 2n + 1$.

Provided you know the first term, and in this case $u_1 = 3$, it is now possible to find all the terms in the sequence.

$$u_1 = 3 \Rightarrow u_2 = u_1 + 2 \times 2 + 1 = 3 + 4 + 1 = 8$$

$$u_2 = 8 \Rightarrow u_3 = u_2 + 2 \times 3 + 1 = 8 + 6 + 1 = 15$$

> Continue this process and verify that $u_5 = 35$.

This agrees with the answer for $u_3$ in Worked example 13.1 when you were given the formula.

The **inductive definition** for this sequence is

$$u_1 = 3, \quad u_n = u_{n-1} + 2n + 1.$$

Notice you need two things: the first term and an expression relating one term to the previous term.

## Worked example 13.2

Find the first four terms of the sequence defined inductively by $u_1 = 2, u_n = u_{n-1} + 3n^2$.

## Solution

$u_1 = 2 \Rightarrow u_2 = u_1 + 3 \times 2^2 = 2 + 12 = 14$

$u_2 = 14 \Rightarrow u_3 = u_2 + 3 \times 3^2 = 14 + 27 = 41$

$u_3 = 41 \Rightarrow u_4 = u_3 + 3 \times 4^2 = 41 + 48 = 89$

The first four terms are 2, 14, 41, 89

You can produce sequences of this type very easily on a spreadsheet.

| | A | B |
|---|---|---|
| 1 | 1 | 2 |
| 2 | 2 | 14 |
| 3 | 3 | 41 |
| 4 | 4 | 89 |
| 5 | 5 | 164 |
| 6 | 6 | 272 |
| 7 | 7 | 419 |
| 8 | 8 | 611 |
| 9 | 9 | 854 |
| 10 | 10 | 1154 |

| | A | B |
|---|---|---|
| 1 | 1 | 2 |
| 2 | =A1+1 | =B1+3*A2^2 |
| 3 | =A2+1 | =B2+3*A3^2 |
| 4 | =A3+1 | =B3+3*A4^2 |
| 5 | =A4+1 | =B4+3*A5^2 |
| 6 | =A5+1 | =B5+3*A6^2 |
| 7 | =A6+1 | =B6+3*A7^2 |
| 8 | =A7+1 | =B7+3*A8^2 |
| 9 | =A8+1 | =B8+3*A9^2 |
| 10 | =A9+1 | =B9+3*A10^2 |

## EXERCISE 13A

**1** Use the formula $s_n = n^2$, to find $s_1$, $s_2$ and $s_3$.

**2** Use the formula $t_n = 3^n - 1$, to find $t_1$, $t_3$ and $t_5$.

**3** Write down the first five terms of each of the following sequences:

**(a)** $u_n = 2n + 1$,    **(b)** $u_n = n^2 - 1$,    **(c)** $u_n = n(n-1)$,

**(d)** $u_n = n^3 + 1$,    **(e)** $u_n = 2^n$,    **(f)** $u_n = 3^n - 1$.

**13**

**4** Find the first five terms of the following sequences which are defined inductively:

**(a)** $u_1 = 4$, $u_n = u_{n-1} + 3$,  **(b)** $u_1 = 20$, $u_n = u_{n-1} - 2$,

**(c)** $u_1 = 3$, $u_n = u_{n-1} + n^2$,  **(d)** $u_1 = 2$, $u_n = u_{n-1} + 3n - 2$,

**(e)** $u_1 = 1$, $u_n = u_{n-1} + 5n^2$,  **(f)** $u_1 = 100$, $u_n = u_{n-1} - 2n^2$.

**5** For each of the following sequences, find $u_n - u_{n-1}$ simplifying your answer where possible.

**(a)** $u_n = 3n + 2$,  **(b)** $u_n = 5n - 3$,

**(c)** $u_n = 3 - 2n$,  **(d)** $u_n = n^2$,

**(e)** $u_n = n^2 - 3$,  **(f)** $u_n = 3n^2 + 2$,

**(g)** $u_n = n(3n + 1)$.

**6** Find a possible formula for the $n$th term of each of the following sequences:

**(a)** $1, 3, 5, 7, 9, \ldots$,  **(b)** $2, 4, 8, 16, 32, \ldots$,

**(c)** $6, 5, 4, 3, 2, \ldots$,  **(d)** $\dfrac{1}{2}, \dfrac{2}{3}, \dfrac{3}{4}, \dfrac{4}{5}, \ldots$

**7** Write down the first four terms of each of the following sequences and try to find a formula for $u_n$.

**(a)** $u_1 = 5$, $u_n = u_{n-1} + 2$,  **(b)** $u_1 = 40$, $u_n = u_{n-1} - 3$,

**(c)** $u_1 = 4$, $u_n = u_{n-1} + 2n - 1$, **(d)** $u_1 = 2$, $u_n = u_{n-1} + n$.

# 13.4 Arithmetic sequences

A sequence with an inductive relation of the form

$$u_n = u_{n-1} + d$$

is called an **arithmetic sequence**.

The sequence increases by a constant amount from one term to the next (or decreases by a constant amount if $d$ is negative).

The quantity $d$ is called the **common difference**.

Examples of arithmetic sequences are

$3, 7, 11, 15, \ldots$ where the common difference is 4,

$20, 17, 14, 11, \ldots$ where the common difference is $-3$.

> Sometimes an arithmetic sequence is called an **arithmetic progression**.

The first term is usually denoted by $a$ and so the full inductive definition for an arithmetic sequence is

$$u_1 = a, \ u_n = u_{n-1} + d.$$

Writing out the first few terms of the sequence gives

$$a, a + d, \ a + 2d, \ a + 3d, \ ...$$

> The tenth term, for example would be $a + 9d$.

 The $n$th term of an arithmetic sequence is $a + (n - 1)d$.

## Worked example 13.3

The third term of an arithmetic sequence is 11 and the seventh term is 23. Find the first term and the common difference.

### Solution

Let the first term be $a$ and let the common difference be $d$.

The $n$th term would be $a + (n - 1)d$.

The third term is $a + 2d$ and this must equal 11.

$$\Rightarrow a + 2d = 11. \qquad\qquad (A)$$

Similarly since the seventh term is equal to 23

$$\Rightarrow a + 6d = 23. \qquad\qquad (B)$$

Solving $A$ and $B$ simultaneously, $(B) - (A) \Rightarrow 4d = 12 \Rightarrow d = 3$.

Substituting $d = 3$ into $(A) \Rightarrow a + 6 = 11 \Rightarrow a = 5$

> Checking in (B)
> $5 + 6 \times 3 = 23.$ ✓

The first term is 5 and the common difference is 3.

# 13.5 Arithmetic series

> When the terms of a sequence are added together you produce a **series**.

Whereas 1, 4, 9, 16, ... is a sequence
$1 + 4 + 9 + 16 + ...$ is a series.

You can use the formula for the $n$th term to find the number of terms in an **arithmetic series**.

**13**

## Worked example 13.4 _____

Find the number of terms in the arithmetic series

$$13 + 17 + 21 + \ldots + 93.$$

## Solution

The formula for the $n$th term is $a + (n - 1)d$.

In this series, the first term $a = 13$
and the common difference $d = 4$

> because each term is obtained from the previous one by adding 4.

Hence $13 + (n - 1)4 = 93$

$$\Rightarrow 4(n - 1) = 80 \Rightarrow n - 1 = 20$$
$$\Rightarrow n = 21 \text{ so the series has 21 terms.}$$

## Worked example 13.5 _____

An arithmetic series has first term 6 and common difference $2\frac{1}{2}$.
Find the least value of $n$ for which the $n$th term exceeds 1000.

## Solution

The formula for the $n$th term is $a + (n - 1)d = 6 + 2.5(n - 1)$.

You need to solve the inequality $6 + 2.5(n - 1) > 1000$

$$\Rightarrow 2.5(n - 1) > 994$$
$$\Rightarrow (n - 1) > \frac{994}{2.5} \Rightarrow (n - 1) > 397.6$$
$$\Rightarrow n > 398.6$$

Since $n$ must be a whole number, the number of terms must be at least 399 for the $n$th term to exceed 1000.

# 13.6 Sum of the first $n$ natural numbers

In 1786 Carl Friedrich Gauss living in Brunswick Germany was just 9 years old. His teacher wanted to keep the class occupied and asked them to calculate the sum $1 + 2 + 3 + \ldots + 100$. The teacher had barely finished explaining the assignment when Gauss wrote the single number 5050 on his slate and deposited it on the teacher's desk. How did he get the answer so quickly?

He realised that you could pair off numbers from the beginning and end, $1 + 100$, $2 + 99$, $3 + 98$ and so on. Each pair sums to 101 and there are 50 pairs. The total is $50 \times 101 = 5050$.

This method can be extended to find the sum of

$$1 + 2 + 3 + 4 + \ldots + n, \text{ where } n \text{ is any positive integer.}$$

Let $S = 1 + 2 + 3 + 4 + \ldots + n$

and writing in reverse order

$$S = n + (n - 1) + (n - 2) + (n - 3) + \ldots + 1$$

Adding the two series together as pairs

$$2S = [n + 1] + [(n - 1) + 2] + [(n - 2) + 3] + [(n - 3) + 4] + \ldots [n + 1]$$

But the total inside each square bracket is $n + 1$ and there are $n$ terms in square brackets.

$$\Rightarrow 2S = n(n + 1)$$

$$\Rightarrow S = \frac{1}{2}n(n + 1)$$

The sum of the first $n$ natural numbers is $\frac{1}{2}n(n + 1)$

Use this formula to check that the sum $1 + 2 + 3 \ldots + 100 = 5050$.

## Worked example 13.6

Find the sum of all the positive integers from 1000 to 2000 inclusive.

## Solution

You can find the sum from 1 to 2000 and subtract the sum from 1 to 999 using the given formula.

$$1 + 2 + 3 + \ldots + 2000 = \frac{1}{2} \times 2000 \times 2001 = 2\,001\,000$$

$$1 + 2 + 3 + \ldots + 999 = \frac{1}{2} \times 999 \times 1000 = 499\,500$$

Hence

$$1000 + 1001 + 1002 + \ldots + 2000 = 2\,001\,000 - 499\,500 = 1\,501\,500$$

## EXERCISE 13B

**1** Calculate the sum of the first **(a)** 10, **(b)** 20, **(c)** 70 natural numbers.

**2** Determine the sum of the series:

    **(a)** $20 + 21 + 22 + \ldots + 100$,

    **(b)** $100 + 101 + 102 + \ldots + 1000$,

    **(c)** $201 + 202 + 203 + \ldots + 400$,

    **(d)** $97 + 98 + 99 + \ldots + 700$.

13

3 The first term of an arithmetic sequence is 17 and the common difference is 5.
Find **(a)** the third, **(b)** the seventh, **(c)** the twenty-fifth term.

4 The second term of an arithmetic sequence is 12 and the common difference is 9.
Find **(a)** the first, **(b)** the tenth, **(c)** the twenty-first term.

5 The first term of an arithmetic sequence is 9 and the common difference is 7. Find the value of $n$ if the $n$th term is 380.

6 The 17th term of an arithmetic sequence is 50 and the first term is 2. Find the common difference.

7 Find the first term of an arithmetic sequence with common difference 6 and tenth term equal to 50.

8 The fifth term of an arithmetic sequence is 10 and the eighth term is 19. Find the first term and the common difference.

9 The twelfth term of an arithmetic sequence is 60 and the sixteenth term is 70. Find the first term and the common difference.

10 The sixth term of an arithmetic sequence is equal to twice the fourth term and the tenth term is equal to 48. Find the first term and the common difference.

11 The first term of an arithmetic series is 8 and the common difference is 13. Find the value of $n$ for which the $n$th term first exceeds 1000.

12 The first term of an arithmetic series is $-3$ and the common difference is 7. Find the value of $n$ for which the $n$th term first exceeds 650.

# 13.7 Sum of the first $n$ terms of an arithmetic series

Let $S_n$ represent the sum of the first $n$ terms of an arithmetic series with first term $a$ and common difference $d$.

It is sometimes convenient to represent the $n$th term or last term of the series by $l$, so that $l = a + (n - 1)d$.

Using a method similar to that in the last section

$$S_n = a + (a + d) + (a + 2d) + (a + 3d) + \ldots + (l - d) + l.$$
$$S_n = l + (l - d) + (l - 2d) + (l - 3d) + \ldots + (a + d) + a.$$

> Writing the terms in reverse order.

Adding the two equations gives

$$2S_n = [a + l] + [(a + d) + (l - d)] + [(a + 2d) + (l - 2d)] + \ldots + [a + l].$$

Each of the square brackets has value $a + l$ and there are $n$ terms so $2S_n = n(a + l)$.

> The sum of the first $n$ terms of an arithmetic series with first term $a$ and last term $l$ is $\frac{1}{2}n(a + l)$.

## Worked example 13.7

Find the sum of the arithmetic series $23 + 26 + 29 + \ldots + 113$.

### Solution

You know that $a = 23$ and that $l = 113$.

You need to find $n$ but the formula for the $n$th term is $a + (n - 1)d$.

Therefore, since $d = 3$, you can write
$$23 + 3(n - 1) = 113 \Rightarrow 3(n - 1) = 90 \Rightarrow (n - 1) = 30 \Rightarrow n = 31.$$

The sum is equal to

$$\frac{1}{2}n(a + l) = \frac{1}{2} \times 31 \times (23 + 113) = 31 \times 68 = 2108$$

## Alternative formula for $S_n$

An alternative formulae may be used for $S_n = \frac{1}{2}n(a + l)$.

Since $l = a + (n - 1)d \Rightarrow a + l = 2a + (n - 1)d$.

> The sum of the first $n$ terms of an arithmetic series with first term $a$, common difference $d$ is $\frac{1}{2}n[2a + (n - 1)d]$.

## Worked example 13.8

The sum of the first 25 terms of an arithmetic series is 500. The tenth term of the series is 19. Find the first term and the common difference.

### Solution

Let the first term be $a$ and the common difference $d$.

$$\frac{25}{2}(2a + 24d) = 500$$

$$a + 12d = 20 \qquad (A)$$

Tenth term is $19 \Rightarrow a + 9d = 19 \qquad (B)$

> Using $S_n = \frac{1}{2}n[2a + (n - 1)d]$.

**13**

Solving the simultaneous equations $(A) - (B)$ gives

$$3d = 1$$

$$\Rightarrow d = \frac{1}{3}$$

substituting into $(A)$ gives $a + 4 = 20 \Rightarrow a = 16$

Therefore the first term is 16 and the common difference is $\frac{1}{3}$.

## EXERCISE 13C

1 Find the sum of the 20 terms of the arithmetic series with first term 3 and last term 17. Find also the common difference of this series.

2 The first term of an arithmetic series is 6 and the common difference is 5. Find the sum of the first **(a)** ten, **(b)** twenty terms of this series.

3 The twentieth term of an arithmetic series is 50. The sum of the first 20 terms is 200. Find the first term of the series.

4 The sum of the first 30 terms of an arithmetic series with first term 7 is equal to 450. Find the thirtieth term.

5 Find the sum of the following arithmetic series:
   **(a)** $3 + 5 + 7 + 9 + \ldots + 47$,
   **(b)** $22 + 26 + 30 + \ldots + 422$,
   **(c)** $17 + 20 + 23 + \ldots + 167$,
   **(d)** $41 + 38 + 35 + \ldots + (-19)$,
   **(e)** $123 + 107 + 91 + \ldots + (-197)$.

6 Using the formula for the sum of the first $N$ positive integers, write down a formula for $1 + 2 + 3 + 4 + 5 + \ldots + (n - 1)$.

   Hence, by rewriting

   $S_n = a + [a + d] + [a + 2d] + \ldots + [a + (n - 1)d]$ in the form
   $S_n = a + a + \ldots + a + d[1 + 2 + 3 + \ldots + (n - 1)]$,

   prove that $S_n = \frac{1}{2}n[2a + (n - 1)d]$.

# 13.8 Sigma notation

A shorthand notation for finding sums is to use the Greek capital letter sigma, $\Sigma$. This is particularly useful in statistics where there are lots of data values to be added together.

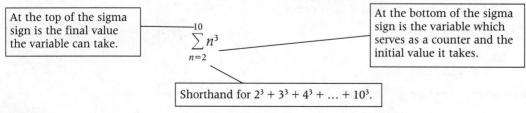

At the top of the sigma sign is the final value the variable can take.

At the bottom of the sigma sign is the variable which serves as a counter and the initial value it takes.

$$\sum_{n=2}^{10} n^3$$

Shorthand for $2^3 + 3^3 + 4^3 + \ldots + 10^3$.

## Worked example 13.9

Write each of the following in full and hence find the value of:

**(a)** $\displaystyle\sum_{k=2}^{7} k^2$,   **(b)** $\displaystyle\sum_{r=4}^{8}(2r+1)$,   **(c)** $\displaystyle\sum_{n=1}^{4}\frac{n}{n+1}$.

## Solution

**(a)** The expression to be summed here is $k^2$.
You need to substitute $k = 2$ then $k = 3$ ... up to $k = 7$
adding the terms together.

$$\sum_{k=2}^{7} k^2 = 2^2 + 3^2 + 4^2 + 5^2 + 6^2 + 7^2$$

$$= 139$$

**(b)** This time the summation expression is $2r + 1$ with
$r$ ranging from 4 to 8.

$$\sum_{r=4}^{8}(2r+1) = 9 + 11 + 13 + 15 + 17$$

$$= 65$$

> Note that different letters may
> be used *within* the summation
> such as $k$, $r$, $n$ etc and yet the
> final answer does not involve any
> of these variables.

**(c)** Substituting $n = 1, 2, 3, 4$ and summing gives

$$\sum_{n=1}^{4}\frac{n}{n+1} = \frac{1}{2} + \frac{2}{3} + \frac{3}{4} + \frac{4}{5} = \frac{30 + 40 + 45 + 48}{60} = \frac{163}{60}$$

## Worked example 13.10

Use appropriate formulae to evaluate **(a)** $\displaystyle\sum_{k=5}^{500} k$, **(b)** $\displaystyle\sum_{r=1}^{50} 3r - 5$

## Solution

**(a)** $\displaystyle\sum_{k=5}^{500} k = 5 + 6 + 7 + ... + 500$

You can use the formula for the sum of the first $n$ natural
numbers

$$1 + 2 + 3 + ... + n = \frac{1}{2}n(n+1)$$

$$\Rightarrow 1 + 2 + 3 + ... + 500 = 250 \times 501 = 125\,250$$

$$\Rightarrow 5 + 6 + 7 + ... + 500 = 125\,250 - (1 + 2 + 3 + 4) = 125\,240$$

**(b)** $\displaystyle\sum_{r=1}^{50} 3r - 5 = -2 + 1 + 4 + ... + 145$

You should recognize this as an arithmetic series with
first term $a = -2$, common difference $d = 3$ and last
term $l = 145$.

**13**

Because the 'counter' $r$ starts at 1 and goes up in steps of 1 to 50, there are 50 terms so $n = 50$.

Using the formula for the sum of the first $n$ terms of an arithmetic series $\frac{1}{2}n(a + l)$ gives

$$25 \times (-2 + 145) = 3575$$

Again, you may find it interesting to set some of these problems up on a spreadsheet to check your answers.

### EXERCISE 13D

**1** Write each of the following in full and hence find the value of:

**(a)** $\displaystyle\sum_{k=3}^{7} k,$

**(b)** $\displaystyle\sum_{r=6}^{9} (3r - 11),$

**(c)** $\displaystyle\sum_{n=1}^{5} n^2,$

**(d)** $\displaystyle\sum_{r=4}^{7} (5r - 19),$

**(e)** $\displaystyle\sum_{k=2}^{4} k^3,$

**(f)** $\displaystyle\sum_{n=2}^{6} (n - 2)(n - 3).$

**2** Find the sum of each of the following by using appropriate formulae:

**(a)** $\displaystyle\sum_{k=13}^{100} k,$

**(b)** $\displaystyle\sum_{r=3}^{102} (2r - 5),$

**(c)** $\displaystyle\sum_{n=11}^{299} n,$

**(d)** $\displaystyle\sum_{k=10}^{99} 2 + 3k,$

**(e)** $\displaystyle\sum_{r=13}^{122} 2r,$

**(f)** $\displaystyle\sum_{n=10}^{509} 4n - 37.$

## 13.9 Sums of squares and cubes

You have already seen that $1 + 2 + 3 + 4 + \ldots + n = \frac{1}{2}n(n + 1)$ which can be written in sigma notation as

$$\sum_{r=1}^{n} r = \frac{1}{2}n(n + 1).$$

Of course any letter (other than $n$) could be used instead of $r$ in the summation.

There are similar formulae for the sums of the squares and cubes of the first $n$ natural numbers. The formulae will be proved in a later text but you need to be able to use these formulae in this section.

## Sums of squares

$$1^2 + 2^2 + 3^2 + 4^2 + \ldots + n^2 = \sum_{r=1}^{n} r^2 = \frac{1}{6}n(n+1)(2n+1)$$

## Sums of cubes

$$1^3 + 2^3 + 3^3 + 4^3 + \ldots + n^3 = \sum_{r=1}^{n} r^3 = \frac{1}{4}n^2(n+1)^2$$

## *Worked example 13.11*

Evaluate **(a)** $\displaystyle\sum_{r=11}^{50} r^2$, **(b)** $\displaystyle\sum_{k=100}^{200} k^3$.

## *Solution*

**(a)** $\displaystyle\sum_{r=11}^{50} r^2 = \sum_{r=1}^{50} r^2 - \sum_{r=1}^{10} r^2$

$$= \frac{1}{6} \times 50 \times 51 \times 101 - \frac{1}{6} \times 10 \times 11 \times 21$$

$$= 42\,540$$

> Now you can use the formulae above with $n = 50$ and $n = 10$.

**(b)** $\displaystyle\sum_{k=100}^{200} k^3 = \sum_{k=1}^{200} k^3 - \sum_{k=1}^{99} k^3$

$$= \frac{1}{4} \times 200^2 \times 201^2 - \frac{1}{4} \times 99^2 \times 100^2$$

$$= 379\,507\,500$$

Sometimes a combination of these formulae needs to be used.

**Note.** $\displaystyle\sum_{r=1}^{n} 1 = \underbrace{1 + 1 + 1 + \ldots + 1}_{n \text{ terms}} = n$

> A common mistake is to think this is equal to 1.

You can split up a complicated summation into separate sums,

For example,

$$\sum 3k^2 + 2k = \sum 3k^2 + \sum 2k$$

You can take a constant outside the sigma sign as a common factor so that $\sum 3k^2 + \sum 2k = 3\sum k^2 + 2\sum k$ and then you can use the standard formulae to evaluate the summation.

**13**

## Worked example 13.12 _____

Find the value of $\sum\limits_{r=1}^{25} 2r^2 - 5r + 4$.

## Solution

$$\sum_{r=1}^{25} 2r^2 - 5r + 4 = \sum_{r=1}^{25} 2r^2 - \sum_{r=1}^{25} 5r + \sum_{r=1}^{25} 4 = 2\sum_{r=1}^{25} r^2 - 5\sum_{r=1}^{25} r + 4\sum_{r=1}^{25} 1$$

$$\sum_{r=1}^{25} r^2 = \frac{1}{6} \times 25 \times 26 \times 51 = 5525;$$

$$\sum_{r=1}^{25} r = \frac{1}{2} \times 25 \times 26 = 325;$$

$$\sum_{r=1}^{25} 1 = 25$$

$$\Rightarrow \sum_{r=1}^{25} 2r^2 - 5r + 4 = 2 \times 5525 - 5 \times 325 + 4 \times 25 = 9525$$

## Worked example 13.13 _____

Find $\sum\limits_{k=1}^{n} 4k^3 - 12k$ and factorise your answer.

## Solution

$$\sum_{k=1}^{n} 4k^3 - 12k = 4\sum_{k=1}^{n} k^3 - 12\sum_{k=1}^{n} k$$

$$= 4 \times \frac{1}{4} \times n^2 \times (n+1)^2 - 12 \times \frac{1}{2} \times n \times (n+1) = n(n+1)\{n(n+1) - 6\}$$

$$= n(n+1)(n^2 + n - 6) = n(n+1)(n+3)(n-2)$$

### EXERCISE 13E _____

1 Find the value of each of the following:

(a) $\sum\limits_{r=1}^{25} r$,    (b) $\sum\limits_{r=1}^{20} r^2$,    (c) $\sum\limits_{r=1}^{40} r^3$,

(d) $\sum\limits_{r=51}^{100} r^2$,    (e) $\sum\limits_{r=101}^{130} r^3$.

**2** Evaluate

**(a)** $\sum_{k=1}^{10} k^2,$ **(b)** $\sum_{k=1}^{60} k^3,$ **(c)** $\sum_{k=16}^{30} k^2,$

**(d)** $\sum_{k=15}^{50} k^3,$ **(e)** $\sum_{k=1}^{10} 3,$ **(f)** $\sum_{k=1}^{20} k^2 + 3k,$

**(g)** $\sum_{k=1}^{30} k^3 + 7k^2,$ **(h)** $\sum_{k=1}^{20} 3k^3 - 6k^2 + 7.$

**3** Find the value of each of the following and factorise your answers.

**(a)** $\sum_{r=1}^{n} 4r^3 + 2r,$ **(b)** $\sum_{r=1}^{n} 6r^2 + 4r,$ **(c)** $\sum_{r=1}^{n} 8r^3 - 2r,$

**(d)** $\sum_{r=1}^{n} 8r^3 - 6r^2,$ **(e)** $\sum_{r=1}^{n} 12r^3 + 8r,$ **(f)** $\sum_{r=1}^{n} 6r^2 - 6.$

**4** Find the value of $\sum_{k=13}^{50} 2k^3 - 12k^2 - 7.$

**5** Evaluate: **(a)** $\sum_{k=1}^{20} (2k - 3)^2,$ **(b)** $\sum_{k=11}^{40} (3k - 2)^2.$

**6** Find the least value of $n$ for which $\sum_{r=1}^{n} r^3 > 10\,000.$

## WORKED EXAMINATION QUESTION

The sum of the first five terms of an arithmetic series is 5 and the sum of the **next** five terms is 105. Find the first term and the common difference. [A]

## Solution

$S_5 = 5 \Rightarrow 5 = \frac{5}{2}(2a + 4d)$

$S_{10} = 110 \Rightarrow 110 = \frac{10}{2}(2a + 9d)$

Using $S_n = \frac{1}{2}n[2a + (n - 1)d]$.

There are several ways of dealing with the second condition, e.g. $[a + 5d] + [a + 6d] + [a + 7d] + [a + 8d] + [a + 9d] = 105$

You now have two simultaneous equations equivalent to $a + 2d = 1$ and $2a + 9d = 22$, which can be solved to give $a = -7, d = 4.$

First term is −7; common difference is 4.

13

## MIXED EXERCISE

1 An arithmetic sequence has fifth term 10 and seventeenth term 31. Find the first term and the common difference of the sequence. [A]

2 In an arithmetic series, the ninth term is 7, and the twenty-ninth term is equal to twice the fifth term.

   (a) Determine the first term and the common difference of the series.

   (b) Calculate the sum of the first 200 terms of the series. [A]

3 The ninth term of an arithmetic series is 17 and the sum of the first five terms is 10. Determine the first term and the common difference of the series. [A]

4 The first term of an arithmetic series is 3. The seventh term is twice the third term.

   (a) Find the common difference.

   (b) Calculate the sum of the first 20 terms of the series. [A]

5 An arithmetic sequence with first term 37 has common difference 29. Find the value of $n$ for which the nth term first exceeds 5000.

6 An arithmetic series has first term 12. The sum of the first 15 terms is equal to four times the twenty-eighth term. Find the common difference.

7 Calculate (a) the sum of, (b) the sum of the squares of, the integers from 500 to 1000 inclusive.

8 Find the value of $\sum\limits_{k=1}^{20} 4k^3 - 36k^2 - 10$.

9 Obtain an expression in terms of $n$ for $\sum\limits_{k=1}^{n} 20k^3 + 2k$ and factorise your answer.

## Key point summary

**1** A sequence is a set of numbers separated by commas following a particular rule.  *pp215,216*

An example of a sequence is 1, 4, 9, 16, … .

**2** A sequence may be defined by a formula such as $u_n = 3n^2 - 7$,  *p216*

**3** A sequence may be defined inductively by giving one of the terms and a rule which relates one term to the previous term such as $u_1 = 5$; $u_n = u_{n-1} + 4n^3$.  *p217*

**4** An arithmetic sequence with common difference $d$ has the inductive definition $u_1 = a$; $u_n = u_{n-1} + d$.  *p218*

**5** The $n$th term of an arithmetic sequence is given by $u_n = a + (n - 1)d$ and this formula must be learnt off by heart.  *p219*

**6** When the terms of a sequence are added together they form a series. For example $1 + 8 + 27 + \ldots + 2197$ is a series.  *p219*

**7** An arithmetic series is of the form  *p219*

$$a + [a + d] + [a + 2d] + [a + 3d] + \ldots + [a + (n - 1)d].$$

**8** The sum of the first $n$ terms of an arithmetic series is  *p221*

$$S_n = \frac{1}{2}n[2a + (n - 1)d].$$

This formula must be learnt off by heart.

**9** Sigma notation can be used as a shorthand for series.  *p226* The sum of the first $n$ natural numbers is given by

$$\sum_{r=1}^{n} r = \frac{1}{2}n(n + 1).$$

This formula must be learnt off by heart.

**10** The following formulae can be used to find sums of other series:  *p226*

$$\sum_{r=1}^{n} 1 = n; \quad \sum_{r=1}^{n} r = \frac{1}{2}n(n + 1); \quad \sum_{r=1}^{n} r^2 = \frac{1}{6}n(n + 1)(2n + 1);$$

$$\sum_{r=1}^{n} r^3 = \frac{1}{4}n^2(n + 1)^2.$$

**13**

| Test yourself | What to review |
|---|---|
| **1** Write down the first five terms of the sequence defined by $u_n = 2n^3 - 1$. | *Section 13.2* |
| **2** A sequence has the following inductive definition: $u_1 = 3;\ u_n = 3u_{n-1} - 7$. Find the first five terms. | *Section 13.3* |
| **3** The twentieth term of an arithmetic sequence is 100 and the first term is 43. Find the common difference. | *Section 13.4* |
| **4** The sum of the first 16 terms of an arithmetic series is 48. The tenth term is 6. Find the first term and the common difference. | *Section 13.7* |
| **5** Calculate the sum of all the natural numbers from 150 to 250 inclusive. | *Section 13.6* |
| **6** Find the sum of the following series:<br>**(a)** $\displaystyle\sum_{k=13}^{40} k^3$,      **(b)** $\displaystyle\sum_{r=1}^{50} 3r^2 - 2r - 20$. | *Section 13.9* |

**Test yourself** ANSWERS

**1** 1, 15, 53, 127, 249.

**2** 3, 2, −1, −10, −37.

**3** $d = 3$.

**4** $a = -12,\ d = 2$.

**5** 20 200

**6 (a)** 666 316, **(b)** 125 225.

# Exam style practice paper

Time allowed 1 hour 15 minutes

Answer all questions

**1** Express $\dfrac{8}{(\sqrt{5}+1)^2}$ in the form $a + b\sqrt{5}$, where

a and b are integers. *(4 marks)*

**2** Evaluate

$$\sum_{11}^{100}(r^3 + 3).$$ *(4 marks)*

**3** The gradient of a curve at the point $(x, y)$ is $\dfrac{6(\sqrt{x} - 2x)}{x}$.

(a) Write the gradient in the form $p + qx^{-\frac{1}{2}}$, where $p$ and $q$ are constants to be determined. *(1 mark)*

(b) Use integration to find the equation of the curve, given that it passes through the point $(4, 3)$. *(4 marks)*

**4** The point $A$ has coordinates $(3, 5)$, $B$ is the point $(-5, 1)$ and $O$ is the origin.

(a) Find, in the form $y = mx + c$, the equation of the perpendicular bisector of the line segment $AB$ . *(3 marks)*

(b) This perpendicular bisector cuts the $y$-axis at $P$ and the $x$-axis at $Q$.

   (i) Show that the line segment $BP$ is parallel to the $x$-axis. *(2 marks)*

   (ii) Find the area of triangle $OPQ$. *(2 marks)*

**5** The function f is defined for all real values of $x$ by

$$f(x) = (x + 5)(2x - 3).$$

   **(a)** Find the value of $f'(2)$.        *(4 marks)*

   **(b)** Find the set of values of $x$ for which

$$f(x) < 6x - 9.$$

                                                  *(4 marks)*

**6 (a)** Prove the identity

$$\frac{3 + \cos^2 \theta}{2 + \sin \theta} \equiv 2 - \sin \theta.$$     *(3 marks)*

   **(b)** Hence find all solutions of the equation

$$\frac{3 + \cos^2 2x}{2 + \sin 2x} = \frac{9}{5}$$

   in the interval $0° \leqslant x \leqslant 180°$, giving your answers correct to the nearest $0.1°$.    *(5 marks)*

**7** The function f is defined for all real values of $x$ by

$$f(x) = x^2 - 4x + 16.$$

   **(a)** Express $f(x)$ in the form $(x + a)^2 + b$, finding the values of $a$ and $b$.    *(2 marks)*

   **(b)** Hence, or otherwise,

      **(i)** find the range of f;    *(1 mark)*

      **(ii)** describe the single transformation by which the graph of $y = f(x)$ can be obtained from the graph of $y = x^2$;    *(2 marks)*

      **(iii)** state whether the inverse of f exists, giving a reason for your answer.    *(1 mark)*

   **(c)** The curve $y = x^2 - 4x + 16$ crosses the curve

$$y = \frac{12}{2 - x} \text{ at the point where } x = k.$$

   Prove that $1.06 < k < 1.07$.    *(3 marks)*

**8** The curve $C$ has equation

$$y = 3x + \frac{12}{x^2}.$$

**(a) (i)** Prove that the curve $C$ has just one
stationary point. *(4 marks)*

**(ii)** Show that this stationary point is a minimum and
find its coordinates. *(3 marks)*

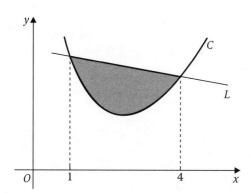

The diagram shows part of the curve $C$ and a line $L$.

**(b)** The line $L$ intersects the curve $C$ at the points $(1, 15)$ and
$(4, 12\frac{3}{4})$. Find the equation of the line $L$ giving your
answer in the form $y = mx + c$, where the values of $m$
and $c$ are to be found. *(3 marks)*

**(c)** Show that the area of the shaded region bounded

by the curve $C$ and the line $L$ is $\dfrac{81}{8}$. *(5 marks)*

# Answers

## 1 Indices

### EXERCISE 1A

| | | | | | | | |
|---|---|---|---|---|---|---|---|
| **1** | $6m^5$, | **2** | $2b^3$, | **3** | $24p^3q^2$, | **4** | $r^9$, |
| **5** | $56t^8$, | **6** | $36a^3b^6$, | **7** | $54a^{12}$, | **8** | $24a^{12}b^5$, |
| **9** | $60p^5q^4$, | **10** | $10p^{10}q^8$, | **11** | $36a^4p^3q^4$, | **12** | $m^{15}$, |
| **13** | $m^{15}$, | **14** | $a^{10}b^{10}$, | **15** | $8x^6$, | **16** | $a^6b^{12}$, |
| **17** | $3p^9q^8$, | **18** | $10m^6n^7$, | **19** | $4r^{11}t^7$, | **20** | $20p^{14}q^{11}$. |

### EXERCISE 1B

**1** $a^3$,

**2** $4p^2$,

**3** $5t$,

**4** $10$ or $10h^0$,

**5** $x^3$,

**6** $3a^3$,

**7** $\frac{1}{3}pq$ or $\frac{pq}{3}$,

**8** $\frac{1}{2}a^8$,

**9** $2pq^3$,

**10** $\frac{5}{6}b$,

**11** $10t^4$,

**12** $10a^8$,

**13** $2p^4q^3$,

**14** $x^{11}y^{-1}$ or $\frac{x^{11}}{y}$,

**15** $mn^{-2}$ or $\frac{m}{n^2}$,

**16** $\frac{1}{3}a^0c^{-5}$ or $\frac{1}{3c^5}$,

**17** $\frac{3}{4}m^{-1}n^3$ or $\frac{3n^3}{4m}$,

**18** $x^0y^0$ or $1$,

**19** $30xyz^{-1}$ or $\frac{30xy}{z}$,

**20** $2a^2b^5c^{-5}$ or $\frac{2a^2b^5}{c^5}$.

### EXERCISE 1C

**1** **(a)** $2^4$, **(b)** $3^3$, **(c)** $5^3$, **(d)** (any prime)$^0$,
　 **(e)** $7^2$, **(f)** $2^{-3}$, **(g)** $3^{-4}$, **(h)** $3^{-1}$,
　 **(i)** $11^{-2}$, **(j)** $17^{-2}$, **(k)** $2^{-7}$.

**2** **(a)** $\frac{1}{2}$, **(b)** $1$, **(c)** $625$, **(d)** $\frac{1}{49}$,

　 **(e)** $1$, **(f)** $-\frac{1}{125}$, **(g)** $\frac{1}{12}$, **(h)** $\frac{1}{9}$,

　 **(i)** $\frac{1}{25}$, **(j)** $9$.

**3 (a)** $\frac{1}{2}$,  **(b)** $\frac{1}{81}$,  **(c)** 3,

  **(d)** $\frac{1}{25}$  **(e)** $\frac{4}{9}$,  **(f)** $\frac{1}{64}$.

**4 (a)** $x^{-10}$ or $\frac{1}{x^{10}}$,  **(b)** $a^{21}$,  **(c)** 1,

  **(d)** $c^{-15}d^{20}$ or $\frac{d^{20}}{c^{15}}$,  **(e)** $x^{-12}$ or $\frac{1}{x^{12}}$,  **(f)** $a^{-2}$ or $\frac{1}{a^2}$,

  **(g)** $p^{-11}$ or $\frac{1}{p^{11}}$,  **(h)** $5p^{12}$,  **(i)** $4a^2$,

  **(j)** $13a^{-4}$ or $\frac{13}{a^4}$,  **(k)** $7a^{-6}$ or $\frac{7}{a^6}$,  **(l)** 2,

  **(m)** $4y^{12}$,  **(n)** $7x^2$,  **(o)** $3p^{-3}q^{-4}$ or $\frac{3}{p^3q^4}$,

  **(p)** $3a^7b^{-6}c^4$ or $\frac{3a^7c^4}{b^6}$,  **(q)** $3a^{-10}b^2$ or $\frac{3b^2}{a^{10}}$,  **(r)** $32a^{-4}b^0c^{-5}$ or $\frac{32}{a^4c^5}$,

  **(s)** $\frac{3}{2}a^{-2}bc^3$ or $\frac{3bc^3}{2a^2}$,  **(t)** $6x^{-8}y^{-1}z^{-2}$ or $\frac{6}{x^8yz^2}$.

**5 (a)** $x^5$,  **(b)** $y^{-3}$ or $\frac{1}{y^3}$,  **(c)** $p^{-1}$ or $\frac{1}{p}$,

  **(d)** $r^{-6}$ or $\frac{1}{r^6}$.  **(e)** $t^{-8}u^2$ or $\frac{u^2}{t^8}$,  **(f)** $p^3q^{-1}$ or $\frac{p^3}{q}$,

  **(g)** $a^{-1}b^{-1}$ or $\frac{1}{ab}$.

## EXERCISE 1D

**1 (a)** 8  **(b)** 100 000,  **(c)** 9,

  **(d)** 10 000,  **(e)** 32,  **(f)** 4.

**2 (a)** $\frac{1}{4}$,  **(b)** $\frac{1}{8}$,  **(c)** $\frac{1}{625}$,

  **(d)** $\frac{7}{2}$,  **(e)** $\frac{25}{4}$,  **(f)** $\frac{4}{3}$,

  **(g)** $\frac{5}{4}$,  **(h)** $\frac{9}{16}$,  **(i)** $\frac{13}{9}$.

**3 (a)** $x^2$,  **(b)** $a^5$,  **(c)** $x^5$,

  **(d)** $y$,  **(e)** $a^{\frac{7}{12}}$,  **(f)** 2.

**4 (a)** $x = -1$,  **(b)** $x = \frac{4}{5}$,  **(c)** $x = \frac{1}{3}$,  **(d)** $x = \frac{11}{6}$.

**5** $x = \frac{13}{6}$.

## 2 Surds

**EXERCISE 2A**

| | | | | | | | |
|---|---|---|---|---|---|---|---|
| **1** | Irrational. | **2** | Rational. | **3** | Irrational. | **4** | Rational. |
| **5** | Rational. | **6** | Rational. | **7** | Irrational. | **8** | Irrational. |
| **9** | Rational. | **10** | Irrational. | | | | |

**EXERCISE 2B**

| | | | | | | | |
|---|---|---|---|---|---|---|---|
| **1** | $2\sqrt{2}$. | **2** | $2\sqrt{3}$. | **3** | $2\sqrt{5}$. | **4** | $5\sqrt{3}$. |
| **5** | $2\sqrt{13}$. | **6** | $2\sqrt{30}$. | **7** | $7\sqrt{5}$. | **8** | $6\sqrt{7}$. |
| **9** | $8\sqrt{3}$. | **10** | $10\sqrt{10}$. | **11** | $\sqrt{3}$. | **12** | $\sqrt{2}$. |
| **13** | 5. | **14** | $2\sqrt{7}$. | **15** | $7\sqrt{5}$. | **16** | 45. |

**17** $30\sqrt{2}$.    **18** $\dfrac{\sqrt{6}}{3}$.

**19** (a) $4\sqrt{2}$,    (b) $7\sqrt{7}$,    (c) $-\sqrt{3}$.

**20** $\sqrt[6]{17}$, $\sqrt[3]{13}$, $\sqrt[10]{170}$, $\sqrt[3]{5}$.

**EXERCISE 2C**

| | | | | | | | |
|---|---|---|---|---|---|---|---|
| **1** | $-2\sqrt{7}$. | **2** | $3\sqrt{3}$. | **3** | $-\sqrt{5}$. | **4** | $6\sqrt{2} + 2\sqrt{3}$. |
| **5** | $5\sqrt{2}$. | **6** | $5\sqrt{3}$. | **7** | $-2\sqrt{5}$. | **8** | $3\sqrt{6}$. |
| **9** | $33\sqrt{5}$. | **10** | $9\sqrt{7} + 42\sqrt{2}$. | **11** | $3\sqrt{5}$. | **12** | $6\sqrt{7}$. |

**13** (a) $\sqrt{41}$,    (b) $2\sqrt{3}$.

**EXERCISE 2D**

| | | | | | | |
|---|---|---|---|---|---|---|
| **1** | $30\sqrt{2}$. | **2** | $60\sqrt{5}$. | **3** | $\sqrt{30} - 2\sqrt{5}$. |
| **4** | 12. | **5** | $6\sqrt{5} + 60$. | **6** | $21 - 3\sqrt{3} + 7\sqrt{2} - \sqrt{6}$. |
| **7** | 2. | **8** | $4 + 5\sqrt{42}$. | **9** | 6. |

**10** $132 + 8\sqrt{11} - 6\sqrt{33} - 4\sqrt{3}$.

**EXERCISE 2E**

**1** $\dfrac{\sqrt{10}}{10}$.    **2** $\dfrac{3\sqrt{2}}{2}$.

**3** $\dfrac{\sqrt{35}}{10}$.    **4** $\sqrt{2} + 1$.

**5** $\dfrac{\sqrt{21} + 3}{4}$.    **6** $\dfrac{2\sqrt{5} + 2\sqrt{2}}{3}$.

**7** $\dfrac{\sqrt{14} - 2}{2}$.    **8** $2 - \sqrt{2}$.

**9** $\dfrac{7 - \sqrt{21} + 5\sqrt{7} - 5\sqrt{3}}{4}$.    **10** $\dfrac{23 + 3\sqrt{21}}{68}$.

**11** $\dfrac{9 + \sqrt{65}}{4}$.    **12** $\dfrac{20\sqrt{3} + 10}{11}$.

**13** $\dfrac{37 + 8\sqrt{10}}{27}$.    **14** $-8 - 2\sqrt{14}$.

## MIXED EXERCISE

**1 (a)** $5\sqrt{3}$,  **(b)** $10\sqrt{3}$,  **(c)** $8\sqrt{2}$,
  **(d)** $0$,  **(e)** $11\sqrt{2}$,  **(f)** $\sqrt{6}$.

**2 (a)** $5\sqrt{3} - 6$,  **(b)** $3\sqrt{5} + 15$,  **(c)** $4$,
  **(d)** $5\sqrt{3} - 11$,  **(e)** $-17\sqrt{5} - 13$,  **(f)** $12\sqrt{3} + 21$.

**3 (a)** $\dfrac{7\sqrt{15}}{5}$,  **(b)** $\dfrac{\sqrt{3} + 1}{2}$,  **(c)** $\dfrac{\sqrt{5} + 3}{2}$,

  **(d)** $\dfrac{\sqrt{13} + \sqrt{11}}{2}$,  **(e)** $\dfrac{7 - 3\sqrt{3}}{2}$,  **(f)** $\dfrac{33 - 17\sqrt{3}}{3}$,

  **(g)** $27 - 19\sqrt{2}$,  **(h)** $\dfrac{2 + \sqrt{2}}{2}$.

**4 (a)** $11 - 6\sqrt{2}$,  **(b)** $\dfrac{11}{49} + \dfrac{6}{49}\sqrt{2}$.

**5 (a) (i)** Any rational number between 4 and 5.
    **(ii)** Any irrational number between 4 and 5.
  **(b)** 1, this is rational so the student is incorrect.

**6 (a)** $-32 + 11\sqrt{7}$,  **(b)** $11 + 4\sqrt{7}$.

## 3 Linear equations and inequalities

### EXERCISE 3A

**1** $x = \dfrac{18}{5}$.  **2** $x = \dfrac{9}{2}$.  **3** $x = \dfrac{16}{7}$.

**4** $x = -13$.  **5** $x = -\dfrac{26}{3}$.  **6** $x = \dfrac{31}{5}$.

**7** $x = 3$.  **8** $x = 6$.  **9** $x = 2$.

**10** $x = \dfrac{44}{29}$.  **11** $x = 3$.  **12** $x = \dfrac{34}{21}$.

**13** $x = \dfrac{41}{8}$.  **14** 21.  **15** 43.

### EXERCISE 3B

**1** $x = 1, y = 3$.  **2** $x = 2, y = -1$.
**3** $x = -2, y = -3$.  **4** $x = -4, y = 1$.

**5** $x = \dfrac{46}{13}, y = -\dfrac{4}{13}$.  **6** $x = \dfrac{1}{17}, y = \dfrac{7}{17}$.

**7** $x = -\dfrac{29}{13}, y = \dfrac{11}{13}$.  **8** $x = -\dfrac{27}{35}, y - \dfrac{11}{35}$.

**9** $x = \dfrac{5}{2}, y = 0$.  **10** $x = 2, y = -2$.

## EXERCISE 3C

**1** $x = -\sqrt[3]{4}$.

**2** $x = -\sqrt[5]{2}$.

**3** $x = \dfrac{3}{2}, -\dfrac{3}{2}$.

**4** No real solutions.

**5** $x = 2$.

**6** $x = 9$.

**7** $x = -64$.

**8** $x = -\dfrac{19}{27}$.

**9** $\dfrac{3\sqrt{3} + 29}{22}$.

**10** $x = \dfrac{136 - 27\sqrt{7}}{59}$.

## EXERCISE 3D

**1** $x < 16$.

**2** $x \geqslant -\dfrac{7}{2}$.

**3** $x < 12$.

**4** $x > -\dfrac{10}{19}$.

**5** $x > 53$.

**6** $x \geqslant \dfrac{31}{5}$.

**7** $x > \dfrac{61}{23}$.

**8** $x \leqslant 37$.

**9** $x < 3$.

**10** $x > \dfrac{5}{2}$ and $x < 15$.

## 4 Coordinate geometry

## EXERCISE 4A

**1 (a)** 5,　　**(b)** $\sqrt{17}$,　　**(c)** $\sqrt{34}$,　　**(d)** $\sqrt{29}$,　　**(e)** $\sqrt{5}$,

　**(f)** $\sqrt{18}$,　　**(g)** $\sqrt{89}$,　　**(h)** $\sqrt{73}$,　　**(i)** 5,　　**(j)** 12.5

**2 (a)** $AB = 6$, $AC = 5$, $BC = 5$, not right-angled.

　**(b)** $AB = \sqrt{68}$, $AC = \sqrt{136}$, $BC = \sqrt{68}$, yes right-angled.

　**(c)** $AB = \sqrt{8}$, $AC = \sqrt{26}$, $BC = \sqrt{18}$, yes right-angled.

**3** $p = \pm 4$.

**4 (a)** $PQ = \sqrt{18}$, $PR = \sqrt{18}$, $QR = 6$　　**(c)** $S(1, 0)$　　**(d)** $T(1, -3)$

## EXERCISE 4B

**1 (a)** $(5, 2)$,　　**(b)** $(1, 0.5)$,　　**(c)** $(3, 2)$,　　**(d)** $(-2, 4.5)$,

　**(e)** $(3.5, 2)$,　　**(f)** $(-4.5, -0.5)$,　　**(g)** $(0, 2)$,　　**(h)** $(2, 1)$,

　**(i)** $(1, 3)$,　　**(j)** $(0.25, 0.5)$.

**2 (a)** $(4, 5)$　　**(b)** $(4, 5)$,　　**(c)** $(0, 7)$,

　**(d)** $(8, 5)$,　　**(e)** $(4, 1)$,　　**(f)** $(6, -6)$.

**3 (a)** $(7, 3)$

## EXERCISE 4C

**1 (a)** Yes; gradients are 2 and 2,

　**(b)** No; gradients are $-0.5$ and $0.5$,

　**(c)** Yes; gradients are 0 and 0,

　**(d)** Yes; gradients are 1/7 and 1/7.

**3 (a)** 6/11, 1/3 and 4/5,　　　　**(b)** $AC$.

## EXERCISE 4D

**1** (a) $-5/2$, (b) 3, (c) $-1/4$, (d) $2/7$, (e) $-4/9$.

**2** (a) $-1/3$, (b) 3.

**3** (d) 20.

## EXERCISE 4E

**1** (a) $2x - y - 3 = 0$, (b) $2x + 3y - 6 = 0$, (c) $x + 2y + 6 = 0$.

**2** Answers are in form gradient; $y$-intercept.

(a) 3, 2, (b) 2, $-2.5$, (c) 0.5, 1.75, (d) $-2/3$, 8/3,
(e) 1.25, $-2$, (f) 8, $-6$, (g) 3/5, $-2/5$, (h) $-3/2$, 2,
(i) 2, $-1.2$, (j) 0, 2.

## EXERCISE 4F

**1** $y = 2x + 4$.

**2** $3y + x = 6$.

**3** $2y = x + 5$.

**4** $3x - 2y + 3 = 0$.

**5** $6y = 4x + 23$.

**6** (b) $D(-1, -2)$, (c) $y = 5x + 3$.

**7** 40 square units.

## EXERCISE 4G

**3** (a) $y + x = 4$, (b) $k = 1$.

**4** (a) $2y = 5x + 16$, (b) No.

**5** (a) $(-6, -5)$, (b) $(1, 2)$, (c) $(4, -2)$, (d) $(8, 64)$,
(e) $(34, -7)$, (f) $(3, 12)$, (g) $(4/3, -1)$, (h) $(-7, -4)$.

## MIXED EXERCISE

**1** (a) $AB$: $y = -5x + 4$, $BC$: $5y = x - 6$, (c) 52 square units,
(d) $(0, 30)$.

**2** (b) $B(2\frac{1}{2}, -1)$, $D(5\frac{1}{2}, 5)$

**3** (b) $y = -5x + 33$, (c) $k = 1\frac{1}{2}$.

**4** (a) $\dfrac{5}{6}$ square unit, (b) $12y + 5x = 0$, (c) $AB = \dfrac{13}{6}, \dfrac{10}{13}$.

**5** (a) $y = x + 1$, (b) $B(-2, -1)$.

**6** (b) 20 square units, (c) (i) $P(3, 6)$, (ii) $Q(2, -1)$.

**7** (a) $D(5, 6)$, (b) 65 square units.

**8** (a) $P(1, 1\frac{1}{3})$,

(b) gradient of $AP$ is $\dfrac{4}{3(1 - h)}$, gradient of $BP$ is $\dfrac{4 - 3k}{3}$.

**9 (a)** $B(3, -1)$, **(b)** $AC$: $6y + x = 11$, $CD$: $3x + 4y = 19$,

**(c)** $D(1, 4)$, **(d)** 14 square units.

**10 (a)** $A(2, 0)$, $C(0, 6)$, $B(9, 3)$,

**(c)** **(i)** 27 square units,

**(d)** $P(7, 9)$

## 5 Functions and graphs

### EXERCISE 5A

**1** $\{2, 3, 6, 11\}$.

**2** $\{-132, -34, -8, -6, 20\}$

**3** $\left\{\dfrac{10}{9}, \dfrac{5}{4}, 2\right\}$

**4 (a)** $-1$, **(b)** $-1$, **(c)** $-1$ **(d)** $-7$ **(e)** $-25$.

**5 (a)** $\dfrac{1}{27}$, **(b)** $\dfrac{1}{64}$, **(c)** $\dfrac{1}{125}$,

**(d)** $\dfrac{1}{8}$, **(e)** $1$, **(f)** $-1$,

**(g)** $1\,000\,000$, **(h)** $(b + 3)^{-3}$, **(i)** $a^{-3}$.

**6 (a)** $\sqrt{5}$, **(b)** $\sqrt{7}$, **(c)** $3$, **(d)** $\sqrt{3}$, **(e)** $1$.

### EXERCISE 5B

**1** $6 \leqslant g(x) \leqslant 11$. **2** $2 < f(x) < 10$.

**3** $-7 \leqslant q(x) \leqslant 2$. **4** $g(x) \geqslant -2$.

**5** $-1021 \leqslant f(x) < 4$. **6** $-25 \leqslant h(x) < 10$.

**7** $3 < f(x) \leqslant 4$. **8** $0 < g(x) < 2$.

**9** $\dfrac{4}{3} \leqslant f(x) \leqslant 2$. **10** $3.25 < h(x) < 4$.

### EXERCISE 5C

**1** $x \in \mathbb{R}, x \neq 1$, **2** $x \geqslant -3$,

**3** $x \in \mathbb{R}, x \neq 2$, **4** $x \in \mathbb{R}, x \neq -1$,

**5** $\mathbb{R}$, **6** $x > 2$,

**7** $x \in \mathbb{R}, x \neq 1, x \neq 2$, **8** $x < 4, x \neq 0$.

### EXERCISE 5D

**1** Many–one function. **2** Not.

**3** One–one function. **4** One–one function.

**5** Many–one function. **6** Not.

## EXERCISE 5E

**1** Even.     **2** Neither.     **3** Odd.     **4** Neither.

**5** Even.     **6** Neither.     **7** Even.     **8** Even.

**9** Neither.     **10** Odd.

## EXERCISE 5F

**1 (a)** $fg : x \mapsto 4 - 2x$,     **(b)** $fg : x \mapsto (2 + x)^2 - 3$,

   **(c)** $fg : x \mapsto (3x - 1)^3 + 1$,     **(d)** $fg : x \mapsto (x + 1)^8 - 2$.

**2 (a)** $gf : x \mapsto 7 - 2x$,     **(b)** $gf : x \mapsto x^2 - 1$,

   **(c)** $gf : x \mapsto 3x^3 + 2$,     **(d)** $gf : x \mapsto (x^4 - 1)^2$.

**3 (a)** $9x^2$,     **(b)** $6x - 3x^2 - 2$.

**4 (a)** $-1$,     **(b)** $4a - 9 : a = 3$.

**5 (a)** $4k - 2 - 3kx$,     **(b)** $10 - 3kx, k = 3$.

**6** $fg(x) = (5 + x)^2$, $gf(x) = 5 + x^2$, $x = -2$.

## EXERCISE 5G

**1 (a)** $f^{-1} : x \mapsto \dfrac{x - 7}{5}$,     **(b)** $f^{-1} : x \mapsto \sqrt[3]{x} - 2$,

   **(c)** $f^{-1} : x \mapsto \dfrac{6x - 1}{2}$,     **(d)** $f^{-1} : x \mapsto \dfrac{x^3 + 1}{2}$,

   **(e)** $f^{-1} : x \mapsto \dfrac{5x - 3}{-2} = \dfrac{3 - 5x}{2}$,     **(f)** $f^{-1} : x \mapsto \dfrac{7 - 4x}{3}$.

**2 (a) (i)** $f(x) \geqslant -64$,     **(ii)** $f^{-1} : x \mapsto \dfrac{\sqrt[3]{x} + 1}{3}, x \geqslant -64$,

   **(iii)** $f^{-1}(x) \geqslant -1$,     **(b) (i)** $-1 \leqslant g(x) < 1$,

   **(ii)** $g^{-1} : x \mapsto \dfrac{2}{1 - x}, -1 \leqslant x < 1$,     **(iii)** $g^{-1}(x) \geqslant 1$,

   **(c) (i)** $h(x) > 243$,     **(ii)** $h^{-1} : x \mapsto \dfrac{\sqrt[5]{x} - 3}{2}, x > 243$,

   **(iii)** $h^{-1}(x) > 0$,     **(d) (i)** $0 < q(x) < 1$,

   **(ii)** $q^{-1} : x \mapsto \dfrac{5}{x - 1}, 0 < x < 1$,     **(iii)** $q^{-1}(x) < 5$,

   **(e) (i)** $-2 \leqslant r(x) < 0$,     **(ii)** $r^{-1} : x \mapsto 3 - \dfrac{4}{x}, -2 \leqslant x < 0$,

   **(iii)** $r^{-1}(x) \geqslant 5$.

**3 (a)** f is many–one, e.g. $f(-2) = f(2)$,

   **(b)** g is one–one – domain excludes negative values
     $g^{-1}(x) = \sqrt{x - 3}$; since range of g is $g(x) \geqslant 4$, domain of $g^{-1}$ is
     $x \geqslant 4$ and range is $g^{-1}(x) \geqslant 1$.

**4 (a)** h is one–one since domain has only negative values of $x$.

   **(b)** $h^{-1}(x) = -\sqrt{x + 3}$; domain of $h^{-1}$ is $x > -3$; range is $h^{-1}(x) < 0$.

## MIXED EXERCISE

**1** **(a)** $-3 < f(x) < 0$, **(b)** $f^{-1}(x) = 4 - \dfrac{3}{x}$.

**2** **(a)** $fg : x \mapsto \dfrac{3}{x^2} + 4, x \in \mathbb{R}, x \neq 0$, **(b)** $f^{-1} : x \mapsto \dfrac{x-4}{3}, x \in \mathbb{R}$.

**3** **(a)** $\dfrac{1}{2} \leqslant f(x) < 2$, **(b)** $f^{-1}(x) = \dfrac{3}{2-x}$.

**4** **(a)** $g(x) \geqslant 1$, **(b)** $fg(x) = \dfrac{3}{2x^2 + 1}$; range $0 < x < 3$.

**5** **(b)** f is one–one; domain of $f^{-1}$ is $x > 0$; $f^{-1}(x) = 2 + \dfrac{1}{x^2}$.

**6** **(a)** $0 < f(x) \leqslant 4$, **(b)** $f^{-1}(x) = \dfrac{8}{x} - 2$, **(c)** $x = 2$.

**7** **(a)** $0 \leqslant f(x) < 1$, **(b)** one–one; $0 \leqslant x < 1$; $f^{-1}(x) = \dfrac{2}{1-x}$.

## 6 Introduction to differentiation

### EXERCISE 6A
**1** 7. **2** 20. **3** $-6$. **4** 3. **5** $-4.75$.

### EXERCISE 6B
**1** 16.4

**2** 4.641.

**3** **(a)** 6.1051,
   **(b)** 5.101 005 01,
   **(c)** 5.010 010 005. Gradient at $x = 1$ is 5.

**4** Gradient at $x = 2$ is 24.

### EXERCISE 6C
**1** Gradient of chord $= 10 + 5h$, gradient of curve at $P$ is 10.

**2** **(a)** Gradient of chord $= -4 - 2h$, gradient of curve at $P$ is $-4$.
   **(b)** Gradient of chord $= -8 - 2h$, gradient of curve at $P$ is $-8$.
   **(c)** Gradient of chord $= -4a - 2h$, gradient of curve at $P$ is $-4a$.

**3** Gradient at $P = -\dfrac{1}{25}$.

**4** **(a)** $h^3 + h^2 - 8h - 12$, **(b)** gradient at $P$ is $-8$.

### EXERCISE 6D
**1** **(a)** 8, **(b)** $10x$, **(c)** $8x + 2$, **(d)** $2x$,

   **(e)** $6x^2$, **(f)** $12x^2$, **(g)** $3x^2 - 3$, **(h)** $-\dfrac{1}{x^2}$.

## EXERCISE 6E

**1 (a)** $0,$     **(b)** $9x^2 - 14x,$     **(c)** $6x^5 - 8x + 5,$

**(d)** $6x^5 + 3x^2,$     **(e)** $10x - 2,$     **(f)** $21x^2,$

**(g)** $8x - 27x^2,$     **(h)** $80x^9 - 42x^5,$     **(i)** $16x + 4,$

**(j)** $12x - 4,$     **(k)** $7x^6 - 6x + 2,$     **(l)** $4x^3 - 9x^2 - 1.$

**2 (a)** $x^2,$     **(b)** $30x^4 - 16x + \dfrac{x}{3},$     **(c)** $14x - \dfrac{1}{5},$

**(d)** $4x^5 - 6x^7,$     **(e)** $\dfrac{15x^4}{4} - \dfrac{10x}{9},$     **(f)** $8x^{11} - \dfrac{7x^2}{2} + \dfrac{5}{4}.$

**3 (a)** $\dfrac{\mathrm{d}p}{\mathrm{d}q} = 18q^2 - 7,$     **(b)** $\dfrac{\mathrm{d}y}{\mathrm{d}t} = 27t^8 - 0.4,$

**(c)** $\dfrac{\mathrm{d}m}{\mathrm{d}n} = \dfrac{8n}{3} - \dfrac{4}{7},$     **(d)** $\dfrac{\mathrm{d}r}{\mathrm{d}s} = 21s^2 - \dfrac{1}{4},$

**(e)** $\dfrac{\mathrm{d}t}{\mathrm{d}w} = \dfrac{3w}{2} - 4w^6,$     **(f)** $\dfrac{\mathrm{d}z}{\mathrm{d}p} = 15p^2 - 2p^7 + 2.$

## EXERCISE 6F

**1 (a)** $9x^2 + \dfrac{2}{x^2},$     **(b)** $5 + \dfrac{8}{3x^3},$

**(c)** $-\dfrac{4}{7x^2} - \dfrac{6}{5x^3} - 16x,$     **(d)** $-\dfrac{35}{x^8} + \dfrac{2x}{5} - 27,$

**(e)** $-\dfrac{25}{x^6} - \dfrac{6}{x^7} - 7,$     **(f)** $-\dfrac{8}{5x^3} + \dfrac{2}{3x^2} + \dfrac{8}{3},$

**(g)** $-\dfrac{3}{2x^2} - \dfrac{4}{x^4} - 6x^2,$     **(h)** $\dfrac{x^6}{2} - \dfrac{40}{x^5}.$

**2 (a)** $\dfrac{5}{2\sqrt{x}},$     **(b)** $\dfrac{1}{3x^{\frac{2}{3}}},$     **(c)** $\dfrac{1}{x^{\frac{2}{3}}} + \dfrac{2}{5x^{\frac{4}{5}}},$

**(d)** $21x^2 + \dfrac{1}{2x^{\frac{3}{2}}},$     **(e)** $-\dfrac{24}{5x^5} - \dfrac{3x^2}{5},$     **(f)** $-\dfrac{1}{x^{\frac{4}{3}}} + \dfrac{4}{x^{\frac{7}{5}}},$

**(g)** $12x - \dfrac{3\sqrt{x}}{2} + \dfrac{4}{x^3},$     **(h)** $-\dfrac{4}{5x^{\frac{6}{5}}} - \dfrac{9\sqrt{x}}{2}.$

**3 (a)** $12x^2 - \dfrac{18}{5x^4},$     **(b)** $\dfrac{3}{\sqrt{x}} - 3,$     **(c)** $-4 + \dfrac{6}{x^3},$

**(d)** $-\dfrac{10}{x^3} - \dfrac{15}{x^6},$     **(e)** $\dfrac{3}{4x^{\frac{1}{4}}} + \dfrac{5x^{\frac{1}{4}}}{4},$     **(f)** $12x^3 + \dfrac{3}{5x^{\frac{6}{5}}} - \dfrac{8}{5x^3},$

**(g)** $\dfrac{4}{x^3} - \dfrac{5}{2\sqrt{x}},$     **(h)** $\dfrac{2}{\sqrt[5]{x^4}} - \dfrac{-4}{\sqrt[3]{x^5}}.$

**4 (a)** $\dfrac{dz}{dx} = 6x + \dfrac{8}{x^5}$,

**(b)** $\dfrac{dv}{dt} = 3 + \dfrac{7}{t^3} + \dfrac{3}{2\sqrt{t}}$,

**(c)** $\dfrac{dp}{db} = -\dfrac{12}{b^4} - \dfrac{9}{b^{13}} - 56b^6$,

**(d)** $\dfrac{dy}{dz} = \dfrac{3}{25z^{\frac{2}{5}}} - \dfrac{10}{z^3} - 27$,

**(e)** $\dfrac{ds}{dt} = -\dfrac{72}{t^7} - \dfrac{2}{t^3}$,

**(f)** $\dfrac{dh}{dc} = \dfrac{1}{3c\sqrt{c}} + \dfrac{4}{3\sqrt{c}} - \dfrac{8}{5c^3}$.

## MIXED EXERCISE

**1** 51.  **2** 1.  **3 (a)** $-10$,  **(b)** 128,  **(c)** $-1$.

**4 (a)** $-2$,  **(b)** $10, -10$.

**5** $(7, 19)$.  **6** $(-2, 9)$.  **7** $(3, 21.5)$ and $\left(-2, -\dfrac{53}{3}\right)$.

**8 (a)** $(3.5, -2.25)$,  **(b)** $(2, -9)$.

**9 (a)** $-7$,  **(b)** $\dfrac{5}{3}$.

**10** $(2, 17)$ and $(4, 13)$.  **11** 0, tangent is parallel to the $x$-axis.

## 7 Quadratics

### EXERCISE 7A

**1 (a)** $(x - 1)(x - 2)$,  **(b)** $(x + 1)(x - 8)$,  **(c)** $(x + 3)(x + 4)$,
**(d)** $(2x - 3)(x + 1)$,  **(e)** $(3x - 1)(x - 2)$,  **(f)** $(4x - 3)(x + 1)$,
**(g)** $(1 - 2x)(7 + x)$,  **(h)** $(3x - 2)(2x + 3)$,  **(i)** $(2 - x)(3 + 4x)$,
**(j)** $x(5 - 2x)$,  **(k)** $(3 + 4x)(7 - x)$,  **(l)** $(5 + 2x)(3 - 4x)$,
**(m)** $(6 - x)(2 + 3x)$,  **(n)** $x(3 + 4x)$,  **(o)** $(6 - 5x)(9 + 5x)$.

**2 (a)** $1, 2$,  **(b)** $-1, 8$,  **(c)** $-4, -3$,
**(d)** $-1, 1\frac{1}{2}$,  **(e)** $\frac{1}{3}, 2$,  **(f)** $-1, \frac{3}{4}$,
**(g)** $-7, \frac{1}{2}$,  **(h)** $-1\frac{1}{2}, \frac{2}{3}$,  **(i)** $-\frac{3}{4}, 2$,
**(j)** $0, 2\frac{1}{2}$,  **(k)** $-\frac{3}{4}, 7$,  **(l)** $-2\frac{1}{2}, \frac{3}{4}$,
**(m)** $-\frac{2}{3}, 6$,  **(n)** $-\frac{3}{4}, 0$,  **(o)** $-\frac{9}{5}, \frac{6}{5}$.

**3 (i)** $\cup$,  **(ii)** $\cap$, straight line.

**4 (a)** $x = 1\frac{1}{2}$,  **(b)** $x = 3\frac{1}{2}$,  **(c)** $x = -3\frac{1}{2}$,

**(d)** $x = \dfrac{1}{4}$,  **(e)** $x = \dfrac{7}{6}$,  **(f)** $x = -\dfrac{1}{8}$,

**(g)** $x = -\dfrac{13}{4}$,  **(h)** $x = -\dfrac{5}{12}$,  **(i)** $x = \dfrac{5}{8}$,

**(j)** $x = \dfrac{5}{4}$,  **(k)** $x = \dfrac{25}{8}$,  **(l)** $x = -\dfrac{7}{8}$,

**(m)** $x = \dfrac{8}{3}$,  **(n)** $x = -\dfrac{3}{8}$,  **(o)** $x = -\dfrac{3}{10}$.

**5 (a)** $y = (x - 3)(x - 5)$,  **(b)** $y = (x - 3)(x + 2)$,

**(c)** $y = 2(x - 4)(x - 6)$,  **(d)** $y = (x + 1)(1 - x)$,

**(e)** $y = \dfrac{1}{2}(x - 2)(x - 3)$,  **(f)** $y = -3(x + 2)(x + 5)$.

## EXERCISE 7B

**1 (a)** $(x + 4)^2 + 3$,  **(b)** $(x + 2)^2 + 9$,  **(c)** $(x + 5)^2 - 11$,

**(d)** $(x - 5)^2 + 5$,  **(e)** $(x - 4)^2 - 13$,  **(f)** $\left(x + \dfrac{3}{2}\right)^2 + \dfrac{3}{4}$,

**(g)** $\left(x + \dfrac{1}{2}\right)^2 + \dfrac{3}{4}$,  **(h)** $\left(x - \dfrac{5}{2}\right)^2 + \dfrac{3}{4}$,  **(i)** $\left(x - \dfrac{1}{2}\right)^2 + \dfrac{7}{4}$,

**(j)** $\left(x - \dfrac{7}{2}\right)^2 - \dfrac{57}{4}$.

**2 (a)** $y = (x + 2)^2 + 8$, vertex $(-2, 8)$, axis $x = -2$,

**(b)** $y = (x + 6)^2 + 4$, vertex $(-6, 4)$, axis $x = -6$,

**(c)** $y = (x - 3)^2 - 7$, vertex $(3, -7)$, axis $x = 3$,

**(d)** $y = (x + 4)^2 - 11$, vertex $(-4, -11)$, axis $x = -4$,

**(e)** $y = (x - 1)^2 - 4$, vertex $(1, -4)$, axis $x = 1$,

**(f)** $y = (x - 7)^2 - 17$, vertex $(7, -17)$, axis $x = 7$,

**(g)** $y = \left(x + \dfrac{1}{2}\right)^2 + \dfrac{11}{4}$, vertex $\left(-\dfrac{1}{2}, \dfrac{11}{4}\right)$, axis $x = \dfrac{1}{2}$,

**(h)** $y = \left(x - \dfrac{3}{2}\right)^2 - \dfrac{1}{4}$, vertex $\left(\dfrac{3}{2}, -\dfrac{1}{4}\right)$, axis $x = \dfrac{3}{2}$,

**(i)** $y = \left(x - \dfrac{5}{2}\right)^2 - \dfrac{21}{4}$, vertex $\left(\dfrac{5}{2}, -\dfrac{21}{4}\right)$, axis $x = \dfrac{5}{2}$,

**(j)** $y = \left(x - \dfrac{9}{2}\right)^2 - \dfrac{21}{4}$, vertex $\left(\dfrac{5}{2}, -\dfrac{21}{4}\right)$, axis $x = \dfrac{5}{2}$,

**3 (a)** $-2 \pm \sqrt{7}$,  **(b)** $-3 \pm \sqrt{5}$,  **(c)** $4 \pm \sqrt{11}$,

**(d)** $1 \pm \sqrt{5}$,  **(e)** $5 \pm 2\sqrt{7}$,  **(f)** $7 \pm 3\sqrt{5}$,

**(g)** $\dfrac{1}{2} \pm \dfrac{\sqrt{5}}{2}$,  **(h)** $-\dfrac{3}{2} \pm \dfrac{\sqrt{29}}{2}$,  **(i)** $\dfrac{3}{2} \pm \dfrac{\sqrt{5}}{2}$,

**(j)** $\dfrac{7}{2} \pm \dfrac{\sqrt{53}}{2}$,  **(k)** $\dfrac{5}{2} \pm \dfrac{\sqrt{13}}{2}$,  **(l)** $\dfrac{1}{2} \pm \dfrac{\sqrt{13}}{2}$.

## EXERCISE 7C

**1 (a)** $3(x + 1)^2 - 5$,  **(b)** $5(x + 4)^2 - 73$,  **(c)** $2(x + 3)^2 - 19$,

**(d)** $4(x + 1)^2 - 15$,  **(e)** $5\left(x + \dfrac{1}{2}\right)^2 + \dfrac{39}{4}$,  **(f)** $3\left(x + \dfrac{3}{2}\right)^2 - \dfrac{59}{4}$,

**(g)** $2\left(x + \dfrac{5}{4}\right)^2 - \dfrac{17}{8}$,  **(h)** $3\left(x + \dfrac{2}{3}\right)^2 + \dfrac{17}{3}$,  **(i)** $4\left(x + \dfrac{7}{8}\right)^2 - \dfrac{81}{16}$,

**2 (a)** $3(x-2)^2 - 7$, $A = 3$, $B = 2$, $C = 7$,

   **(b) (i)** $-7$,  **(ii)** $0$,

   **(c) (i)** $x = 2$,  **(ii)** $x = 2 \pm \sqrt{\dfrac{7}{3}}$.

**3 (a)** $a = 26$, $b = 5$,     **(b)** $26$, $x = -\dfrac{5}{3}$.

**4** $\left(-\dfrac{b}{2a}, c - \dfrac{b^2}{4a}\right)$.

**5 (a)** $k = 9$,    **(b)** $a = 3$, $b = 2$, $c = -1$,    **(c)** $-1$, $x = -2$.

**6 (a)** $d^2 = 5x^2 + 10x + 50$; least distance $= 3\sqrt{5}$,

   **(b)** $d^2 = 2x^2 + 8x + 10$; least distance $= \sqrt{2}$,

   **(c)** $d^2 = 2x^2 - 16x + 34$; least distance $= \sqrt{2}$,

**7** $25 - (x - 5)^2$, $25$, $x = 5$.

**8** $1800 - 2(x - 30)^2$, $1800$, $x = 30$.

**9** $x + y = 25$, $350$ square units.

## EXERCISE 7D

**1 (a)** $\dfrac{3}{2} \pm \dfrac{\sqrt{13}}{2}$,    **(b)** $-\dfrac{7}{4} \pm \dfrac{\sqrt{57}}{4}$,    **(c)** no real roots,

   **(d)** $\dfrac{5}{8} \pm \dfrac{\sqrt{57}}{8}$,    **(e)** no real roots,    **(f)** $-\dfrac{3}{10} \pm \dfrac{\sqrt{29}}{10}$,

   **(g)** $\dfrac{5}{4} \pm \dfrac{\sqrt{17}}{4}$,    **(h)** no real roots,    **(i)** $-\dfrac{7}{4}$, $1$.

**2 (a)** $-0.236$, $4.24$,    **(b)** $-3.39$, $0.886$,    **(c)** $0.446$, $2.80$,

   **(d)** $-0.531$, $1.13$,    **(e)** $-0.360$, $-1.39$,    **(f)** $-1.53$, $0.131$,

   **(g)** $0.734$, $4.77$,    **(h)** $-1.43$, $-0.232$,    **(i)** $0.133$, $-1.88$.

## EXERCISE 7E

**1 (a)** $64$, rational,    **(b)** $49$, rational,    **(c)** $37$, irrational,

   **(d)** $17$, irrational,    **(e)** $81$, rational,    **(f)** $1$, rational,

   **(g)** $9$, rational,    **(h)** $41$, irrational,    **(i)** $2436$, irrational,

**2 (a)** $k > -1$,    **(b)** $k < -2$,    **(c)** $k > -\dfrac{25}{24}$,

   **(d)** $k > -\dfrac{113}{32}$,    **(e)** $k < \dfrac{109}{40}$,    **(f)** $k < \dfrac{37}{36}$.

**3 (a)** $p = \pm\dfrac{5}{2}$,    **(b)** $p = 2$,    **(c)** $p = \pm\dfrac{4}{\sqrt{3}}$,

   **(d)** $p = 3$,    **(e)** $p = 7$, $-9$,    **(f)** $p = 2$, $-8$.

**4 (a)** $2$,    **(b)** $0$,    **(c)** $1$,    **(d)** $2$,    **(e)** $1$,

   **(f)** $2$,    **(g)** $2$,    **(h)** $2$,    **(i)** $2$,    **(j)** $0$.

## EXERCISE 7F

**1 (a)** $(2, -6)$, **(b)** $\left(-\dfrac{1}{2}, -\dfrac{21}{4}\right)$, **(c)** $\left(\dfrac{2}{3}, -\dfrac{35}{9}\right)$.

**2 (a)** $(-2, 0), (3, 5)$, **(b)** $(1, 3), (2, 2)$, **(c)** $(7, 7)\left(-\dfrac{1}{2}, -\dfrac{17}{4}\right)$,

**(d)** $(0, -6), \left(-\dfrac{10}{3}, \dfrac{32}{3}\right)$, **(e)** $(2, 0), \left(-\dfrac{23}{15}, \dfrac{106}{45}\right)$.

**3 (a)** 1, **(b)** 2, **(c)** 0, **(d)** 0, **(e)** 2.

**4 (a)** $(1, -3)$, **(b)** none, **(c)** $(1, 2)$,

**(d)** $(3, 16), (-2, 21)$, **(e)** none, **(f)** $(1, 3), \left(-\dfrac{1}{2}, \dfrac{27}{4}\right)$,

**(g)** $(0, 3), \left(\dfrac{1}{2}, \dfrac{13}{4}\right)$.

**5 (a)** $2 \pm 2\sqrt{2}$, **(b)** $\dfrac{3}{4} \pm \dfrac{\sqrt{57}}{4}$, **(c)** $\dfrac{5}{2} \pm \dfrac{\sqrt{5}}{2}$,

**(d)** $-\dfrac{3}{4} \pm \dfrac{\sqrt{17}}{4}$, **(e)** $\dfrac{3}{4} \pm \dfrac{\sqrt{33}}{4}$.

**6** Line is a tangent to the curve.

**7** $k < \dfrac{5}{3}$.

## 8 Further differentiation

## EXERCISE 8A

**1 (a)** $6x - 6$, **(b)** $20x - 9$, **(c)** $24x + 19$,
**(d)** $72x - 36$, **(e)** $4x + 5$, **(f)** $40x^3 + 70x + 25$,
**(g)** $\dfrac{3\sqrt{x}}{2} + \dfrac{2}{\sqrt{x}}$, **(h)** $1 - 3\sqrt{x}$.

**2 (a)** $12x^3 + 16x$, **(b)** $\dfrac{4x^2 - 2x}{3}$, **(c)** $9x^2 + 4 - \dfrac{6}{x^3}$,

**(d)** $\dfrac{12}{x^2}$, **(e)** $1 + \dfrac{12}{x^2}$, **(f)** $\dfrac{3}{10x^2} - \dfrac{2}{5x^5}$,

**(g)** $-\dfrac{25}{2x^3\sqrt{x}} - 12x^3$, **(h)** $\dfrac{18}{x^4} - \dfrac{1}{x^2} - \dfrac{2}{x^3}$.

**3 (a)** 21, **(b)** $-12$, **(c)** 2.5

**4 (a)** $112x^6 - 32x^7$,

**(b)** $\dfrac{-18}{x^{\frac{5}{2}}} - \dfrac{1}{2x^{\frac{3}{2}}}$,

**(c)** $3\sqrt{x} + 9 - \dfrac{7}{3x^{\frac{2}{3}}}$,

**(d)** $\dfrac{20x^{\frac{2}{3}}}{3} - \dfrac{7}{6x^{\frac{5}{6}}} + \dfrac{3}{x^2}$.

## *EXERCISE 8B*

**1**

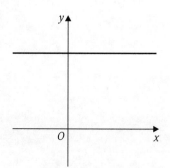

**2**

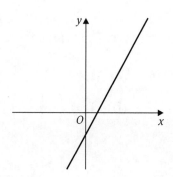

**3**

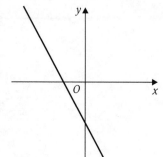

**4**

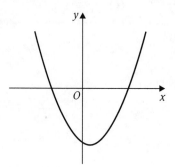

**5**

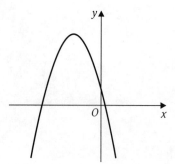

**6**

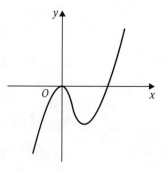

## *EXERCISE 8C*

**1** Minimum at $(3, -2)$.

**2** Greatest value of 18.5 at $x = 2.5$; range is $f(x) \leqslant 18.5$

**3 (a)** $(2.5, -3.75)$ minimum,
**(b)** $(1.5, 16)$ maximum,
**(c)** $(4, 32)$ minimum, $(-4, -32)$ maximum.

**4 (a)** (0, 0) maximum, (2, −8) minimum,

 **(b)** (4, −62) minimum, (6, −58) maximum,

 **(c)** (3, 54) minimum.

**5** (4, 8) maximum.

**6 (a)** $A(-1, 9)$, $B(3, -23)$,

 **(b)** $f(-2) = 2$; $f(6) = 58$, range: $-23 \leqslant f(x) \leqslant 58$.

**7** Maximum height 14.0625 metres.

## EXERCISE 8D

**1** (0, 16) inflection.

**2** (1, 2) inflection.

**3 (a)** (−2, −11) maximum, (−1, −12) minimum,

 **(b)** (−2, −11) minimum, (2, 21) maximum.

**4 (a)** (0, 0) minimum, $(-\frac{1}{3}, \frac{1}{9})$ maximum,

 **(b)** $(\frac{1}{4}, 8)$ minimum, $(-\frac{1}{4}, -8)$ maximum.

 **(c)** (0, 0) inflection, (1, −1) minimum.

**5** (3, −216) minimum, (−3, 216) maximum crosses axes at (0, 0) $(3\sqrt{3}. 0)$ and $(-3\sqrt{3}, 0)$.

## MIXED EXERCISE

 **1** −1.

 **2 (a)** $5h^2 + 18h + 9$,  **(b)** $18 + 5h$,  **(c)** 18.

 **3 (a)** $8x - 3$,  **(b)** $-\dfrac{3}{x^2}$.

 **4 (a)** $18x^2 - 10x + 1$,  **(b)** $5x^2 + 8x - \frac{1}{2}$,  **(c)** $28x^3 - 16x$.

 **5 (a)** $\dfrac{2}{x^2} - \dfrac{8}{x^3} + 4$,  **(b)** $\dfrac{3}{\sqrt{x}} + \dfrac{7}{x^3}$,  **(c)** $\dfrac{3\sqrt{x}}{2} - \dfrac{3}{2\sqrt{x}} - \dfrac{1}{x\sqrt{x}}$.

 **6 (a)** 2,  **(b)** 1,  **(c)** −18,  **(d)** $\frac{5}{9}$.

 **7** (5, −80.5), (−2, 21).

 **8** 12, $(-\frac{1}{2}, -10)$.

 **9 (a)** $2x + 3$,  **(b)** $-16x - \dfrac{4}{x^3}$,

 **(c)** $\dfrac{81\sqrt{x}}{2} + 12$,  **(d)** $12x^2 + 4 - \dfrac{1}{x^2}$.

**10** (0, −19), (0.5, −19.25).

**11 (a)** $A = 4, B = -3$,  **(b)** maximum of $\dfrac{4}{3}$ when $x = \dfrac{2}{3}$.

**12** (4, −128) minimum, (−4, 128) maximum.

**13 (a)** $(\frac{1}{4}, -1\frac{3}{8})$,  **(b)** 9.684 (to three decimal places).

**14** $\dfrac{dy}{dx} = 2x + \dfrac{54}{x^2}$, (−3, 27) minimum.

## 9 Integration

***EXERCISE 9A***

**1** **(a)** $y = 2x^6 + c,$      **(b)** $y = \dfrac{x^4}{2} + c,$

    **(c)** $y = \dfrac{x^8}{2} + c,$      **(d)** $y = 12x + c,$

    **(e)** $y = x^3 - x^2 + 5x + c,$      **(f)** $y = x^6 - 6x^3 - \dfrac{x^2}{2} + c,$

    **(g)** $y = \dfrac{x^8}{2} - 2x^6 - 4x + c,$      **(h)** $y = \dfrac{-2}{x^3},$

    **(i)** $y = 4x^{\frac{3}{4}} + c,$      **(j)** $y = \dfrac{1}{x} - \dfrac{1}{x^3} + c,$

    **(k)** $y = 4x\sqrt{x} + c,$      **(l)** $y = 4\sqrt{x} + c.$

**2** **(a)** $f(x) = 2x^3 - 2x^2 + 5x + c,$    **(b)** $f(x) = x^3 + 5x^2 + 4x + c,$

    **(c)** $f(x) = 2x^5 - \dfrac{1}{2}x^6 + 7x + c,$    **(d)** $f(x) = x^{10} - 2x^4 + x + c,$

    **(e)** $f(x) = \dfrac{1}{x^3} - \dfrac{2}{x} + c,$      **(f)** $f(x) = \dfrac{3}{x^4} - \dfrac{2}{x^5} - \dfrac{7}{x} + c,$

    **(g)** $f(x) = c - \dfrac{1}{x^3} - \dfrac{2}{x^5},$      **(h)** $f(x) = \dfrac{3}{x^4} - \dfrac{1}{x^2} + c,$

    **(i)** $f(x) = \dfrac{2}{x^7} - \dfrac{2}{x^9} + c,$      **(j)** $f(x) = 4x\sqrt{x} - \dfrac{6}{x\sqrt{x}} + c.$

**3** $f(x) = 4x^3 + 4x^2 - 3x - 8.$

**4** $y = 2x^4 - 4x^3 + 3x - 1.$

**5** $y = 31 - \dfrac{4}{x} - 4x^2 + 5x.$

**6** **(a)**            **(b)**            **(c)**

 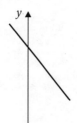 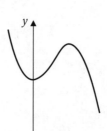

**7** $y = 2x\sqrt{x} + 4x^2\sqrt{x} - 133.$

**8** $y = 6x^{\frac{4}{3}} - 3x^{\frac{2}{3}} - 455.$

**9** $n = -1.$

## EXERCISE 9B

**1 (a)** $y = x^3 - x^2 + c$,

**(b)** $y = 2x^5 + \dfrac{3x^4}{2} + c$,

**(c)** $y = x^8 + 2x^6 + c$,

**(d)** $y = -x^{-3} - 2x^{-4} + c$,

**(e)** $y = \dfrac{5}{2}x^2 - x^3 - 2x + c$,

**(f)** $y = \dfrac{x^4}{4} + \dfrac{x^3}{3} - 3x^2 + c$,

**(g)** $y = \dfrac{x^5}{5} + \dfrac{3x^4}{4} + \dfrac{2x^3}{3} + c$,

**(h)** $y = c - \dfrac{1}{3x^3} - \dfrac{2}{x^4} - \dfrac{3}{x^5}$,

**(i)** $y = c - \dfrac{2}{x} - \dfrac{11}{2x^2}, - \dfrac{4}{x^3}$,

**(j)** $\dfrac{6x^{\frac{5}{2}}}{5} + \dfrac{4x^{\frac{3}{2}}}{3} - 16x^{\frac{1}{2}} + c$.

**2 (a)** $f(x) = c - \dfrac{4}{3}x^3 + 8x^2 - 15x$,

**(b)** $f(x) = 2x\sqrt{x}(x-1) + c$,

**(c)** $f(x) = 2x^6 - 3x^4 + c$,

**(d)** $f(x) = 4x\sqrt{x} - x^2 + c$,

**(e)** $f(x) = \dfrac{x^3}{3} - 3x - \dfrac{7}{x} + c$,

**(f)** $f(x) = \dfrac{2}{5}x^{\frac{5}{2}} - 2x^{\frac{3}{2}} + 10x^{\frac{1}{2}} + c$,

**(g)** $f(x) = \dfrac{12}{5}x^{\frac{5}{3}} - \dfrac{15}{2}x^{\frac{2}{3}} + c$,

**(h)** $f(x) = x - \dfrac{8}{3}x^{\frac{3}{2}} + 12x^{\frac{1}{2}} + c$.

**3** $y = 5x^5 - 4x^4 + 12$.

**4** $y = \dfrac{x^4}{4} - 3x - \dfrac{2}{x} + 1$.

**5** $y = \dfrac{2}{x} - \dfrac{11}{2x^2} + \dfrac{5}{x^3} + \dfrac{1}{2}$.

**6** $y = \dfrac{2}{5}x^{\frac{5}{2}} - 2x^{\frac{3}{2}} + 14x^{\frac{1}{2}} + \dfrac{1}{5}$.

**7** $y = \dfrac{3}{4}x^{\frac{8}{3}} - 3x^{\frac{5}{3}} - \dfrac{9}{2}x^{\frac{2}{3}} - \dfrac{7}{4}$.

## EXERCISE 9C

**1** $2x^6 + c$.

**2** $4x^5 + c$.

**3** $\dfrac{-1}{x^2} + c$.

**4** $x^4 + 2x^3 + c$.

**5** $8x^{11} + c$.

**6** $\dfrac{-20}{3x^3} + c$.

**7** $-3x^{-1} + c$.

**8** $-4x^{-1} + x^6 + c$.

**9** $-\dfrac{5}{3}x^{-3} + c$.

**10** $2x^{\frac{3}{2}} + c$.

**11** $\dfrac{-1}{2x^2} + c$.

**12** $-\dfrac{4}{x} - \dfrac{3}{x^2} + c$.

**13** $x^3 + 4x^2 + 5x + c$.

**14** $2x^3 - \dfrac{11}{2}x^2 + 5x + c$.

**15** $9x - \dfrac{3}{2}x^2 - \dfrac{2}{3}x^3 + c$.

**16** $\dfrac{9}{2}x^2 - x^3 - \dfrac{x^4}{2} + c$.

**17** $9x + 6x^2 + \dfrac{4}{3}x^3 + c$.

**18** $4x - 6x^2 + 3x^3 + c$.

**19** $\dfrac{2}{7}x^{\frac{7}{2}} + c$.

**20** $\dfrac{x^2}{2} - \dfrac{4}{3}x^{\frac{3}{2}} + x + c$.

**21** $\dfrac{2}{5}x^{\frac{5}{2}} - 2x^{\frac{1}{2}} + c$.

**22** $\dfrac{3}{13}x^{\frac{13}{3}} - \dfrac{3}{4}x^{\frac{4}{3}} + c$.

**23** $25x - 30x^2 + 12x^3 + c$.

**24** $x^2 - \dfrac{1}{x^2} + c.$      **25** $4x^4\sqrt{x} + c.$      **26** $\dfrac{x^2}{2} + 4x\sqrt{x} + 9x + c.$

**27** $\dfrac{2}{7}x^{\frac{7}{2}} + 6x^{-\frac{1}{2}} + c.$    **28** $\dfrac{x^8}{8} - \dfrac{2x^5}{5} + \dfrac{x^2}{2} + c.$    **29** $\dfrac{2}{5}x^{\frac{5}{2}} - 2x^{-\frac{5}{2}} + c.$

**30** $\dfrac{x^3}{3} - \dfrac{12x^2\sqrt{x}}{5} + \dfrac{9x^2}{2} + c.$

## EXERCISE 9D

**1** 3.      **2** 484.      **3** 48.      **4** 127.5      **5** $-12.$

**6** $\dfrac{4}{3}.$      **7** $-\dfrac{7}{2}.$      **8** $-42.$      **9** $\dfrac{2}{3}.$      **10** $\dfrac{2}{3}.$

**11** $-\dfrac{1}{4}.$      **12** 64.      **13** 81.      **14** $\dfrac{23}{6}.$      **15** 18.

**16 (a)** $\dfrac{125}{6}.$      **(b)** $\dfrac{45}{8}.$      **(c)** $\dfrac{19}{4}.$

## EXERCISE 9E

**1** $(1, 2), (2, 5); \dfrac{1}{6}.$      **2** $(0, 18), (6, 0); 36.$

**3** $(3, 6), (-2, 11); \dfrac{125}{6}.$      **4** $(1, 9), (4, 24); 9.$

**5** $(0, 3); (-1, 6) \dfrac{1}{3}.$      **6** $(-3, 0), (2, 0); \dfrac{125}{6}.$

**7** $F(5, 0); \dfrac{125}{2}.$      **8** $\dfrac{9}{2}.$

**9** $A(4, 2); \dfrac{4}{3}.$      **10** $(3, 7), (-\frac{1}{2}, 15\frac{3}{4}); \dfrac{343}{24}.$

**11** $\dfrac{5}{12} + \dfrac{8}{3} = \dfrac{37}{12};$ part of region lies below $x$-axis.

**12 (a)** $A(-2, 0), B(2, 0), C(-1, -3);$      **(b)** $\dfrac{9}{2}.$

## 10 Further equations and quadratic inequalities

## EXERCISE 10A

**5** Between $-2$ and $-1$.

**6** Between 2 and 3.

**7** Between 1.80 and 1.85.

**8 (b) (i)** No, there may be an even number of roots in this interval.
    **(ii)** $g(-\frac{1}{2}) = -2.53125$ and $g(1\frac{1}{2}) = -12.90625$. At least one root lies between $-1$ and $-0.5$ and between 1.5 and 2.

**9 (a)** $\sqrt[3]{16} - \sqrt[3]{4}$,   **(b)** $\sqrt[3]{4} - \sqrt[3]{2}$   **(c)** $(14\sqrt{2} + 20)^{\frac{1}{3}} + (20 - 14\sqrt{2})^{\frac{1}{3}} = 4.$

**10** $f(0) = -1$ and $f(1) = 1$. No, the function has a discontinuity when $x = \frac{1}{2}$ and is therefore not continuous between 0 and 1. No conclusion can be made about roots in this interval.

## EXERCISE 10B

**1** $(2, 10)$, $(-\frac{10}{3}, -6)$.

**2** $(2, 1)$, $(1, 2)$.

**3** $(3, -1)$, $(-\frac{2}{3}, -\frac{25}{3})$.

**4** $(6, 1)$, $(4\frac{1}{6}, -\frac{5}{6})$

**5** Quadratic does not have real roots.

**6 (a)** Does not intersect, **(b)** $(3, 0)$, $(5, 4)$, **(c)** Does not intersect.

**7** $-4 \pm \sqrt{21}$.

**8** $3 \pm \sqrt{2}$.

## EXERCISE 10C

**8 (a)** $-0.58 < a < -0.57$, **(b)** $1.36 < c < 1.37$.

## EXERCISE 10D

**1** $-3\frac{1}{2} < x < 3$.      **2** $x \leqslant 1, x \geqslant 1\frac{1}{2}$.      **3** $x > 3, x < -2$.

**4** $-1 < x < 6$.      **5** $x \leqslant -5, x \geqslant 2$.      **6** $-4 < x < -3$.

**7** $x > 1, x < -\frac{1}{2}$.      **8** $x > 4, x < -4$.      **9** $-\frac{2}{3} \leqslant x \leqslant 2$.

**10** $x > 1, x < \frac{1}{4}$.      **11** $x < -1\frac{1}{2}, x > 3$.      **12** $-5 \leqslant x \leqslant 5$.

**13** $x \geqslant 3, x \leqslant -1$.      **14** $x > 1, x < \frac{3}{5}$.      **15** $x < -1, x > 1\frac{3}{4}$.

**16** $\frac{3}{8} < x < 1$.      **17** $x > \frac{1}{2}, x < -3$.      **18** $-\frac{11}{12} < x < 2$.

**19** $x > \frac{1}{2}, x < \frac{3}{10}$.      **20** $x \leqslant \frac{1}{3}, x \geqslant 1\frac{2}{3}$.

## EXERCISE 10E

**1** $3 - \sqrt{13} < x < 3 + \sqrt{13}$.

**2** $-4 - \sqrt{13} \leqslant x \leqslant -4 + \sqrt{13}$.

**3** $x > 2 + \sqrt{5}, x < 2 - \sqrt{5}$.

**4** $1 - \sqrt{6} < x < 1 + \sqrt{6}$.

**5** $x \geqslant 5 + \sqrt{22}, x \leqslant 5 - \sqrt{22}$.

**6** $\frac{1}{2}(-3 - \sqrt{5}) < x < \frac{1}{2}(-3 + \sqrt{5})$.

**7** $x > 1 + \sqrt{\frac{3}{2}}, x < 1 - \sqrt{\frac{3}{2}}$.

**8** $x > 1 + \sqrt{\frac{10}{3}}, x < 1 - \sqrt{\frac{10}{3}}$.

**9** $2 - \sqrt{\frac{17}{3}} \leqslant x \leqslant 2 + \sqrt{\frac{17}{3}}$.

**10** $x > \frac{3}{2} + \sqrt{\frac{3}{2}}, x < \frac{3}{2} - \sqrt{\frac{3}{2}}$.

## EXERCISE 10F

**1** $-\frac{4}{7} \leqslant k \leqslant 4$.      **2** $k \leqslant -2, k \geqslant -1\frac{1}{13}$.

**3** $k > 2, k < \frac{2}{9}$.      **4** $-\frac{15}{8} < k < 1$.

**5** $1\frac{6}{7} < k < 3$.      **6** $-1\frac{16}{23} \leqslant k \leqslant -1$.

**7** $\frac{1}{2} < k < \frac{5}{6}$.      **8** $k \geqslant 6\frac{1}{2}, k \leqslant \frac{1}{2}$.

## 11 Trigonometry

### EXERCISE 11A

**1 (a) (i)** sine positive;  **(ii)** cosine positive,
  **(b) (i)** sine positive;  **(ii)** cosine negative,
  **(c) (i)** sine negative;  **(ii)** cosine positive,
  **(d) (i)** sine negative;  **(ii)** cosine negative,
  **(e) (i)** sine negative;  **(ii)** cosine positive,
  **(f) (i)** sine negative;  **(ii)** cosine negative.

**2 (b) (i)** $\theta = -340°, -200°, 20°, 160°,$  **(ii)** $-230°, 50°, 130°.$

**3 (b) (i)** $\theta = -410°, -50°, 50°, 310°,$  **(ii)** $\theta = 140°, 220°, -220°$

### EXERCISE 11B

**1 (a)** $\theta = -310°, -230°, 130°,$    **(b)** $\theta = -160°,$
  **(c)** $\theta = -270°,$              **(d)** $\theta = -180°, 180°,$
  **(e)** $\theta = -350°, -190°, 10°,$   **(f)** $\theta = -50°, 230°, 310°.$

**2 (a)** $\theta = 40°,$    **(b)** $\theta = 290°,$    **(c)** $\theta = 250°,$
  **(d)** $\theta = -360°,$  **(e)** $\theta = 270°,$    **(f)** $\theta = -20°.$

**3 (a)** $\theta = 35°,$    **(b)** $\theta = 20°,$     **(c)** $\theta = 180°,$
  **(d)** $\theta = 225°,$   **(e)** $\theta = 230°,$    **(f)** $\theta = 135°.$

### EXERCISE 11C

**1 (a)** $\theta = 14.5°, 50°, 165.5°,$
  **(b)** $x = -323.1°, -36.9°, -20°, 36.9°,$
  **(c)** $x = -336.4°, -203.6° , 23.6° , 90°, 156.4°,$
  **(d)** $\theta = -225.6°, -134.4°, 134.4°, 0°, 225.6°,$
  **(e)** $x = 170°, -287.5°, -72.5°,$
  **(f)** $\theta = -130°, 210.0°, 330.0°,$
  **(g)** $x = 180.0°,$
  **(h)** $\theta = -360°, 0°, 360°.$

**2 (a)** $\theta = -40°, 30.0°, 150.0°, 390.0°, 510.0°,$
  **(b)** $x = 70°, 214.8°, 325.2°, 574.8°, 685.2°,$
  **(c)** $x = 110°, 113.6°, 246.4°, 473.6°, 606.4°,$
  **(d)** $\theta = 0°, 191.5°, 348.5°, 551.5°, 708.5°,$
  **(e)** $\theta = 48.2°, 90°, 311.8°, 408.2°, 671.8°,$
  **(f)** $x = 20°, 41.8°, 138.2°, 401.8°, 498.2°.$

**3 (a)** $\theta = 0°, 120°, 240°,$           **(b)** $\theta = 0°, 19.5°, 160.5°, 180°,$
  **(c)** $\theta = 0°, 180°,$                 **(d)** $\theta = 90°, 101.5°, 270°, 258.5°,$
  **(e)** $\theta = 30°, 150°, 199.5°, 340.5°,$ **(f)** $\theta = 75.5°, 284.5°,$
  **(g)** $\theta = 70.5°, 120°, 240°, 289.5°,$ **(h)** $\theta = 14.5°, 165.5°, 270°.$

**4 (a)** $x = 51.8°, 308.2°,$   **(b)** $x = 189.9°, 350.1°,$
  **(c)** $x = 47.1°, 132.9°,$   **(d)** $x = 73.1°, 286.9°,$
  **(e)** $x = 35.5°, 144.5°,$   **(f)** $x = 145.1°, 214.9°.$

*EXERCISE 11D*

1  $\theta = 26°, 66°, 146°$.

2  $x = 12.4°, 77.6°, 192.4°, 257.6°$.

3  $\theta = -137.7°, -102.3° -17.7°, 17.7°$.

4  $\theta = -172.8°, -97.2°, 7.2°, 82.8°$.

5  $\theta = -76.1°, -43.9°, 43.9°, 76.1°$.

6  $\theta = 25°, 205°$.

7  $x = 38.7°, 111.3°, 218.7°, 291.3°$.

8  $\theta = -80.5°, -12.8°, 39.5°$.

9  $x = -138.2°, -96.8°, 41.8°, 83.2°$.

10  $x = 11.5°, 87.2°, 131.5°$.

11  $\theta = 5.6°, 101.0°, 125.6°$.

12  $x = 16.3°, 61.7°, 88.3°, 133.7°, 160.3°$.

13  $\theta = 34.9°, 325.1°$.

14  $x = 169.3°$.

15  $\theta = 156.4°, 683.6°$

*EXERCISE 11E*

1  (a)  $-130°, 50°, 230°,$          (b)  $160°, 340°,$
   (c)  $-240°, -60°, 120°,$        (d)  $-340°, -160°,$
   (e)  $-130°, 50°, 230°,$         (f)  $-240°, -60°, 120°$.

2  (a)  $x = 26.6°, 206.6°,$
   (b)  $\theta = 45°, 225°,$
   (c)  $x = 0°, 180°, 360°,$
   (d)  $x = 9.5°,$
   (e)  $\theta = -16.7°, 163.3°$.

3  (a)  $\theta = -153.4°, -26.6°, 153.4°, 26.6°, 206.6°,$
   (b)  $x = -84.3°, -76.0°,$
   (c)  $\theta = -116.6°, -45°, 63.4°, 135°,$
   (d)  $\theta = 17.4°, 72.6°, 197.4°, 252.6°,$
   (e)  $x = -51.6°, -165.2°, 14.8°, 128.4°$.

4  (a)  $x = 22.5°, 112.5°,$
   (b)  $\theta = 32.4°, 92.4°, 152.4°,$
   (c)  $\theta = -151.8° -61.8°, 28.2°, 118.2°,$
   (d)  $\theta = -170°, -80°, 10°, 100°,$
   (e)  $x = -35.5°, 24.5°, 84.5°,$
   (f)  $x = 26.7°, 116.7°,$
   (g)  $\theta = -86.2°, -26.2°, 33.8°,$
   (h)  $x = 168.9°,$
   (i)  $\theta = -230.4°, 309.6°$.

**EXERCISE 11F** _____

**1 (a)** $\tan \theta = -\frac{4}{3}$, **(b)** $\tan x = \frac{12}{5}$, **(c)** $\sin \theta = \frac{5}{13}$,

**(d)** $\sin x = -\frac{4}{5}$, **(e)** $\tan x = -\frac{7}{24}$, **(f)** $\cos \theta = \frac{7}{25}$,

**(g)** $\cos x = -\frac{4}{5}$.

**3 (a)** $x = 133.3°, 226.7°$,

**(b)** $\theta = 67.5°, 292.5°$,

**(c)** $x = -343.0°, -197.0°, 17.0°, 163.0°$,

**(d)** $x = -141.8°, -38.2°$,

**(e)** $\theta = 45.0°, 135.0°\ 225.0°\ 315.0°$.

**4 (a)** $18.2°, 78.2°, 138.2°$, **(b)** $55.9°, 145.9°$.

**5 (a)** $3 + \sin \theta$, **(b)** $x = 105°, 165°, 285°, 345°$.

**6 (b)** $7.9°, 52.1°, 127.9°, 172.1°, 247.9°, 292.1°$.

**7 (c)** $38.2°, 141.8°$.

**8** $210°, 330°$.

## 12 Transformations of graphs

**EXERCISE 12A** _____

**1 (a)** $\begin{bmatrix} 7 \\ 0 \end{bmatrix}$ **(b)** $\begin{bmatrix} -1 \\ 0 \end{bmatrix}$ **(c)** $\begin{bmatrix} 6 \\ 0 \end{bmatrix}$ **(d)** $\begin{bmatrix} -2 \\ 0 \end{bmatrix}$

**(e)** $\begin{bmatrix} 1 \\ 5 \end{bmatrix}$ **(f)** $\begin{bmatrix} -2 \\ 3 \end{bmatrix}$ **(g)** $\begin{bmatrix} 1 \\ -7 \end{bmatrix}$ **(h)** $\begin{bmatrix} -8 \\ 3 \end{bmatrix}$

**2 (a)** $y = x - 4$, **(b)** $y = 3 + x$,

**(c)** $y - 5 = x - 2$ or $y = 3 + x$, **(d)** $y = (x + 1)^2 - 1$,

**(e)** $y = (x - 3)^2 + 2$, **(f)** $y = (x + 1)^5 - 3$,

**(g)** $y = (x + 3)^7 - 4$, **(h)** $y + 5 = \sqrt{x - 1}$,

**(i)** $y = 4 + \dfrac{2}{x - 3}$.

**3** Translation of **(a)** $\begin{bmatrix} 1 \\ 0 \end{bmatrix}$, **(b)** $\begin{bmatrix} -2 \\ 0 \end{bmatrix}$, **(c)** $\begin{bmatrix} -2 \\ 3 \end{bmatrix}$, **(d)** $\begin{bmatrix} 3 \\ 2 \end{bmatrix}$, **(e)** $\begin{bmatrix} 1 \\ -2 \end{bmatrix}$.

**4** Translation of **(b)** $\begin{bmatrix} 10° \\ 0 \end{bmatrix}$, **(c)** $\begin{bmatrix} -70° \\ 0 \end{bmatrix}$, **(d)** $\begin{bmatrix} 30° \\ 2 \end{bmatrix}$.

**5** Translation of **(b)** $\begin{bmatrix} -120° \\ 0 \end{bmatrix}$, **(c)** $\begin{bmatrix} 50° \\ 0 \end{bmatrix}$, **(d)** $\begin{bmatrix} 80° \\ -3 \end{bmatrix}$.

**6** Translation of **(b)** $\begin{bmatrix} -20° \\ 0 \end{bmatrix}$, **(c)** $\begin{bmatrix} 30° \\ 0 \end{bmatrix}$, **(d)** $\begin{bmatrix} 30° \\ 5 \end{bmatrix}$.

**7** 270, 630, 900; translation of 270°, etc., in $x$-direction maps $y = \sin x$ onto $y = \cos x$.

## EXERCISE 12B

**1** **(a)** Reflection in $y = 1$, **(b)** translation of $\begin{bmatrix} 0 \\ 2 \end{bmatrix}$,

**(c)** reflection in $x = 2$, **(d)** reflection in $x = -1$,

**(e)** reflection in $y = x$, **(f)** reflection in $y = 4$,

**(g)** reflection in $x = 1$, **(h)** reflection in $y = 5$.

**2** **(a)** $y = 4 - x$, **(b)** $y = (2 - x)^5$,

**(c)** $y = (x - 1)^4 + 2$, **(d)** $y = \sqrt[7]{x}$,

**(e)** $x + y + 1 = 0$, **(f)** $y = (6 - x)^5 + (6 - x)$,

**(g)** $y = x^5 + 4$, **(h)** $y = 2x - x^3$.

**3** **(a)** reflection in $x = 20°$,

**(b)** reflection in $x = 45°$,

**(c)** reflection in $y = 1$.

**4** **(a)** reflection in $x = 60°$, **(b)** translation of $\begin{bmatrix} 0 \\ 2 \end{bmatrix}$,

**(c)** reflection in $y = 3$.

## EXERCISE 12C

**1** **(a)** **(i)** $\frac{1}{2}$, **(ii)** 4, **(b)** **(i)** $\frac{1}{2}$, **(ii)** 8,

**(c)** **(i)** $\frac{4}{3}$, **(ii)** $\frac{9}{16}$, **(d)** **(i)** $\frac{1}{3}$, **(ii)** $\sqrt{3}$.

**2** **(a)** translation $\begin{bmatrix} 15° \\ 0 \end{bmatrix}$ followed by a stretch SF $= 3$ in $y$-direction,

**(b)** a stretch SF $= \frac{1}{3}$ in $x$-direction followed by a translation $\begin{bmatrix} 0 \\ 2 \end{bmatrix}$,

**(c)** a stretch SF $= \frac{1}{5}$ in $x$-direction followed by a reflection in $y = 2$,

**(d)** reflection in $x = 10°$ followed by a stretch SF $= 5$ in $y$-direction.

**3** **(a)** translation $\begin{bmatrix} 15° \\ 0 \end{bmatrix}$ followed by a stretch SF $= 5$ in $y$-direction,

**(b)** a stretch SF $= \frac{2}{3}$ in $x$-direction followed by a translation $\begin{bmatrix} 0 \\ 7 \end{bmatrix}$,

**(c)** a stretch SF $= \frac{1}{2}$ in $x$-direction followed by a reflection in $y = \frac{1}{2}$,

**(d)** reflection in $x = 10°$ followed by a stretch SF $= 3$ in $y$-direction.

**4** **(a)** $y = 5(4 - x)^2$, **(b)** $y = 2 - \dfrac{x^2}{4}$, **(c)** $y = 4(8 - x)^2$,

**(d)** $y = 3(4 + x)^2$, **(e)** $y = 3 + (4 - x)^2$.

**5** **(a)** $y = 2 - (4 - x)^3$, **(b)** $y = 10 - (6 - x)^3$, **(c)** $y = 8(8 - x)^3$,

**(d)** $y = -3(x + 4)^3$, **(e)** $y = \sqrt[3]{(2 - x)}$.

## EXERCISE 12D

**1** **(a)** 3, **(b)** 4, **(c)** 10, **(d)** 2, **(e)** 6, **(f)** 1.

**3** **(a)** 60°, **(b)** 1440°, **(c)** 24°, **(d)** 480°,

**(e)** 120°, **(f)** 72°, **(g)** 45°.

**6 (b) (i)** 1.25, **(ii)** 1.2.

**7 (c) (i)** 1.75, **(ii)** 1.75. **(iii)** 2.5.

## 13 Sequences and series

### EXERCISE 13A

**1** 1, 4, 9.

**2** 2, 8, 14.

**3 (a)** 3, 5, 7, 9, 11, **(b)** 0, 3, 8, 15, 24,
   **(c)** 0, 2, 6, 12, 20, **(d)** 2, 9, 28, 65, 126,
   **(e)** 2, 4, 8, 16, 32, **(f)** 2, 8, 26, 80, 242.

**4 (a)** 4, 7, 10, 13, 16, **(b)** 20, 18, 16, 14, 12,
   **(c)** 3, 7, 16, 32, 57, **(d)** 2, 6, 13, 23, 36,
   **(e)** 1, 21, 66, 146, 271, **(f)** 100, 92, 74, 42, $-8$.

**5 (a)** 3, **(b)** 5, **(c)** $-2$, **(d)** $2n - 1$,
   **(e)** $2n - 1$, **(f)** $6n - 2$.

**6 (a)** $2n - 1$, **(b)** $2^n$, **(c)** $7 - n$, **(d)** $\dfrac{n}{n + 1}$.

**7 (a)** 5, 7, 9, 11; $2n + 3$, **(b)** 40, 37, 34, 31; $43 - 3n$,
   **(c)** 4, 7, 12, 19; $n^2 + 3$, **(d)** 2, 4, 7, 11; $1 + \dfrac{n}{2}(n + 1)$.

### EXERCISE 13B

**1 (a)** 55, **(b)** 210, **(c)** 2485.

**2 (a)** 4860, **(b)** 495 550, **(c)** 60 100, **(d)** 240 694.

**3 (a)** 27, **(b)** 47, **(c)** 137.

**4 (a)** 3, **(b)** 84, **(c)** 183.

**5** 54.     **6** $d = 3$.

**7** $-4$.     **8** $a = -2, d = 3$.

**9** $a = 32.5, d = 2.5$.     **10** $a = -6, d = 6$.

**11** 78.     **12** 95.

### EXERCISE 13C

**1** 200, $\frac{14}{19}$.

**2 (a)** 285, **(b)** 1070.

**3** $a = -30$.

**4** 23.   **5 (a)** 575, **(b)** 22 422, **(c)** 4692, **(d)** 231, **(e)** $-777$.

## EXERCISE 13D

**1** (a) 25, (b) 46, (c) 55,
(d) 34, (e) 99, (f) 20.

**2** (a) 4972, (b) 10 000, (c) 44 795,
(d) 14 895, (e) 14 850, (f) 500 500.

## EXERCISE 13E

**1** (a) 325, (b) 2870, (c) 672 400,
(d) 295 425, (e) 47 002 725.

**2** (a) 385, (b) 3 348 900, (c) 8215, (d) 1 614 600,
(e) 30, (f) 3500, (g) 282 410, (h) 115 220.

**3** (a) $n(n + 1)(n^2 + n + 1)$, (b) $n(n + 1)(2n + 3)$,
(c) $n(n + 1)(2n^2 + 2n - 1)$, (d) $n(n + 1)(2n^2 - 1)$,
(e) $n(n + 1)(3n^2 + 3n + 4)$, (f) $n(n - 1)(2n + 5)$.

**4** 2 731 516.

**5** (a) 9140, (b) 186 735.

**6** 14.

## MIXED EXERCISE

**1** $a = 3, d = 1.75$. **2** (a) $a = 5, d = 0.25$, (b) 5975.

**3** $a = -3, d = 2.5$. **4** (a) $d = 1.5$, (b) 345.

**5** 173. **6** $d = 44$.

**7** (a) 375 750, (b) 292 291 750.

**8** 72 880. **9** $n(n + 1)(5n^2 + 5n + 1)$.

## Answers to practice paper

**1** $3 - \sqrt{5}$.

**2** 25 499 745.

**3** (a) $-12 + 6x^{-\frac{1}{2}}$, (b) $y = -12x + 12\sqrt{x} + 27$.

**4** (a) $y = -2x + 1$, (b) (ii) 0.25.

**5** (a) 15, (b) $-2 < x < \dfrac{3}{2}$.

**6** (b) 5.8° and 84.2°.

**7** (a) $(x - 2)^2 + 12$.
(b) (i) $f(x) \geqslant 12$,
(ii) Translation of $\begin{bmatrix} 2 \\ 12 \end{bmatrix}$.
(iii) $f^{-1}$ does not exist since f is many–one, e.g. f(3) = f(1).

**8** (a) (ii) (2, 9), (b) $y = -\frac{3}{4}x + 15\frac{3}{4}$.

# Index